A Glimpse In
Of Kenneth W. Simpson

"People change, but not much."

"A man promising what he can't deliver will fail."

"Anybody can see what is; it's seeing what could be that makes the difference."

"When a man has a second family, he usually forgets the first."

"If you do business with a liar, you can never win."

"Old men send young men to fight wars. All wars should be fought by mature individuals. It would end wars."

"Hollywood has made it look easy to get wounded fellow soldiers off the battlefield. Just toss them over your shoulder and get out. It's not that easy."

"Military medals never meant much to me. I saw too many guys getting medals for things they didn't do, and not enough getting them for the things they did."

"World War II was a big war fought by ordinary people."

"I was in lots of fights. Did I win most of them? I have no idea. The objective wasn't winning or losing. The ob jective was making sure the other guy knew you were in the fight and that you'd never back down."

"You have to have the right people in the right places if you're going to be successful."

"There's so little to be proud of in war. You always have the feeling you could have done more."

"Being a hero is an accident created by the need to do the right thing."

About the Cover

The cover of Warrior was created by Dave Shaffer from a concept offered by the author. The elements of the cover represent the sweep of years in the life of Ken Simpson. The right side of the image was taken from a snapshot of First Lieutenant Simpson taken in Korea when Ken was 23 years old. The left side is from a photo shot in the early autumn of 2010 when Ken was 81.

To: Beth - Dec 25, 2014
From: Sue
Kenneth is the grandson of Pala's (William Clvis Davis, b 14 Oct 1887 d 2 Jan 1980) sister, Susan Francis Davis James, b 5 Feb. 1881, d 25 Oct 1947

WARRIOR

FROM GRENADES TO GREETING CARDS, THE TRUE STORY OF AN AMERICAN FIGHTING MAN

WARRIOR

FROM GRENADES TO GREETING CARDS, THE TRUE STORY OF AN AMERICAN FIGHTING MAN

WILT BROWNING

Alabaster Book Publishing
North Carolina

Published by Alabaster Book Publishing
P.O. Box 401
Kernersville, North Carolina 27285

Book and Cover Design by
David Shaffer

First Edition

ISBN 13: 978-0-9846320-6-0
ISBN 10: 0-9784620-6-9

Library of Congress Control Number:
2010916081

With Gratitude to:

Harold Simpson, my late brother who from childhood was my role model.

The late Nan Falkenheiner, more than Just a friend who challenged me to "put it in writing."

The late Alan Goldston, always a friend who dreamed of this project.

The late Anne Hetrick Kennedy, who said that she was teaching history while I was off making history.

Ron Campbell, who was with me every step of the way.

Bert Rovens, a great salesman and friend whose enthusiasm remains infectious.

CEOs Thomas Cooney and Ben Sotille, two men who gave me the freedom to be me.

Ken Simpson

Acknowledgement

On a day on which the winter of 2010 showed the first warm promise of the spring to come, Dr. Herb Appenzeller returned to his Summerfield, North Carolina, home to find a recorded telephone message waiting. He pressed the "Play" button and heard a voice he did not recognize.

"Herb," the voice said. "You and I go back a long way. Give me a call." The caller left a phone number and area code Appenzeller did not recognize.

Now, Dr. A is a stickler about returning phone calls, even from people he doesn't know. Whether he would do the bidding of this one was never in doubt. The news of Appenzeller's selection and impending induction into the North Carolina Sports Hall of Fame had brought calls from a number of people, some with whom he had not been in touch for more than a few years.

So, he dialed the number the unknown voice had left.

"Hello," came that same voice, still not a familiar one.

"This is Herb Appenzeller," he said (he also seldom refers to himself as "Doctor" Appenzeller, which he certainly is).

"You were my football coach back in high school," the voice announced. "Do you remember the white shorts?"

"I remember some white shorts," Appenzeller confirmed. "But what's your name."

"I'm Ken Simpson. Played when you were coaching for the first time down in Wake County. I also was a fighter and you loaned me some white shorts when I was going to compete in the Golden Gloves tournament in Raleigh."

The mention of the white shorts revived a faint memory for Appenzeller. Indeed, the white shorts he remembered had a history. Appenzeller had been a running back on the football team of legendary Wake Forest coach D.C. "Peahead" Walker, but also ran track as an unattached athlete since the Deacons in those days did not field a track and field team. Appenzeller specialized in the sprints, but he too needed proper clothing to compete in the North Carolina collegiate meet then being held in Chapel Hill. When Appenzeller asked his coach if there were in the athletic department clothing suitable for track competition, Walker came up with a knit shirt and a pair of white shorts.

By studying the starter and learning the man's rhythm with his trigger finger on the starter's pistol, Appenzeller got great jumps on the field and won the first two heats in the 60-yard dash. But on the third and final heat, the starter crossed Appenzeller up and Wake Forest's lone competitor finished second.

"I remember those shorts, but how'd they do in the Golden Gloves?" he asked Simpson.

"I won my first two fights – knocked the first man out in just over a minute – but lost the third one on a decision the crowd didn't like. They thought I had won and almost booed the referee out of the place. So, they came in second there.

"I just never did get a chance to thank you for those shorts," Simpson said. "I live in Maggie Valley now and I want you and your wife to come up and see us."

The Appenzellers made the trip and returned to North Carolina's Triad without the white shorts from long ago, but with a recommendation that Ken Simpson's life is the stuff of legend. And I thank them for passing their thoughts on to me and, in very large part, making this book possible. I owe Dr. A and his wife, Ann, so much far beyond the scope of this book. I offer my most sincere gratitude.

I also am indebted to Ken and his wife, Laura, perfect hosts beginning with that first visit which we used to get a sort of bird's eye view – the kind the Simpsons get on the world from their home atop Walker Bald, a Blue Ridge Range peak – of the life this warrior has known in more than eighty-two years of living. Ken and Laura never wavered in their kindness on all those visits that were necessary in gathering the material for this book.

And Ken was an open book in the figurative sense of the expression and never wavered in his willingness to share the remarkable story of his life. He made the preliminary work in the creation of this book easier than one would have expected, despite continuing health problems that have been visited upon him in recent years, and for that he has my deep appreciation.

The contributions of a couple of business giants in their time made perspective possible when viewing Ken's life as a businessman himself. His own former boss, Benjamine Sotille, for a time the Chief Executive Officer of the Gibson Greeting Card Company, and Randy Barfoot, who was Director of Non-Foods for Winn-Dixie during a period of robust growth by the grocery chain, offered invaluable perspectives. Both now retired, they shared their memories freely and brought balance to the pages of this book. I am indebted to them for that.

Jane Roscoe, a retired public school teacher, is known as "Mrs. Coach" around Northern Guilford High School where her husband, Johnny, is the very successful football coach. She skillfully coached me as my editor from beginning to end, and her work was critical to this work. She has my gratitude.

And finally I thank North Carolina Congressman Howard Coble for offering me his excitement and encouragement for this writing project documenting the life of an American fighting man.

INTRODUCTION

Ken Simpson epitomizes what Tom Brokaw, in his highly acclaimed book, called "the greatest generation any society has produced." Ken experienced the Great Depression and he served his country as a fighting man in two great conflicts, World War II, as an underage seaman in the United States Navy, and the Korean War, as a commissioned officer in the United States Army. He was a fighter before the wars and he remains a fighter. Only the battlefields have changed for this man who is now an octogenarian.

Though he has had skirmishes with skin cancer in late 2010 and early 2011, his last major battle came in 2009 in the form of an aortic valve and quadruple bypass surgery in which doctors also diffused an aneurism "the size of a hand grenade" before it could explode. The cardiac battle waged at Mission Hospital in Asheville, North Carolina, left Ken uncertain of his steps and

The Simpsons, Ken and Laura (2005)

with the certain knowledge that physically his fighting days are over.

That was a strong dose of reality for a fighting man who, incongruous though it may seem, became a conqueror in the greeting card business. The truth is that, in a fighting sense, Ken started a revolution in the business. He did it by running his operation with the same zeal, intensity and tenacity with which in the early 1950s he hunted down North Korean soldiers on frozen hills a world away from his North Carolina roots, a world where at the time most of the hills bore numbers instead of names. Ken's warrior attitude became his battle cry in both the shooting wars he knew and the corporate ones he later waged. He succeeded on both fronts.

Ken has lived for the last twenty-eight years on a hill that has no number, but a distinctive name, Walker Bald. Laura, his wife, has lived there for the last fifteen years. Their battles now are ones that come with naturally occurring events, such as the snows of winter that sometimes reach drifts taller than Ken. These days Laura mans the front line. Her attack vehicle is a snow plow bolted to the nose of a four-wheel drive Bronco, when it comes to wintry weather.

Otherwise, few battles remain to be waged, nor should there be at this stage of life for Ken and Laura in the paradise they call home. To get to their front door is a mountain adventure all its own played out on a narrow, curving, always climbing road. Along the way one passes in the ascent to the top a sign that reads: "Chicken Turnaround." "That's where, before I paved the road, people who didn't want to go any further would turn around," Ken said. "People who were too chicken to keep going."

Those who have kept going to the top have been awesomely rewarded with a mountain view like no other. Home is a place called "The White House" because it can be seen gleaming atop the distant mountain long before one arrives at the last curve on the winding ribbon of asphalt that is the Simpsons' driveway. There are places just off Interstate 40 in western North Carolina from where "The White House" can be seen from as far away as a distance of twenty miles. The Simpsons look down upon the expanse of the Blue Ridge Range from atop Walker Bald Mountain. Though he cannot be absolutely certain, Ken counts his as the highest permanent residence east of the Mississippi River. "We're at 5,400 feet in elevation," he says. "There aren't many mountains that reach this elevation east of the Mississippi, and almost all of the ones that do have no houses on top."

The Simpsons are surrounded by mountains including to the west the gorgeous Great Smokys. On a clear day, it is likely that they can see more of the Blue Ridge Range at one time than anyone and they have come to know the names of many of the peaks that seem to strain to attain the elevation of their own. Mount Mitchell, the loftiest peak in the eastern United States, rises in the distance to the northeast. Mount Pisgah, that from a distance seems a perfectly inverted cone shape, stands out to the south. To the immediate west and on winter evenings, the mountains glow with the lights illuminating Cataloochee's ski slopes. And looking south and slightly easterly, it is possible on a perfectly clear day to see Asheville's famous Biltmore House, once the American castle home of the Vanderbilts. From this distance, the massive Biltmore seems smaller than a Monopoly board game house.

It is in this home and in this slice of Heaven that Ken from time to time recounts the battles he has known, military and corporate, and the fights he has both won and lost. The setting could not be more perfect.

A life-size 500-pound bronze of a Japanese Samurai warrior of uncertain vintage stands guard on the main level of the home. His attire is held together by the perfectly knotted *obi* and his *haori* is adorned with stylized chrysanthemum blooms emblematic of the Chrysanthemum Throne of Japan which the Samurai is sworn to defend, apparently even this far removed from Nippon.

There are no chrysanthemums here other than those etched into the bronze. This is a home where orchids, rich in color, bloom to the bidding of the sun streaming through large windows with an eastern exposure. Beyond the windows and across much of the crest of the mountain stand an array of blue spruce still reaching for the sky from the rocky soil in which Ken planted them more than a decade ago.

At an elevation slightly lower than the main house are two guest houses, one built by Ken and the other he has rebuilt several times. A third house is the home of one of Ken's two former wives who has become friends with Laura and who occasionally calls Ken to ask him to come down the hill and encourage black bears who also make their home on Walker Bald to vacate her sunny, front porch.

Simpson, the family's gentle German shepherd, is apparently happily living out his own golden years here as well. His personal battle is with the encroachment of hip problems common to large breeds. Simpson is a canine of privilege and never was a common mongrel; he is a descendant of champions, both paternal and maternal. His large, regal face is evidence of his lofty bloodline. Fittingly, Simpson has his own home, built a few years ago, just beyond the paved apron upon which guests park after the torturous climb from Maggie Valley more than three miles down the mountain. But, Simpson has never moved into his custom-built pad preferring instead accommodations in the main house. He knows that he is, after all, an important member of the family. Sometimes grudgingly, Simpson shares the home not only with Ken and Laura, but also with sister Siamese cats named Thelma and Louise, one of whom mostly ignores Simpson.

Ken and Laura, once his "right arm" when both worked for Gibson Greeting Cards, are still active in their own business. Now in his ninth decade there still is a love for high-performance automobiles in Ken's surgically repaired heart. His own automobile is a twelve-cylinder 1999 Mercedes 600SL hard top convertible with less than 20,000 miles on the odometer and capable of incredible speeds. The Mercedes remains mostly in the protection of a garage where it is admired frequently by Ken. Laura's vehicle of choice is a more utilitarian Chevrolet Tahoe, white as though to match the color of the home. It is considered Simpson's car. In early 2011, a new Chevrolet Tahoe moved as well into the three-car garage now that the older Tahoe some time ago passed the 160,000-mile mark.

More than once, personal and business acquaintances have seen in this man a parallel to the public notion of what the American warrior was through most of the Twentieth Century – brave, strong, gallant, dedicated, resourceful, patriotic and skilled. Unquestionably, Ken has embodied all of that. His has been a life uniquely remarkable in all its drama. Through the years, he has been advised to put his memories of that singular life "in writing."

In September 2010, just as the first blush of fall was beginning to paint the mountain tapestry around him, Ken decided to do just that. This is his story. These are his memories. The scars he carries are ones he earned. The embedded shrapnel that still stubbornly clings to its hiding places in his body is his unhappy inheritance. In large part, this is the inspiring legacy he offers to Laura, his children, grandchildren and friends.

After reading this book, hopefully you will agree that it also is inspirational for all of us who owe so much to American fighting men such as Ken Simpson.

TRAIN TO OBLIVION

The three sons of cotton mill workers, the oldest not yet ten, waited expectantly in the gathering darkness of the summer evening. Neither spoke, each intently listening to the sounds of the night, listening for a particular sort of sound.

And there it was, that lonesome, soulful moan of a passenger train's warning horn being sounded far away. The sort of sound that makes grown men cry and about which woeful songs have been written for generations. The sound came as always through the night, not so regularly one could set a watch by it, but it was predictable enough that young Ken Simpson, Raymond Tilley and a local tough kid, Bozo Benningfield, knew when locomotives were likely to be rumbling their way. It was of no importance that the trains were known by magical-sounding names such as the *Southern States Special*, *Orange Blossom Special*, the *Silver Meteor* or other wonderful such designations. It was more important that they regularly rumbled both north and south through the rolling hills of the North Carolina farm region to and from exotic destinations in Florida so that their arrivals could, to some degree, be anticipated. And the boys knew from experience when to begin listening for the mournful sounds well before the thundering beasts came snorting through their part of the world.

For the three, the sound was something more than a rhapsody in three discordant notes. Each boy imagined that the sound like that of Gabriel's trumpet in triplicate might mean the difference in living and dying. And, indeed, for this trio that was the case.

Once the horn sounded, it was as though a sequence of events must – almost by rule - be put into place, that they had no option other than to react. And when those events had been played out, they determined whether each boy lived another day or perished in a violence so vile as to be almost unimaginable.

There always was a solitary witness, Ken's older brother Harold, who trembled at the thought of what might happen. It was as though Harold sought to honor his role as his younger sibling's protector, yet he was powerless to stop this insanity. Harold, never the daredevil himself, could only watch, always in horror, from the side of the track as though he was there to literally pick up the pieces if the unthinkable tragedy were to befall any of the three, particularly Ken.

As the thundering locomotive approached the Main Street crossing in Youngsville, North Carolina, a bit more than three miles from where the three pals stood listening intently in that summer of 1937, the engineer would send a blast of deafening sound through the night air. It was a warning to stand clear of the Main Street railroad crossing where the town's principal thoroughfare intersected with the appropriately named Railroad Street. Everyone in town knew the *Palmland* or some other train was coming through, its steel wheels striking showers of sparks occasionally from the steel rails of the Seaboard Line, its rumble growing more loudly as it approached, and then fading away as it rolled on through the night.

But for the three boys in Wake Forest, the next town down the line from Youngsville and in those days a college town of some note, it was a signal of another kind. Once the report of the train's klaxon reached their young ears, the three would have only just enough time to hurry across White Street which ran parallel with the tracks through their town, and then up the berm upon which rested the heavy gravel bed for the tracks. From that gentle elevation of the tracks, the three viewed much of the village made up of small, spare houses owned by the textile manufacturing company, Glen Royall Mill. Would this be the last they would see of those white houses in which hard-working people lived and died, God-fearing folk trying to claw their way out of the Depression? Would Harold soon be rushing home to deliver the devastating news of Ken's violent demise to Grandmother James?

Once the sound of the train reached their ears, the three adventurers had to hurry. To have arrived too early might have been enough time that they would have been found out and sent back to shocked parents and, in Ken's case, grandparent before this folly could be played out. This was a game best attempted in the dark of night. Quickly, the three hurried onto the tracks and took their places sitting almost shoulder to shoulder on a crosstie connecting the glistening steel rails. They arrived just in time to see the distant train whose name was of no interest to them come into sight as it came out of a long curve that turned the line from due south to slightly southwest on its final run into Wake Forest where it would not stop. Nor would it even throttle down to a more cautious speed as it approached Brick Street, a pattern that added even more drama to the actions of the three.

The rapidly shrinking distance between the boys sitting there on the tracks and the speeding train at this point was so great – perhaps more than a mile – that each had ample time to consider his resolve, his bravery, and whether he would be the first to "chicken out" and abandon the tracks. In Ken's case, he had just enough time to wonder even if anyone would truly miss him if he were to perish beneath the wheels of the approaching train.

The train's sweeping, blinding headlight seemed to tantalize the three who sat unmoved on the tracks. This was a game, a dangerous game, for the daredevils, the object of which was to determine the answer to a simple question: which of the three was the bravest? The last to abandon the tracks as the speeding train with all its passenger cars drew near would be the winner. If even one of the three waited too long to leap to safety, he still would win, but would die in the effort. It was a game more about death than about trains.

Ken would remember years later the sensation – some would say the terror – of the game. "It was like that big headlight was lighting up the world," he said as he recalled looking down the track at the big beacon of brilliant illumination sweeping left and right again and again, as he challenged a force for which he would have been no match. "And the closer the train came, the more you would feel that you were just absolutely frozen in place so that you could not move."

But one by one, the boys, their hearts now racing, would break free of the spell and scurry to the safety of the shoulder of the track, or if particularly frightened, to a neighborhood yard even further from the track. There they would wait, the elation of having tempted death and gotten away with it washing over them, until the long train had thundered on into the night bound for its stop in Raleigh another twenty minutes down the line. Through the laughter, some of it the nervous kind, they would decide who on this night had been the bravest among them.

In all the months the boys played the dangerous game, the train never won. All the boys who dared test their own mettle – and the three on this night were not the only challengers of trains in a long summer – always managed to escape death just in time. Almost without fail, the last to give in to the force of the train, to break the mesmerizing sensation of the daredevil competition, was Ken. "All of them were close calls," Ken said. "You just had to be the last one to leave the track.

"We lost one on the tracks," Ken remembered years later. "We called him Bozo. Isn't that some name to call somebody? But I never knew his real name. Just Bozo. Bozo Benningfield, the meanest guy in town. Bozo, the guy who once jumped on my back and hit me over the head with a brick.

"Bozo got one of his legs taken off by a train and he eventually died. But Bozo wasn't playing a game when it happened. He was a grown man and he was drunk."

In late September of 2010, the eighty-one-year-old Ken, a knit sweater warming his strong shoulders against a touch of early autumn, said that the boyhood game of "chicken" he played with his pals "was about as foolish a thing as we could have done." This from a man who knows something of risk-taking.

Though Ken emotionally recoils now at the memory of the potentially deadly game, in a sense it would come to define his very life. In the years to come, Ken would again and again challenge the proverbial trains of his life, staying in a sense on the tracks along his colorful journey longer than other men, cheating death so many times he has lost count.

In another life, he might have been a race car driver, a wildcatter in the oil fields, perhaps even a test pilot. He would have been the firefighter rushing without a moment's hesitation into a burning building to save a life. Fear seems to have been a stranger to Ken for his entire life.

"In my lifetime, I've been blown up twice, I've totaled two cars, I've been shot at more than a few times, I've been beaten to a pulp, I've jumped out of airplanes and had bad things happen doing it, and I've lived through corporate wars and won," he said.

"I never really knew fear. I don't really know what fear's about. I just don't have the normal fear that most people have. I'm not a cautious person. What I am … is the luckiest man who ever lived." Not many people have ever disagreed with that claim.

Kenneth Walton Simpson was born in Roanoke Rapids, North Carolina, just ahead of spring, on March 11, 1929. He was the second of four children in a Depression Era family. Edgar Harold, his brother, was two years older. His sisters, Elaine and Donna, were younger. By the autumn of 2010, only Ken remained. Harold had died August 6 from complications of Parkinson's disease, and Donna in 2009 of emphysema. Elaine was long dead, the tragic victim of a 1966 automobile accident in Norfolk, Virginia.

But in the late 1920's and the 1930's, Southern textiles was as Depression-proof as almost any line of work in the country

Annie Simpson flanked by daughters Donna (left) and Elaine (mid-1940s)

and Ken's mother, Annie, spent her career tending spinning frames or winding machines for what was called "the Old Mill" in Roanoke Rapids and Glen Royall in Wake Forest.

The father, Verney Walton Simpson, who abandoned the family in 1935, also worked at New Mill in Roanoke Rapids, but not as a mill hand. Verney was a bookkeeper earning twelve dollars a week. Annie, his wife, brought home eight dollars each week for her labors in the noise and heat of the cotton mill. Verney Simpson had matriculated well beyond the high school level and, in fact, for a time taught in public schools in North Carolina beginning when he was only eighteen. But if there was academic talent embedded in his genes, Ken, his second son, would seem to inherit none of it.

From early in his life, Ken's lot was as a child in a mostly dysfunctional family. Merely knowing what house to call home was no simple matter for the precocious child. His first home was a mill village duplex in Roanoke Rapids, a house with three identical rooms on each side divided by a common partition that ran the length of the house. It was the type of house that would be referred to as a "double shotgun" house. Theoretically, one could open the front and the back doors and fire a shotgun through the house without hitting anything. On one side was the growing Simpson family and on the other was a family presided over by a likable, friendly man named Willie Cutler.

With his family seeming to break up around him with

the departure of his father, Ken wound up calling both Roanoke Rapids and Wake Forest home. Until he had completed the fourth grade, Ken spent the school years in Roanoke Rapids loosely under his father's control, but was dispatched to the home of his grandmother Susan James in Wake Forest for the summer. By the time he began the fifth grade, Ken was finally living in Wake Forest in the Glen Royall Mill community home of his grandmother year around. His mother also lived in Wake Forest, but had other romantic interests in her life. The result was that, despite Ken's youth, both of his biological parents were then only peripherally in his life.

It was his grandmother James who inherited primary

Annie Simpson with sons Ken (with dog) and Harold (circa 1931)

Grandmother Susan James was the stability in Ken's life (1946)

responsibility for raising the young, active male, and Ken's love for his grandmother grew as he grew. "She died in her sixties in 1947," he remembered years later, "and there's no question that she went to Heaven. She was a wonderful, caring woman."

Indeed, Ken's father would remarry and would have other

Ken (left) with big brother Harold (1932)

Annie Simpson (about 1938)

children from that union and once into his early teenage years, Ken would seldom see his father again. "I learned that when a man has a second family," Ken said, "he usually forgets the first."

As a school child, Ken took only grudging interest in academics and came home again and again with unremarkable report cards. "I was mostly a 'C' student, nothing special," he remembers. His older brother, Edgar Harold, known to most people by his second name, did much better academically, underscoring the fact that the two sons in the family were markedly different in interests and motivation. Yet, if there was a bond of love in the family, it was between these two brothers and it would last a lifetime even though Ken suggests that having him for a sibling could not have been easy for his older brother. "I always admired my brother," he said. "He was so straight, was a good student and he had good sense. I didn't have any of those things, especially good sense."

Even in the choices involving organized religion, the boys were different. "We decided to start going to church, me and my brother," Ken said. "But we weren't going to the same church. He went to the Baptist church and I decided I would go to the

Methodist church.

"There was a reason we went to different churches. Harold went to the Baptist church in a sort of plain building and not very interesting from the outside. But the Methodist church had a steeple. I wanted to go to a church with a steeple."

A framed picture of Harold remains on the mantle in Ken's mountain home, and is still treasured as is the memory of his sibling. And Ken still refers to his brother only by his second name though through thirty-two years of military service, his brother was known most often as Ed.

It may be an exaggeration to say that it was necessary for Ken to fight his way through his childhood, but mostly he did it gladly, the black eyes and other bruises he suffered coming without so much as a whimper. "If there was a fight, I was probably in it," he said.

Indeed, if the young Ken were looking for a fight, it would not be long in coming. "There were a bunch of real delinquents in town," he remembered. "And we were always trying to find something to get into." If it wasn't fighting or sitting on the railroad track challenging an approaching train, it was climbing the water tower that served Glen Royall Mill and the surrounding mill village. More than a few times, Ken with various childhood friends, hopped aboard passing freight trains for rides to Franklinton and back ten miles away, just for the adventure.

But fighting apparently was Ken's forte. He discovered early on that not all his boyhood acquaintances had a taste for knuckles and elbows as he did. When his friend, Irvin Brown, wound up battered and bruised, Ken asked how it happened.

"He said that Delk, the preacher's son who was older and bigger, had beaten him up," Ken remembered.

"'C'mon,' I told him. 'It might take two of us, but you're going to get even.'"

Together the pair, the victim and the apparent avenger, marched off to find the preacher's son, and when they did, Irvin apparently decided he already had done enough fighting and fled the scene.

Ken was left alone to fight it out with the bigger, older, heavier antagonist.

Did he win or lose? "I don't know," Ken answered. "I've had lots of fights in my life like that, but I never was in them to win. Winning was immaterial to me. I just wanted whoever I was fighting to know that I had been there and that I'd never back down. That's just the way I was. Actually, it was the way I was all my life."

More and more, as Ken grew into adolescence, he was expected to pull his own weight, as much as possible, in the Simpson family. Every dime coming into the household was precious so that in the summer of 1940, when Ken was eleven and his brother Harold thirteen, they worked chopping tobacco on a farm almost twenty miles from Wake Forest. For Ken to join those working the tobacco, he even had to be, in a sense, willing to fight for the hot, low-paying job.

But when Donald Underwood, a kid from the mill neighborhood and slightly older than Ken, quit early in the summer, Ken once again sought to join Harold in the fields. Finally, grudgingly, the farmer took Ken on as a laborer. The farmer's attitude did not change with time. He had committed to pay Ken fifteen dollars a month, the same as Harold received from the neighboring farmer. But Ken's boss soon adjusted his pay to a mere twelve dollars a month because, he explained, Ken was only eleven years old.

So, Ken worked the tobacco for three months for twelve dollars a month. Because he was older, Harold earned his promised fifteen dollars a month working for a neighboring farmer whose field was in sight of the one in which Ken labored. When the last tobacco leaf had been put up to cure, Ken got thirty-six dollars for his summer of work, nine dollars less than Harold would draw at the end of his work season on the nearby farm. "That farmer would sell his soul for nine dollars," Ken remembered years later. "He was bad news."

Ken, like Donald before him, decided to quit the job. But quitting didn't work. Ken's mother put him in her A Model Ford beside her and drove him back to the tobacco farm. "She wanted me to buy school clothes with the thirty-six dollars I would earn," he said. "So, she took me back to the fields."

If the wage arrangement seemed unfair, the summer of 1943 started more hopefully, but ended dismally. This time the brothers Simpson were hired on to work the tobacco owned by their uncle and aunt, and it seemed a lucrative offer. Together, the two would be given in earnings whatever an acre of tobacco would yield in profit as their pay for the summer, a deal that seemed vastly superior to that of the summer of '40. The profit on an acre of good tobacco should certainly surpass the thirty-six dollars Ken had earned in that pre-war summer.

But late in the growing season, an earth-shaking thunderstorm rolled through the farm country north of Raleigh leaving a section of the tobacco field under water and ruined for the year. "My aunt's husband – I never called him my uncle - told us that our acre had been the one that was hit the hardest and would have no yield. We got gypped every way you can imagine," Ken said.

At the news that there was to be little or no profit for the summer, Harold moved to Morehead City and had a brief career as a hotel bellhop leaving Ken behind to collect any money that may be forthcoming from the tobacco farmer. There would be none immediately though when he returned to Wake Forest, Harold collected fifty dollars for the work of the two of them which he passed along to Grandmother James.

For almost all of his life, Ken could not avoid personally comparing himself to those around him, particularly his brother to whom he was closer than anyone in his family. Ken was different, especially when he considered the calm, studious nature of Harold.

Ken was quick to fight; Harold was far more reluctant. Ken was at best an average grammar school student; Harold, two years ahead, was at the top of his class. Harold was tall and angular with the look of his father; Ken was on the small side and looked like no one in his family.

But like most young males, Ken loved dogs and there was a canine member of the Cutler family, which shared the mill house duplex with the Simpsons, who stole Ken's heart. Bob was the Cutler's German shepherd and the bond between Ken and the neighbor's dog created a memory to last a lifetime.

Together, Ken and Bob followed older brother Harold to school when Ken was only four and five years old. Harold's teacher regularly invited Ken into the classroom and he would sit at a desk in the back of the classroom with Crayons and coloring books while Harold's class was in session. Bob, ever the faithful companion, always waited just outside the school for his pal, Ken, to emerge.

It was the first of the breed Ken ever knew and the two, the boy and the dog, became virtually inseparable. And the love affair never died; other German shepherds would come into Ken's life and he later became an accomplished trainer winning a number of shows with dogs that followed Bob in his life. In 2011, Simpson was the latest royalty in a long line of champion German shepherds for Ken.

SAILOR BOY

Wake Forest, like most of the rest of the South, in the late 1930s and early 1940s was a black and white world, certainly from a racial point of view, and Ken was one of the few who regularly crossed that line. For several years, in the hours before dawn, Ken would deliver the *Raleigh News & Observer* to subscribers in the college town, some of whom lived in the black section.

Almost everyone in the black neighborhoods came to know Ken's name, and if not his name they were keenly aware of his reputation as a fighter.

"I found out the hard way that one white boy against fifteen black boys just didn't work out very well," he said.

Still, through all the conflicts, friendships were made that lasted for years. Among Ken's black friends was one he knew only as "Knee Baby."

"He was kind of like Bozo; I never knew his real name either," Ken said. "But we got along. I saw Knee Baby years ago and introduced him to my daughter. Knee Baby had grown to be a big man, a lot more than a knee baby, 6-feet-4 and more than 200 pounds."

There was another bigger fight brewing in Europe and it had gotten the attention of the slender North Carolina newspaper delivery boy who still was but a child himself. Despite the fact that he was not yet into his teenage years, Ken watched with a strange excitement the developments that led to World War II, and it came to consume him.

Though only twelve years old on December 7, 1941, Ken reacted to the Japanese attack on Pearl Harbor as did Americans everywhere. And he had one question above all others:

Where's Pearl Harbor?

"There was a man who lived in Wake Forest who had been in the Marines," Ken said. "I asked him where it was. He said it was in the Hawaiian Islands. But I didn't know much about the Hawaiian Islands, so that didn't mean much to me either.

"But I had this strong feeling that I ought to do something to help those men who had gotten caught up in the attack at Pearl Harbor. Of course, there wasn't much I could do."

Even from pre-school days, Ken had been interested in the military. "I always thought it would be wonderful to be in the military," he said, though there was one pointed matter about being a soldier or sailor that troubled Ken. "The only thing was," he said, "they gave you shots, and I didn't like the idea of taking those shots."

But, with or without vaccinations, the attack by the Japanese turned that interest in becoming a military man into a virtual obsession. Great Britain was under withering attacks from the Germans. According to the daily headlines in the *News & Observer* he delivered, the Pacific Fleet had been decimated by the sneak attack at Pearl Harbor, and America was at war and looking for fighting men. "I Want You" Uncle Sam posters were popping up everywhere.

Though the fighting war had not come to the shores of the continental United States, it touched the lives of people, including Ken's, across America in a myriad of ways. Young men he had seen in the neighborhood were no longer there; they were going off to war once the United States wound up with a two-front fight of its own. Wartime manufacturing, including that in textiles, was being ramped up. That had an impact on everyone Ken knew because it seemed that everyone he knew worked in the nearby mills, or were members of mill families. More often now, Ken and his buddies watched as military equipment – principally tanks and trucks – came through Wake Forest on flatbed rail cars on the Seaboard Line. And there were times, mostly shortly after nightfall, when the world seemed to grow dark in one of the practice "blackouts" that were staged as part of civil defense drills, and radio stations stopped broadcasting for a time to counter the possibility that German bombers might follow radio frequency beams to the very heart of Wake Forest if not the very street on which Ken lived with his grandmother.

Even the 1942 Rose Bowl football game, Ken read in the *News & Observer*, had been moved to nearby Durham because of the perceived Japanese threat to the West Coast following Pearl Harbor. In all, the news on the home front indicated that the United States was preparing for a difficult global war.

If there was going to be fighting, Ken wanted to be a part of it. Though still far too young to volunteer for military service, Ken plotted ways to do just that. Unquestionably, Ken wanted to be a part of the big fight the war would bring. Though only twelve, he reported to the Armed Services Recruiting Station in Raleigh to sign up. "Nobody wanted me," he said.

"How old are you, son?" one of the recruiters asked Ken.

"Eighteen," he lied.

"Well, we'd be glad to have you," the recruiter said. "All you have to do is go home and get your birth certificate and bring it to me. It has to be a birth certificate that hasn't been altered."

Temporarily prevented from enlisting on that technicality, Ken had no intention of waiting what seemed a lifetime to become a soldier or sailor. Not with a war raging.

Again and again, Ken tried to find a way around his youthful looks and the age problem it represented and almost two years after the attack on Pearl Harbor, his break came.

"My brother said we ought to arrange to get drafted, and that's all I needed," Ken said.

Bernard Dixon, one of Ken's childhood friends, also was

interested in signing up, and the two, neither of whom met the minimum age requirements, stepped up to register for the draft on August 25, 1943. It was a date that Ken had to remember so that the lie that was taking form in his head would not fall apart; he claimed it as his eighteenth birthday, though he was only fourteen years and five months old on that date. But his word was considered his bond, shaky though it was; this time, to merely register, no birth certificate was required and no age-related inquiries were forthcoming.

The first chance to disrupt Ken's plans came when he made an appointment with local physician Dr. Dodd at the Army's direction for a pre-induction physical examination. During the routine checkup, Dr. Dodd marveled at Ken's youthful look. "I never knew you were that old," Dr. Dodd said, accepting as fact that an eighteen-year old male on the verge of manhood stood before him.

Ken did not bother to confirm his true age even to Dr. Dodd.

His preliminary physical now a part of his record, Ken's "greeting" came in the mail in November, 1943. He was to report for induction at Fort Bragg on December 1.

In the hour just before dawn on the appointed day, Ken's grandmother awakened her fourteen-year-old grandson. "I got dressed and she fed me," he recalled. "She fed me a lot. She said she wanted me to weigh all I could weigh, and then got me out the door and on my way.

"She probably was relieved to see me go."

Harold also had hoped to follow his younger brother into the military, but an ear drum problem would eliminate Harold, at least temporarily, from becoming a soldier. Ken was the only one of the three to make it through the induction obstacle course. He was off to war.

But Harold was not far behind. His familiar name changed

to Edgar in keeping with the military tradition that first names are first names, Harold volunteered for the Marine Corps at the age of seventeen and was accepted for induction.

"I never did like for anyone to pick on my brother," Ken said. "But I didn't have to worry about that any more. Anybody who can go through training at Parris Island has to be tough and my brother had become pretty tough himself."

But in early December, 1943, Ken did not yet know with which branch his own military future would lie, if indeed there was to be a military future. He knew that he still faced hurdles because of his youthful looks plus his claim of being eighteen years old.

And it didn't take long for the suspicious military to put Ken to the test once again.

He had thought about the differences between the Army and Navy, and wondered with what service branch his future might lie as he rode the bus to Fort Bragg near Fayetteville, North Carolina, for his pre-induction physical. He had heard that the first requirement of a draftee into the Army was to walk a great distance with a 100-pound pack on his back. On the day he was to face his first physical examination, Ken weighed only 119 pounds.

"I didn't imagine I would get very far carrying a backpack that weighed almost as much as I did," he said. If one could volunteer for specific branches, therefore, he would choose the Navy.

But when at Fort Bragg Ken stripped down and got into line with all the other naked draftees awaiting physical examination, he tried to look as inconspicuous as possible for fear that his true age might betray him. And when someone pulled him out of line and told him an officer needed a word with him, Ken's heart sank. Had his still-developing young body betrayed him?

Still undressed, Ken was shown into a nearby room where an Army officer sat behind a desk. "No matter what he asks me," Ken reminded himself silently as he entered, "I've gotta have the right answers. I've gotta prove to this man that I'm pretty worthless back home."

"How old are you, young man?" the officer asked.

"Eighteen. Eighteen last August 25," Ken lied yet again.

The officer seemed unimpressed. On December 1, 1943, Ken was 5-foot-8, was sleight of build, and still had the look of a child. The officer doubted that Ken was yet shaving. But without clear evidence that Ken was much younger than he claimed to be, the officer had little recourse. Ken was about to become a military man-child.

"Well, tell me about your family," the officer continued. "Any brothers or sisters?"

"One brother, two sisters," Ken said matter-of-factly.

"Older or younger than you?"

"All three younger," he said, catching himself on the verge of telling the truth.

"Well, tell me about yourself," the officer behind the desk continued to press. "How do you feel about getting drafted?"

"It came at a good time for me," Ken responded, now building a story on half-truths. "I've been out of work. The only job I've been able to get was delivering newspapers.

"Plus, my grandmother – I've lived with her the last few years – needed to get me out of the house. I was a lot of trouble to her. Always getting into fights and stuff like that. You know how it is."

"Yeah," the officer said. "I know how it is. You like fighting?"

"I don't run from any fights, if that's what you mean," Ken said truthfully this time.

"Didn't you do anything to help your grandmother?"

"Not much. I just couldn't get a job, except for a paper route, and that wasn't much help."

"Sounds like you're a good man for the Army," the officer said, writing something on a form that lay before him and dismissing Ken to return to the line of naked men awaiting physical examinations.

"That was that," Ken said years later. "All I had to do from that point on was try to get away with it. I kept wondering, are they going to catch me?"

But on the day of his induction, as Ken waited his turn to be probed and inspected, he was not certain whether he had won or lost in the brief exchange with the Army officer.

Though there were more questions about his age from the medical staff that administered the examination, Ken finally passed and could once again get dressed. Then he was shown into a large room in which there were four large desks with the service branches marked over each – Army, Navy, Marines and Coast Guard.

Despite the Army officer's observation that he might be just what the Army was looking for, he quickly got into the line in front of the desk marked Navy. Once he had signed all the papers, Ken was back on the bus for the return trip to Raleigh and the swearing-in ceremony. On December 8, 1943, he would be heading to the Navy Training Center at Bainbridge, Maryland.

As Ken rode north as a military passenger on a train out of Raleigh that would rumble over the very tracks on which he and his buddies once sat testing their bravery, it was almost without question that he was one of the youngest draftees in the United States since the Civil War.

When Ken stepped from the train in Bainbridge, the first of two surprises struck him. "It was cold as hell," he remembered. "There was snow all over the place. I told myself right there that I should have joined the Army. At least I'd be at Fort Bragg right now and I'd be a little warmer."

Just off the train, Ken and all the other newly sworn sailors were issued all the gear they would need while they were in training at Bainbridge. They were ordered to pick up their gear and walk the three miles to their barracks.

"So, there I was, lugging all that gear. And once again I knew I might as well have joined the Army."

Ken was about to face yet another reality. "I kept getting

into trouble at Bainbridge," he said. "The problem was I was fourteen years old trying to think like an eighteen-year-old. Turns out there's a lot of difference in the way you think at fourteen and at eighteen."

Ken, the 14-year-old sailor (1944)

Though suspicions about Ken's true age persisted, he still managed to get through training at Bainbridge, and then was shipped to Norfolk, Virginia, to await orders to deploy with his outfit.

Ken wouldn't be among those shipping out on time, however. In a time when such slogans as "Loose lips sink ships" served as warnings to people with even minute knowledge of troop movements, Ken discovered that misplacing his military identification card was seen as a

Ken's 1944 Bainbridge graduating class (he's on Row 1, third from left)

serious breach of security.

When he reported that his identification card was missing and inquired how he might get a replacement, Ken was ordered to get his gear and return to the personnel office.

"They put me and my gear in the back of a pickup truck and said that I would be temporarily assigned to 'Unit X'," Ken recalled. Unit X turned out to be a prison for all sailors who were under arrest on various charges, some of them serious offenses. Ken would be confined with them for two weeks.

"When I went to jail, there was reason to be concerned because it was my first experience with wild people. Of course, it was a prison in the truest sense of the word. It had a fence around it to keep us in and guards on duty to keep us in line," Ken recalled.

"The worst part about it was that we had to drill from six in the morning until after dark every day," he said. Among the drills was one in which the sailors in ranks were ordered to place their rifles in an "at rest" position in front of them. Yet "at rest" did not mean that the hands and arms could relax. As the moments of "at rest" dragged on, Ken felt the burning in his arms and slightly relaxed his position. What he did not know at the time was that by simply looking down the ranks of sailors, instructors could instantly spot anyone not performing the exercise perfectly, and Ken stood out as a slacker.

He was ordered out of line. "They gave me my sea bag. It was a very heavy bag. And they put me on top of a trash dumpster and told me to stand there without putting the sea bag down, even for a second.

"You could move it around as much as you wanted, but you could never let it touch the top of the dumpster," Ken said. "And they left me there for a long time. It was a pretty good lesson to other sailors who had thought about easing up. By the time they let you come down, you were hurting all over from keeping that heavy sea bag off the dumpster. I thought it was going to kill me.

"Then when I got down, they shaved my head again. The hair had just started to grow out from the last shaving, and they did it again.

"It was a good experience, though. They wanted to toughen me up and it was a good place to go to do that. And in the evening, I'd really enjoy it. I would lay there on that top bunk and listen to all these old sailors talk about places they'd been, ports they had visited, and about the world they had found there. There were stories about Europe, Asia, and particularly China. They were fascinating to the boy sailor.

"There seemed to be a lot of excitement in all of their lives. They told stories of big fights, and getting thrown through windows, and stories of amazing things they had seen. I loved it. It was absolutely wonderful listening to all those stories at night when you're bone-tired."

In the privacy of the top bunk, and at nights for two weeks, Ken could once again be a wide-eyed fourteen-year-old with dreams of sailing off to exotic places. "I just hated getting my head shaved again," he said. "Once I got off the dumpster, I didn't give anybody any more trouble." Ken had been transformed. He was fourteen going on eighteen, a child growing quickly into a man.

Ken's confinement came in a two-week period in which the unit to which he had been originally assigned drew its orders. So, all the familiar faces already were at sea when Ken was released from Unit X. And Ken soon would be with a new group of new sailors.

"I never knew where that original outfit went, or what happened to them," Ken said. "I heard they went to North Africa, but I don't even know that for sure.

"What I am sure of now, looking back, is that those two weeks in the brig changed the course of my life one way or the other. And it might have saved my life."

One-Way Ticket from Leyte

By the time Ken was on the train with 200 other sailors bound for Orange, Texas, the United States had been at war for more than two years and the nation's ability to produce airplanes and ships for battles in the air and on the seas had been phenomenal. Already more than 40,000 bombers and fighter planes for the Army Air Corps had been placed into service in just over two years, and a number of new craft added to the Navy's fleets. At the same time, American manufacturing was, as it had been since 1941, bolstering the British Fleet and its air armada.

One of the new ships scheduled to come on line in early 1944 was the USS *Edwin A. Howard* (DE 346), a destroyer escort named in honor of a Marine corporal. It was the ship to which Ken would be assigned and it would sail for the first time out of Orange and the facilities of the Consolidated Steel Corporation on January 25, 1944.

Within days, the *Howard* would be officially christened and members of the ship's first crew were given printed invitations which they could use to invite friends and relatives to witness the event. Ken mailed his invitation back to Wake Forest and to the eighth grade teacher he had respected so much, Pearl Ray. "I was told that she seriously considered making the trip to witness the christening," he said, "but she wasn't able to."

The *Howard* was a John C. Butler-class destroyer displacing 1,350 tons and armed with two five-inch guns, four forty-millimeter guns, ten twenty-millimeter guns and three torpedo tubes. She also could lay down a pattern of deadly depth charges in the event of German U-boat or Japanese submarine attacks using her eight depth charge projectors, her hedgehog projector and her two depth charge tracks. Her mission was to sail with destroyer convoys bound for Europe and later for the Pacific, and to run escort for merchant shipping through the treacherous waters of the North Atlantic and to Naples and North Africa.

Few of the men on board knew the legend of the man whose name the ship carried. On November 3, 1942, with the war still in its early stages, it had been the duty of Marine Corporal Edwin A. Howard to reestablish vital lines of communication on Guadalcanal under enemy fire. He was mortally wounded in trying to move one of his fellow Marines, who also had been wounded, to safety. Corporal Howard was posthumously awarded the Silver Star.

The Edwin A. Howard (DE-346), Ken's ride into the North Atlantic, the Mediterranean and the Pacific (1944)

The *Howard* would be home to Ken and 200 of his closest friends for just more than a year. For Ken, it would be an eventful year, though less from the war itself than from within. "In 1942, it was hard to get from the United States to Europe without getting sunk," Ken said. "But by 1944, the United States had pretty much cleaned out the U-boat threat. A lot of them were lying on the floor of the Atlantic."

Indeed, it was on one of those first escort assignments for the Howard that the fourteen-year-old child claiming to be eighteen came through once again. The call to battle stations had come in late morning and the 201 enlisted men on board, many of them wearing only their skivvies, hurried to their assigned duties in the event of battle. A German U-boat had been discovered in the area and the Howard was ready to respond.

The thought that this could be the final day he would live never crossed Ken's mind when the call to battle stations came. "Nothing could happen to me," Ken said, referring to his state of mind at the time. "I just didn't think about such things.

"There was never any mental anguish for me. I was the kind who never worried about things. After all, I was just a kid at war."

The *Howard* remained at the ready for hours as the 201 enlisted men and fourteen officers, including Lieutenant Commander F. Denfield who was the first to take the helm of the new ship, searched the sea to the horizon for any sign of German submarine movement.

After six uneventful hours that had for Ken turned into hours of boredom, he slipped away from his forty-millimeter gun battle station and made his way below to the ship's galley. To get to the galley, he had to breach the water-tight seals which were activated soon after the battle station announcement had come. The seals were a part of a system designed to keep the ship afloat even if it were bombed by air or by torpedo. Working alone, Ken forced his way into the dining area which had been abandoned just as the staff had left it when the call to battle stations had come. Ken, himself assigned to kitchen duty, was in familiar surroundings.

Hungry as any teenage boy would be, he found a lemon pie and sat down back of one of the food counters and began to eat the pie. There he was discovered by the engineering officer who had come to investigate the breach in the water-tight seal. The officer threatened to bring court martial charges against Ken and ordered him back to his battle station. No charges ever were filed.

"Well, to tell you the truth, I was never concerned about German submarines," Ken said in 2010. "After all, I'd never been sunk. But that was the way a fourteen-year-old boy thinks.

"The war must have been a lot more exciting in '42 and '43 than it was by the time I got into it in '44.

"But the whole damn war was an adventure for me. It wasn't like I was old enough to be involved in anything but school. But by the time I finally got in, in 1944, it was pretty obvious that the enemy by then was on the run.

"If I could have been in during '42, I really would have been happy."

As it was, acting like a man was a challenge for Ken. "Clearly," he said, "I just couldn't stay out of trouble."

Even merely serving food to shipmates was not without challenges.

Ken was assigned duties as one of the ship's servers in the galley and his job was to place food on trays as the hungry sailors passed down the line. The key to a smooth operation in the galley was in the system, Ken was told. Again and again, the cook in charge of the meal instructed all the servers to keep the line moving.

And usually keeping the line moving was no problem. The challenge for Ken arose when for the first time fried chicken was on the menu.

"Just put a piece of chicken on the tray and tell 'em to keep moving," the cook instructed Ken.

The plan worked fine until a burly sailor from engineering stopped the line to complain about the piece of chicken Ken had placed on his tray.

"Keep moving," Ken said, following the cook's instructions.

"No, sir," the engineer said, "not until you give me that piece of chicken right there." He pointed to a particularly plump breast of chicken.

"You got your chicken," Ken responded. "Keep moving."

Instead of moving on down the line, the engineer reached for the breast of chicken, but his hand never made it that far. Ken buried the tines of the serving fork in the back of the engineer's hand. In an instant, the big engineer went diving across the gleaming steel fixtures where the food had been lined up for serving and clearly had the upper hand in pounding away at Ken until the master of arms came to Ken's rescue and pulled the still-angry, still-bleeding engineer away.

"I'll tell you one thing," the big engineer said, grimacing over the pain as blood trickled from his hand, "this ship ain't but 300 feet long and I'll find you. If you got any guts, I'll see you on the fantail when you're through down here."

Ken's comment weeks earlier on the day of his induction physical back at Fort Bragg that he never ran from a fight was one of the truthful comments he made in those days. And when he was finally off duty in the galley, Ken made his way to the fantail and spotted the engineer, his right hand now wrapped to protect the wound Ken had left there.

Ken tapped the big man on the shoulder.

"I'm here," he announced. For ten minutes, though it seemed more than an hour, the two sailors brawled away with Ken at a distinct size disadvantage. How he accounted himself is not recorded, but when the last punch had been thrown Ken sported an assortment of scrapes and bruises, including two black eyes left swollen and almost closed. His foe had similar reminders that he too had been in a fight, and a now-battered and bandaged right hand to show for his trouble.

Though the two sailors would continue to serve aboard the same ship, there would be no more battles between the two. When the two were released from sick bay, the big engineer came close to offering an olive branch. "You won't have any more trouble with me," he promised Ken.

Ken had collected a scar over his left eye that would for years after remind him of his fight with the big engineer, and he had the satisfaction of having responded to the challenge, which also was typical of the thinking of a fourteen-year-old boy. Seaman Simpson had not backed down.

Apparently, the Navy agreed with Ken's juvenile assessment that the U-boats were not nearly the threat they had been in the opening stages of the war and in the months leading to the United States' entry into the global conflict. It ordered the *Howard* back to the United States after a limited number of escort assignments in the Atlantic and the Mediterranean and it sailed into the Brooklyn Navy Yard near the end of October, 1944.

"That first night, the cook went ashore and didn't come back," Ken remembered. "I had to cook breakfast for 200 men and Lyonnais potatoes were on the menu.

"I'd never fixed Lyonnais potatoes before and had no idea how to do it.

"They turned out like that stuff you use when you make papier mache. And when the line formed for breakfast, there was real trouble," Ken said. "The first obstacle was how to get the spoon out of the stuff. Everything was sticking. And we damn near had a panic in the kitchen because they said everybody's lips were sticking together."

In early November, with the *Howard* berthed in the Brooklyn Navy Yard, Ken passed another personal milestone. Though he was only fifteen years old and technically ineligible to vote in the presidential election of 1944, the ballot was available to servicemen all over the world and Ken cast one illegal vote for Franklin Roosevelt who was seeking a fourth term. It would have been neither the time nor the place to reveal his true age, he reasoned, so Ken cast his ballot.

The crew of the *Howard* survived the breakfast of Lyonnais potatoes, the single vote did not alter the election, and the ship sailed south on November 10 with an experienced cook on board and crossed from the Atlantic to the Pacific through the Panama Canal heading for the Far East and Leyte Gulf in the Philippines where one of the greatest sea battles of the war was yet to take place.

In a sense, though a war was on, the trip to Leyte was the sort of journey that Ken could never have imagined back home in Wake Forest. The *Howard*, which had a fuel range of 6,000 miles, made two refueling stops en route, the first in the Galapagos Islands, though there was no time to study the endemic species that Charles Darwin earlier had discovered there. It also would make a stop in Bora Bora. And Ken did appreciate the species found there, the beautiful women of Bora Bora.

"I had never seen anything like Bora Bora," he said. "All those beautiful women in grass skirts, beautiful lagoons with water so beautiful it was a deep blue, perfect weather, just the kind of setting that I thought looked like a movie set. I expected Dorothy Lamour, the famous actress, to show up at any time.

"Nobody knew where Bora Bora was in those days, and it took them twenty or more years to find out. Now, everybody wants to go to Bora Bora."

But the *Howard* was not on a cruise to paradise. No one knew it at the time, but its destination in the months ahead was more like hell.

The ship's final stop en route to its destination was in Manus in the Admiralty Islands and for the first time Ken got a glimpse of what war was about. There, berthed so close that one theoretically could have walked to the dock across the deck of one warship after the other, was the largest flotilla, from troop carriers to destroyers and escorts, Ken would ever see in one place.

"When I saw that," he said, "I finally realized that this was a big war being fought by small people, and being a part of such a big thing was exciting."

What Ken had seen was the staging operation for the invasion of Luzon in the Philippines. This time, the *Howard* would not be involved in the operation and on January 6, 1945, the *Howard* arrived in Leyte Gulf, The Philippines, for the first time to reinforce Destroyer Squadron 49 on submarine patrol. She also drew the assignment of escorting a convoy through from The Palaus to San Pedro Bay. En route, in stormy weather and rough seas, a message reached the *Howard* that a Japanese submarine was trailing the convoy. The *Edwin A. Howard* was ordered out of the convoy line to possibly engage the submarine.

But as the *Howard* came about in rough seas, she collided with one of the destroyers she was escorting, hitting the bigger vessel mid-ship. The impact threw sleeping sailors out of their bunks and, assuming they had been hit by enemy fire, perhaps a torpedo, they rushed to battle stations. The destroyer was not severely damaged, but the *Howard*, its bow crushed, had to be towed back to Leyte for repairs.

The crippled destroyer escort was tied up opposite the repair ship which was a permanent fixture on Leyte. And as some of the crew, including Ken, watched from the fantail of the *Howard*, they saw a large row boat making its way across the water toward the repair ship. As it drew closer, it was clear that the people in the boat were mostly women. The sailors on the *Howard* watched as the row boat was tied up just aft of the repair ship and the women began to climb aboard. While the *Howard* crew watched, men on the repair ship began to line up for a bit of time with the local females.

"Everybody on the *Howard* was starving for the touch of a woman," said Ken. And when one of the sailors nearby wished out loud that the women would also visit the *Howard*, Ken had an idea.

"I can make that happen," he said.

"And how would you do that, sailor?" a lieutenant asked.

"Well, sir, I could go get their boat and if they want it back they'll have to come over here to get it."

"Why don't you do that, sailor?" the lieutenant suggested.

Ken considered it an order. He quickly pushed his pants to his ankles, kicked them aside and dived off the fantail. Quickly he covered the distance with members of his crew cheering him on and he grabbed the rope and cut the boat free. Hurriedly, he climbed aboard, and then realized he had never piloted a row boat before, and this was a big row boat at that so that reaching oar locks on opposite gunnels was close to impossible for one man. Even if he had managed that problem, Ken knew little about how to keep the boat going in the direction he sought.

There was now another problem. About the time that he climbed aboard, the tide began to recede and it appeared that he would be swept out to sea in the pilfered boat. Another sailor, realizing the problem Ken was facing, then leaped from the *Howard's* fantail and swam quickly to his aid. Together the two sailors finally pulled alongside their ship, secured the row boat there with the shortened rope and climbed back onto deck.

Ken's reign as a ship's hero was short-lived. He was summoned to the bridge to face the ship's executive, Lieutenant Shriver, one of the fourteen officers on board, and after a brief discussion was given a captain's mast, the Navy equivalent of a court martial.

The order called for nothing more than a slap on the wrist. "There wasn't a reduction in rank," Ken said, "because I didn't have enough rank that it could be reduced. And the possibility of spending time in the brig never came up. The captain's mast also never appeared on my official record.

"It was a minor thing," Ken said years later. "I just had to take the boat back and then do six hours extra duty. I expect all the officers kind of laughed about it after I left.

"But those Philippinos were mighty pissed off that I had taken their boat, but they were glad to get it back, too."

Ken could not have known at the time that his assignment to the *Howard* already was drawing to a close as the ship stood in for repairs. When she returned to Leyte from a subsequent escort mission, one of the officers told him that the Department of Navy had confirmed that he had not been truthful about his age when he signed up for the draft and that it had been discovered that he was too young by military standards by almost four years.

Ken never knew how the Navy came to learn his true age, though for a lifetime he has suspected that his Grandmother James, with whom he had lived before the war, had become concerned and had informed the military that he was vastly underage.

Ken nevertheless was handed a document, his orders to leave the ship and to report to the commander of the Western Sea Frontier. He was to find his own way home to Wake Forest, North Carolina, perhaps with the help of the commander of the Western Sea Frontier. Ken was ferried to a dock in one of the *Howard's* whale boats, then walked ashore.

The beach on which Ken came ashore from his last day on the *Howard* was the same beach on which, only slightly more than four months earlier, General Douglas MacArthur had waded ashore fulfilling his famous promise that "I shall return." There were no combat photographers there to snap Ken's picture as he stepped onto a makeshift dock that extended fifteen to twenty feet into the water.

For Ken, it was not a return, but a departure.

"Here I was, carrying my belongings on my back, walking ashore at Leyte," Ken remembered in 2010. "I started to walk into town, wondering what I would do and how I would get home." One of the first buildings he saw was a white structure that had a sign out front: Commander, Western Sea Frontier.

Ken climbed the steps to the building and tried the door. It was locked. He peered through a window. He could see no one there though it was the middle of the day. He found no sign indicating when the building would again be open for business. He sat down on the steps and waited. The wait dragged on for an hour, then two, and finally three hours or more.

Now he began walking, hoping to reach Tacloban, the island's largest town, before dark. "It was the only town I knew anything about, and it was twenty-five miles away," Ken said.

Within an hour, Ken flagged down a truck with as many as

a dozen Navy Seabees riding in back.

Ken tossed his bag in and climbed in after it.

"Where you heading?" one of the Seabees asked.

"Wake Forest, North Carolina," he answered.

"We won't be going that far," one of them laughed.

The truck and its human cargo bumped on along the road for a time and finally Ken noticed a military insignia that seemed a bit familiar.

"What Seabee group are you guys from?" he asked.

"The 61st," one of them answered.

"The 61st?! Did you guys ever hear of a guy with the 61st named McDouglas?"

"You talking about 'Beachhead' McDouglas?" one of the Seabees asked. Ever since Chief Petty Officer Charles McDouglas had been the first American to step ashore on Samar when the Navy arrived, pushing the Japanese at least temporarily out of the important Pacific outpost, he had carried the "Beachhead" nickname.

"Yeah, I guess that's what they call him," Ken answered feeling his way through the exchange.

"He's our boss," the Seabee said. "CPO McDouglas."

"He's my uncle," Ken said quickly, once again not bothering with accuracy. "Beachhead" McDouglas indeed might have at some time become his uncle had not the war come along. He once had dated Ken's Aunt Neva.

"Is uncle McDouglas with you guys now?" he asked.

"Sure is."

"I'd sure like to see him. Where can I find him?"

"He's over on Samar (the island adjacent to Leyte), and that's where we're going," one of the Seabees answered.

"Mind if I ride to Samar with you?"

"Don't see why not. We can't get you to North Carolina, but we can get you to Samar."

CPO Charles "Beachhead" McDouglas was more surprised

to see Ken than Ken had been when he was booted off the *Howard.* "The last time he had seen me, I had been in grammar school back in Wake Forest," Ken said.

"What you doing out here?" "Beachhead" asked the kid with the familiar face.

"I was in the Navy and I was on the *Howard*," Ken answered.

"Man, I didn't know you were that old," "Beachhead" remarked. "Seems like the last time I saw you, you were just a kid. You were in grammar school, weren't you?"

"That's right. When you were dating Aunt Neva."

"So, kid, what are you doing here?"

"Well, they kicked me off the *Howard.* Found out I had lied about my age to get into the Navy. They told me I'd have to find my own way home. How am I going to do that, Beachhead?"

"Something will come up. We'll find a way."

The familiar face and the confident word was what Ken needed.

For two weeks, enough time to find a ship scheduled to return to the United States, Ken stayed with his aunt's former boyfriend. It was a fortunate development in more than one way, not the least of which was that CPO McDouglas was in possession of a marvelous ice machine in a place where ice was like gold.

When word came that a ship, a troop transport called the *USS Monterrey*, would sail out of Leyte bound for San Francisco and had room on board for an underage sailor, Ken said his goodbyes to "Beachhead" and returned to Leyte where he temporarily surrendered his orders and was assigned sleeping quarters in a tent. The ship would sail in the darkness before dawn.

But when Ken awakened the next morning, dawn had just broken in Leyte and he was alone in the big tent. All the other men bound for the United States had departed and Ken's orders, a part of the personnel package for the group, had gone with them.

"They could have awakened me. But nobody gave a damn," Ken said.

Once again he was stranded on Leyte, now without orders

to bring legitimacy to his quest to get home.

"Beachhead's" quarters on Samar seemed the only route open to Ken, and he returned and explained his situation once more to the man who might have been his uncle. There Ken met another chief petty officer whose original orders also had sailed east on the Monterrey, but without him.

"Not a problem," a yeoman said after hearing of Ken's and the CPO's plight. The yeoman sat down at a typewriter and in ten minutes had pounded out two sets of orders back to the United States, orders that were counterfeit, but almost identical to the original ones.

It was a talent that amazed Ken. "I decided right there that if I ever got back into the Navy, I wanted to be a yeoman," he said.

Though fake, the new orders were done well enough to be accepted again at the departure terminal on Leyte, but the problem now was there was nothing scheduled to anywhere on the West Coast of the United States for days, perhaps even weeks.

So, Ken waited, hoping that another troop ship might hold the key to his return home. He checked in regularly. Nothing was available, at least nothing to the U.S.

"How'd you like to go to New Guinea?" a clerk asked Ken. "Got a destroyer heading to New Guinea."

"That's closer to the United States than the Philippines, isn't it?" Ken asked.

"Yeah. A little closer. But not a lot."

"I'll take it."

Using his fake orders, Ken successfully checked in on the destroyer. His berth for the Pacific crossing from Leyte to Hollandia in New Guinea was one of the destroyer's whale boats. Ken then hitched passage on yet another destroyer for the rest of the trip to Manus in The Admiralty Islands, also a part of Papua New Guinea.

Ken remained in Manus for three weeks hoping once again that he would be able to hitch a ride aboard another ship either to the United States or the Hawaiian Islands. Such transports rarely visited The Admiralties.

Finally, an ocean liner that had been requisitioned to transport troops, appeared on the horizon and berthed at Manus. The *SS City of Paris*, once a British luxury liner, would be taking Ken back to the United States.

The *City of Paris* was the third in a line of ocean liners named for the French city of light, and she already had a war history. On September 16, 1939, with 139 passengers aboard, she had struck a mine that had been laid by German submarine U-13 more than a week earlier. Though one person died in the explosion, the *City of Paris* managed to limp to port for repairs and shortly after she became sea-worthy again, the British government had requisitioned her as a troop carrier.

Ken's time on the *City of Paris* started well. He was shown to a stateroom in which he expected to be comfortable for the duration of the trip. But within a day, the crew discovered that he was not an officer but merely a lowly enlisted man and moved him three decks down and left him to find comfort sleeping in a hammock.

The ship sailed from Manus under the direction of what Ken considered an unusual crew. "It was a Hindi ship then," he said. "Its crew was all Hindis. They all wore turbans, went barefooted and all had bad teeth."

If the ship had been of the luxury class before the war, she was hardly the epitome of luxury in 1944. Her decks were made of wood and the only food on board, Ken recalled, was a grease-laden lamb stew cooked daily in large, black pots, similar to those Ken remembered were used in the washing of clothes over backyard fires back in North Carolina in the years before the war.

"I wasn't going to eat that slop," he said.

The only alternative was found in the poorly supplied PX on board. There Ken found English lemonade and hard candy and that became his diet for twenty-eight days as the *City of Paris* steamed slowly eastward toward the Marshall Islands and then on to Hawaii and San Diego.

Along the way, with the *City of Paris* briefly at anchor in the Marshall Islands, Ken celebrated his sixteenth birthday. He was exactly two years too young to be drafted into the military.

Ken, though still but a slender if well-built teenager when the voyage began, lost fifteen pounds by the time the *City of Paris* pulled into port at Camp Elliot in San Diego. But Ken was not ashore in the United States yet. He and other military enlisted men were ordered to scrub down the transport ship prior to their departure.

When Ken finally stepped ashore, it was April 13, 1945. The flags were at half-mast. President Roosevelt had died the day before in Warm Springs, Georgia, and Harry Truman was the new president and commander-in-chief.

Ken would remain at Camp Elliot for two weeks before his discharge from the Navy became official on April 28 and he could begin the last leg of his journey back home.

By comparison to the *City of Paris*, the train seemed very fast indeed. In just five days out of San Diego, he had arrived in Salisbury, North Carolina, and then made a connection that would get him to Raleigh and almost home.

For all the rest of his life, Ken would remember the trip home from Leyte as the most adventuresome part of his life as a World War II sailor. It was the stuff of which most teenage boys could only dream.

Ken's ship, the *Howard*, would have a distinguished role in the war in the Pacific in the months after Ken was sent home. During the famous Battle of Leyte Gulf, the *Howard* screened minesweepers operating off the coast and covered the landings. She then escorted reinforcements from Morotai to the beachheads.

The war over and the battles won, she sailed from Samar on November 28, 1945, for the United States and was placed out of commission and in reserve on September 28, 1946. She was sold for scrap in 1973.

The Battle of Leyte Gulf was seen as the turning point of

the war with Japan and has been called the ultimate naval battle in history. The Japanese Navy was never again the potent power it had been through the early months of the war, and the devastating defeat signaled a change in sea strategy for Japan which from that point until the Enola Gay lifted off with the atomic bomb aboard used kamikaze air strikes as its primary weapon in naval engagements.

Ken was a civilian teenager again. But his military career had only just begun.

No Hero's Welcome

World War II was the last great conflict in which the United States welcomed her returning warriors with great adoration and adulation, especially following VE (Victory in Europe, May 8, 1945) Day and VJ (Victory over Japan, August 14, 1945) Day. Yet, almost no one marked Ken's return to Wake Forest and no one offered to organize a parade in his honor.

By the time Ken had virtually hitchhiked his way from Leyte in the Philippines to North Carolina, the tides of war had changed in Europe in favor of the Allies and soon would be changing similarly in the Pacific with the Battle of Leyte Gulf. But the contributions that Ken had made, though only a child at the time, were not a cause for celebration in Wake Forest.

Yet, though one of the youngest, wasn't he also among the most brave of them all? Barely a teenager, didn't he have more to lose in life expectancy, if nothing else, if he were lost in battle?

While those things may have been true in Ken's case, his return home was decidedly a non-event.

"When I got back to Wake Forest, nobody asked where I'd been," he said in 2010. "I was nothing when I left to go into the military, and I was nothing when I got back.

"I don't think anybody knew where I was when I was in the Navy, and I'm not sure anyone, except maybe my grandmother, cared."

There remain no treasured letters home or hand-written news from friends and relatives, because none was ever written. No one hung a blue star mother's flag in any window in Wake Forest in honor of Ken.

No one knew Ken would be home before the war had run its course and, indeed, few residents of Wake Forest knew he had defied the reality of his age and had signed up for service. And so it was logical that when he arrived in Raleigh by train from Salisbury, then paid his way onto a Greyhound bus for the short ride to Wake Forest, no one was there to meet him at the station. No one to rush to greet him, no flags waving, no one to say how well he looked, and he wasn't offered bits of local gossip to let him know what had been happening since he had been away.

For Ken, it had been a simple matter of elimination that led to his decision to return to Wake Forest. Apparently no one would have come searching for him had he decided to stay in San Diego where the *City of Paris* had finally docked. Or if he had left the train at any point along the five-day journey from the West Coast.

"I was about as independent as a body could be," he said in 2010. But he decided to return to Wake Forest because that's where he had grown up, it was the only place he called home at the time, and it was the place he knew best though there were no strong family ties drawing him back. His family had never been a tight-knit one and it already had disintegrated long before Ken had become an adventuresome teenager going off to war. He had lived with his Grandmother James on White Street before the war and returned to her hearth when he walked home alone from the bus station on his return. It was as though he perhaps merely had stayed a bit long at the corner grocery and was now home once more.

By the time the war had come to an end, both Simpson brothers had served in the Pacific and when the Japanese finally capitulated, Harold was a private first class who served in the

Marine Corps on Okinawa, once the scene of some of the bloodiest fighting of the war on the western front.

Harold Simpson, USMC (1945)

If there were normalcy in Ken's life, it would emerge to some degree again when Harold came marching home from the Marine Corps, first on leave and later permanently. And some aspects of life were much the same as they had been before Ken had gone away.

"When I got back, I did what I wanted to do and I came home when I wanted to come home," Ken recalled. "The only governor I had was in my head."

In that, Ken was most fortunate. "I was smart enough to know that I needed an education," said Ken who had finished only the eighth grade when he had lied his way into the military. It was still an era in which in some families high school educations represented the pinnacle of academia. Though the trend began changing late in World War II, especially with soldiers and sailors getting second chances at educations because of the GI Bill, few young people who grew up in cotton mill villages aspired to continue their education at the college level. Nor did Ken at the time. Still, the Navy experience had become important to Ken as a motivating factor in his decision to continue his high school matriculation; he had taken written examinations early in his Navy enlistment in a roomful of sailors, some of whom, he realized, were fundamentally unable to read test questions.

Back home in Wake Forest, Ken would return to high school as a ninth-grader and in the process take advantage of the GI Bill which paid him seventy-five dollars each month while he was attending classes. "I had lots of friends helping me spend that seventy-five dollars every month," he said. "It never lasted more than a week."

His enthusiasm for school work also was short-lived, though he persevered. "After the adventure I had just experienced, high school seemed awfully dull," he said. "It was boring, being in high school. I had been all over the world already, and I was eager to continue the trip."

The continuation of the trip would have to wait. There were high school classes to mildly challenge Ken, and though he had never been taught the fine points of how to drive an automobile nor did he possess a license to operate the vehicle, he now had a car, a 1937 Packard purchased in the summer of 1945.

"I didn't have any idea you needed a license to drive a car," Ken said. "I'd never heard of such a thing. But then nobody I knew owned a car." Driving a car without a license, he decided, was a bit like joining the Navy before he was old enough. Both could be considered illegal.

And not only was it illegal, in Ken's case it was dangerous. On the day he purchased the car, Ken knew so little about how to operate an automobile that he had not yet learned the art of stopping a car. On occasion he accomplished the task simply by hitting, though softly, the back of the garage at his grandmother's house.

He caught on to the proper use of the brake pedal quickly.

Warned that he could be fined for driving without the proper accreditation, Ken reported to the Highway Patrol testing center. The examiner sat him down before an array of traffic signs.

"OK," the burly sergeant commanded, "tell me what the signs mean."

"They don't mean anything," Ken responded. "None of

them has any writing."

"Don't you know the shapes?" the sergeant asked.

"All I know is they're all different shapes."

He was sent away with a driving handbook in his possession and told to return when he had studied its contents. Being licensed wasn't the only thing Ken did not know about automobiles.

But Ken was a licensed driver in the winter of 1946 when he and a school friend decided to drive the sixteen miles to Raleigh "for no particular reason," he said. En route to Raleigh, Ken's Packard was sideswiped by a Chevrolet containing soldiers from Fort Bragg who were on their way to Pennsylvania. The Packard seemed to have survived the wreck better than the Chevrolet in which the soldiers were riding.

Ken and the soldier driving the Pennsylvania-bound car stood at the side of the road discussing the accident. "How much money do you have?" the soldier asked Ken.

"Eight dollars," Ken answered.

"We'll take the eight dollars," the soldier said.

Already, it was beginning to snow and Ken and his friend were ready to drive back to Wake Forest. It was then, with the soldiers already on their way northbound, that Ken and his passenger discovered that the collision had damaged the headlights as well as causing a scar down the side of the car. Even so, Ken thought the eight dollars was worth quickly sending the soldiers on their way.

Although Ken in later life would develop a love for exotic automobiles, he knew almost nothing about cars when he purchased the Packard. And the Packard taught him important lessons in that regard, among them that automobiles require not only gasoline, but oil as well.

Emotionally, Harold was easily Ken's closest relative. Though the brothers were markedly different in their interests, they shared the memories of their childhoods and teen years well into their retirement years. Among the memories were the scuffles that naturally developed between brothers. And their mother remembered those times as well. She once said, Ken remembered, "that she wished that just once Harold would beat the hell out of me," Ken recalled, "because maybe that would have made a difference in my life.

"We fought often enough that Dad put us in a room together one time and told us to fight it out. He wanted us to get it out of our systems."

And the discussion brought back a rare warm feeling about their father so that the two brothers, who also were close friends, decided to drive the Packard to Roanoke Rapids where their father still lived with his growing second family.

Verney Simpson knew little more about automobiles than his two sons, but when he rode in Ken's Packard, he was curious.

"Is there anything wrong with this car?" he asked.

"We've got troubles, but I don't know how big they are," Ken responded.

The two brothers would find out in a North Carolina snowstorm. They would drive their father back to his home, then started the trip back to Wake Forest as snow began to flit past the windshield in only light flurries. But the snow grew heavier and accumulated on the windshield at a rate faster than the balky wipers could sweep it noisily away. In order to slowly continue on their route to Wake Forest, the brothers had to frequently keep an eye on the snowy road ahead by looking out the driver's side and the passenger side windows. In that numbing condition, the two made it about forty miles back in the direction of Wake Forest until near Macon on U.S. 158 the car seemed to explode then skidded across the road and into a roadside ditch.

The engine, warning for a long time of its doom in a noisy death rattle, had thrown a rod through the engine block. The Packard had come to the end of its journey, but the boys still had much of the trip home ahead and waited in a cold railroad station near Macon for twelve hours for the next passenger train, one that did not stop, as did none of them, in Wake Forest. The brothers would travel on to Raleigh and find a way back home from there.

Three weeks later, Ken and Albert Caudle, a friend of Ken's, drove back to Macon in Albert's A Model Ford. Using a chain on his A Model, Albert towed the dead Packard, with Ken steering, slowly back forty-nine miles to Wake Forest. There, Albert, who was a mechanic, discovered that the engine had blown from the loss of oil caused when the oil pan had not been securely tightened and the precious oil had been left on the highway between Macon and Roanoke Rapids.

It had been a memorable trip. Ken would see his father no more than two more times before Verney Simpson died in 1956.

Ken's return to Wake Forest was not without some special interest. Ken and Sue Carroll had begun the first grade together years earlier and they had remained friends through what Ken called his delinquent years. If no one else, Sue was apparently pleased that Ken was back in town.

The relationship between the two would slowly develop into a serious romance in 1947. But in his first weeks back in town, Ken also was still trying to replace the excitement in his life that his time in the Navy had brought.

Though sports had not been a magnet for Ken in his early years, unless one counts dodging speeding trains a sport, he now sought his excitement in high school football. He saw the game as an outlet, at least temporarily, for his nervous energy. And Ken became a defensive star.

"I guess my aggressive nature made me a contender for anything physical," Ken remembered. Though weighing only 135 pounds, Ken led his team in tackles and overall was the best defensive player on the squad. He was involved in almost half of his team's tackles in his ninth grade season, 1945, and was even more dominant as a tenth grader a season later.

There also was a payoff that Ken had not anticipated. It was on the football field that one of the most important relationships of Ken's life developed. Though the school's football coach, Joe Hinerman, took most of his players under his wing, Ken felt that here was a man who cared about him perhaps more than any male in his life with the exception of his brother Harold. "He took a lot of time with me," Ken said, "and anybody who did that was important to me.

"Joe was the kind of guy that if you ever met him, you were going to like him. He was just a good guy."

Hinerman placed Ken at the blocking back position in the single wing offense and at linebacker on defense, in both cases because Ken seemed to take great satisfaction at hitting other players.

Like several of his players including Ken, Hinerman was a World War II veteran as well and not until Ken was into his own golden years would he discover that his old coach also had heroic war stories to tell.

Hinerman, a captain in the Army Air Corps, had been assigned to the crew of a bomber in Europe during the first half of the war and when his plane was hit by German antiaircraft fire and pitched out of control, Hinerman had bailed out behind enemy lines. A German farmer watched as Hinerman floated down into one of the fields in which the farmer raised crops.

When the farmer, armed with a shotgun, approached Hinerman, he ordered him in broken English to lie on the ground face down. Hinerman had no choice but to comply. As the farmer drew closer in what Hinerman thought would be his final moments, the German farmer saw a distinctive ring on Hinerman's right hand bearing the unmistakable insignia of the Masons.

"Are you a Mason?" the farmer asked, pointing to the ring.

"Yes," Hinerman nodded, hoping to impress the farmer.

"Then I will get you back through the lines and to safety," the farmer promised. And he had kept his promise and Hinerman had survived the jump into German territory and had returned to North Carolina to teach algebra and to coach.

With that sort of perspective impressed upon him from

Wake Forest High 1946 football team. Ken is No. 28 on the second row, Coach Joe Hinerman also is on the second row.

his time over Germany, Hinerman worked to round his football team into shape. He himself had been a product of Wake Forest College just across town from the high school, so he understood first-hand that the high school football team wasn't likely to make much impact upon the local populace with a college team only a stroll away on a perfect autumn day.

People with names such as Brian Piccolo and Norm Snead would eventually make headlines in town as college football players, and the Deacons were coached by the colorful D.C. "Peahead" Walker.

But there was at least one advantage to being so close to a college program. When Wake Forest College purchased new football uniforms for its team, Coach Walker offered the ones being replaced to Hinerman and the high school team. It was a welcomed gift, and Coach Hinerman dispatched Ken and two other players to the college with a wheelbarrow to bring back all the uniforms they could get. It took more than one trip to haul all the uniforms back to the high school gymnasium.

By the time the 1946 high school season had begun, another veteran was home from the Navy and playing football for Wake Forest High School. Bud Wadford was stocky and weighed about 180 pounds and played tackle. He arrived in good shape from his time in the Navy as an athletic instructor. And like Coach

Hinerman, Wadford liked the way Ken hit.

"Ever think about fighting?" Wadford asked Ken.

"Been fighting all my life," Ken answered.

"That's not what I mean. Boxing. Did you ever think about boxing?"

"Not really."

"I can train you and I think you'd do OK in the Golden Gloves."

Ken said he had taken a lot of licks in his life. He even had played in football games since he returned from the Navy when he wasn't sure where he was, perhaps because of concussions. So boxing had an appeal to the tenth grade veteran.

So Bud Wadford had a job coaching a fighter, and Ken knew he always had been a fighter. Spending time in the Navy had not changed that aspect of his personality. And his fighting still was not confined to the ring.

In early January, 1947, Ken wound up in the middle of a classroom fight. "Somebody did something to provoke me," he said, "and I never missed an opportunity to fight. It's funny what you can do when you have a temper like I had."

His history teacher, Anne Hetrick, was not impressed with Ken's temper or his fighting ability. She marched Ken to the principal's office for disciplinary action.

Anne Hetrick (Kennedy), 9th Grade history teacher (mid-1940s)

He was expelled from school for a month. Which worked out well for the young fighter.

"I spent the month working out getting ready for the Golden Gloves tournament in the school gym," he said. "Nobody was mad at me, so they were happy for me to use the gym during my suspension."

(Sixty years later, at a school reunion held at a restaurant that now occupies the building on Main Street where Tom Holden's drug store once served townspeople, Ken met Anne Hetrick Kennedy again. He presented her a gift of Waterford crystal on behalf of the class. From the reunion and until her death in June 2011, Anne Hetrick Kennedy had been a friend of the Simpsons and an annual house guest in their mountain home.)

Ken's training for the Golden Gloves tournament was going well, and as the tournament drew near, he realized he had a problem. He had spent most of a month working out in old knitwear and had no boxing trunks suitable to wear into the ring in Raleigh.

He asked Herb Appenzeller, a former Wake Forest football player who had helped Hinerman as a volunteer coach of the football team, if he happened to have any shorts he could borrow.

Herb had gone to his football coach, Peahead Walker, with just such a request earlier in the autumn when he had hoped to compete in the North Carolina collegiate track meet at Chapel Hill as an unattached sprinter. Coach Walker had tossed him a pair of white shorts.

When Dr. Herb Appenzeller was inducted into the North Carolina Sports Hall of Fame in 2010, Ken read about his selection in a news bulletin mailed to him by one of his former high school teachers, Anne Hetrick Kennedy, a member of the North Carolina Museum of History Associates. He phoned Herb and after sixty-three years thanked him for sharing his white shorts.

"How'd you do in the shorts?" Ken asked Herb.

"Should have won in the sixty-yard dash," Herb responded. "I won the first two heats, but jumped the gun on the third, so on the re-start I was a little flat-footed because the starter made sure I couldn't time the gun, and I finished second.

"How did you do in the Golden Gloves?"

"I finished second too," Ken answered. He won the first two bouts, and then lost a controversial decision in the championship.

The story on the tournament finals appearing in the *Raleigh News & Observer* included this paragraph:

"Eldred Williamson of Whiteville won the junior lightweight title against Kenneth Simpson of Wake Forest on a decision which again set off loud protests from the spectators."

"I guess those shorts finished second twice," Ken said to Herb with a laugh.

Legal at Last

As winter was taking its last shot at North Carolina in 1947, Ken was counting down the days. He long ago had decided that in March he would enlist once again in the Navy, this time legally. He was about to turn eighteen and he could prove it.

This time, he wouldn't have to worry about the tap on the shoulder, the suggestion that he get out of line for questioning, nor the comment that he looked much younger than other young men of the same age. Yet, Ken's return to the military would be no simple matter.

In the re-enlistment process, Ken was asked for his discharge papers from his previous aborted stint in the Navy as an underage seaman. There was a problem. At the age of sixteen, when Ken had made his way home from Leyte he had received a discharge "under honorable conditions." At the time, the three words – "under honorable conditions" – seemed benign. Now, he was being told that in the eyes of the military, there was an important difference in having a discharge "under honorable conditions" and in having an Honorable Discharge.

The turn of events made Ken more angry than disappointed, and he fired off a pointed letter to the Secretary of the Navy protesting the "honorable conditions" designation. The protest worked, and quickly the discharge Ken had received at the age of sixteen was officially changed to "Honorable." There were no more hurdles remaining before signing on once again, this time legally.

(The problem had a silver lining for Ken, however. Now "honorably discharged," he wondered about mustering out pay he should have received at the end of his earlier period of active duty, even though he had been too young. He filed a request for back pay and received a check for $300.)

Ken re-enlisted in the Navy on March 4, 1947, one week exactly before his birthday, and he was to report to the Navy in Norfolk, Virginia, on his special day.

This time, everything went smoothly even if, to Ken, there no longer was the adventure of a shooting war to stoke his enthusiasm. Indeed, many of the ships he had seen in his previous time at sea, including the *Howard*, already had been taken out of commission and placed in reserve. Most would never again sail in the troubled waters of world conflict.

19-year-old Seaman Ken Simpson (1949)

Within days, Ken's world journey was on once again and once again he was outward-bound on a troop ship through the Panama Canal, and then north along the West Coast of the United States to Treasure Island in San Francisco Bay. There those being deployed out of Norfolk, including Ken, would change ships for the long journey to the Western Pacific. Their new military home would be on Guam, a thirty-mile long spit of sand and surf and the largest island of the Marianas chain.

The Japanese had captured Guam on December 8, 1941, only hours after the attack on Pearl Harbor and had held the strategic Pacific outpost for two and a half years. The Japanese were finally forced from the island by invading U.S. forces in 1944 and by the time Ken arrived in 1947, Guam was becoming a choice overseas assignment for American servicemen and their families.

It was the families living in government housing to which Ken was first assigned. Though the war was over, the compound serving the naval base at Sumay was guarded by Navy personnel around the clock. Theoretically, there remained a low-level threat, a holdover from the United States' invasion of Guam. Though the surrender of Japan had long-since been signed on the deck of the *USS Missouri*, Japanese soldiers who had been left behind from time to time came walking out of the inland jungle. And American military installations on Guam sought to prevent such random appearances from taking place in civilian housing compounds through round-the-clock surveillance.

Ken drew the assignment of patrolling the neighborhood at night.

"When almost everybody else was sleeping, I was awake," Ken said.

But these were happier, peaceful times and it was on one of his late rounds that Ken was offered something new to his diet, a slice of pizza from the wife of a Chief Petty Officer who lived in the neighborhood to which Ken was assigned. He had never tasted such a cheesy treat or anything so wonderful, he thought.

Night duty was a schedule that worked well for Ken. It gave him time to resume his schooling which led more quickly than he had expected to qualifying for his high school diploma through the military's General Educational Development (GED) program. If Ken had been only a marginal student back home, he was much more academically inspired on Guam and the diploma came in the mail from Wake Forest High School Principal Rufus

Forrest. With the sheepskin, Ken had taken a necessary step to the Navy rank that most interested him. It made him eligible to apply for temporary duty to the yeoman school at San Diego where he would spend four months learning all sorts of marvelous things that Navy yeoman were expected to be able to accomplish.

Ken had decided almost three years earlier, when the yeoman on Leyte had typed up the counterfeit orders that got him passage on ships home, that he someday wanted to be able to provide that same sort of magic as well.

Already, this second tour of duty had been vastly different for Ken compared to the first when he had gone to sea as a sailor and a vastly underage fighting man. And one of the ways it was different was that letters were being exchanged between Ken and Sue, the girl back in Wake Forest with whom Ken had started the first grade. The relationship was growing warm.

But October 1947 also brought the news of the death of his Grandmother James with whom Ken had lived and whose home was the only stable home he had known in his childhood. He returned to Wake Forest on leave but arrived too late to attend his grandmother's funeral. He used the occasion to visit with Sue.

Even then, there was no discussion with Sue about the future, and whether they would spend it together. "Looking back, I guess we just assumed that someday we would marry," Ken said.

Ken's term in yeoman school would fall in a perfect place on the calendar as well. The school would close down in mid-session for the Christmas 1947 holiday and though in his earlier enlistment there had been little to turn him toward home, there was love now to tug at his emotion. Sue Carroll was still at home back in Wake Forest and the pretty little girl with whom Ken had begun first grade years earlier had become a beauty. Sue and Ken had been writing regularly since he had returned to the Navy and seeing her at Christmas was now possible.

Such a trip wouldn't be easy. But Ken liked challenges and

his cross-country odyssey this time would provide more than an ordinary one.

A friend from back home in Wake Forest, A.R. Perry, was attending college a long way from home, at San Luis Obispo about two hours north of San Diego, and the two friends hatched a plan. Ken knew of three other sailors who were anxious to get home to North Carolina for the holidays, and the five of them would share driving A.R.'s Chevrolet and A.R. would get fifty dollars per man for the trip. In an era before interstate highways, the five set out hoping to average fifty miles an hour. Stopping only for gasoline – at about nineteen cents a gallon – and food, the five made it home for Christmas.

Another Wake Forest sailor, Jackie Brown, also was home for the holidays after completing half of his boot camp introduction to the Navy in San Diego, and he and Ken were scheduled to report back to the California base on the same day. They would make the trip back to the West Coast together hitch-hiking all the way. Getting to Dallas and almost halfway would become the easy part even though the ride they were able to flag down to get from Atlanta to Birmingham was with a bootlegger who thought that having two service men as passengers would be a good thing if revenuers caught him. The trip to Dallas otherwise went smoothly, but on New Year's Eve, it began snowing in the east Texas transportation hub.

The two sailors, hoping for better weather west of Dallas, climbed aboard a Greyhound bus on New Year's Day 1948 bound for Amarillo.

"When we got to Amarillo, there was a foot of snow on the ground. I didn't even know where Amarillo was," Ken said, "except that it was out there somewhere fairly close to New Mexico."

Though it was freezing and the storm showed no sign of relenting, Ken and Jackie start walking and trying to hail a ride from anyone going west through the blizzard. Finally they were successful in stopping an old pickup truck with a radiator wrapped in a burlap bag to keep it from freezing.

"Where you heading?" the driver called to the two snowy sailors.

"Roswell, New Mexico," Ken called back through the gale. If they could only make it to Roswell, they would get help he thought from his brother Harold, then a mechanic in a B-29 bomber maintenance squadron, who was stationed at an Army Air Force installation there.

"Not going that far, but you can ride a ways with me," the driver said.

Now a seasoned hitch-hiker, Ken's philosophy was to never turn down a ride that would get him closer to his destination, and the old truck was heading west through the snow. The two sailors dressed in their Navy garb with Navy pea coats buttoned tightly against the winter and the collars turned up against the savage winter weather, tossed their belongings into the bed of the old truck and climbed into the warm cab.

The ride west ended in the desolation of a lonely crossroads on an Indian reservation in New Mexico. Finally out of the snow, but still in freezing temperatures, the two sailors began walking west.

"We'd walk and hitch a ride, walk some more and hitch another ride, and it went that way all the way to Roswell," Ken said.

"I tell people that it was the time I walked across New Mexico." Finally, they shared a warm meal with Harold in Roswell, but the visit had to be brief; there were too many miles yet to cover and the time for the two to check in back in San Diego was drawing near.

Once more in Roswell, Ken and Jackie, who together had little money for the journey, turned to Greyhound to continue their trip to the coast and Ken read the passing signs flashing past beside the westbound highway.

"You're in Billy 'The Kid' Territory," one of them read.

They rode on through The Kid's country until they reached the end of the line, the most distant point west that their funds would take them. It was yet another place in the Arizona desert, this time west of Phoenix.

"We counted our money," Ken said. "Between us, Jackie and I had eight dollars and twenty-five cents left. And eight dollars would get one of us to San Diego. We flagged down another passing bus and I put him on the bus and I began hitch-hiking alone."

Ken had twenty-five cents in his pocket. He finally walked into a truck stop somewhere in western Arizona.

"The truckers felt sorry for me and kept buying me coffee. I drank that coffee all night hoping for a ride on to San Diego, but none of the truckers were heading in that direction."

Near five in the morning, a car arrived at the lonely truck stop and gassed up.

"You wouldn't be heading to California, would you?" Ken asked the driver.

The driver looked Ken over before answering. Ken still wore a Navy uniform and a Navy pea coat, but both looked as though they had been slept in, as indeed they had. Still, though not certain that he ought to accept that this was a real Navy man so far from a Navy base, the driver finally relented.

"Going as far as El Centro," the driver said.

Ken would be his passenger, and efforts to hitch-hike from El Centro to San Diego would pay off quickly. Ken arrived at his Navy base in time to sign in before he would have been considered Absent Without Leave. Ken had arrived only slightly more than an hour before his deadline to sign in.

Jackie Brown had arrived only an hour earlier by bus.

Once he had graduated from yeoman school, Ken returned once again to Guam where he would serve out his tour of duty, this time as a yeoman to a Chief Petty Officer in the administration building at Sumay.

For Ken, it was a fortunate pairing. His boss had been a boxer and had volunteered to serve as Ken's trainer if Ken were interested in resuming his brief ring career that had begun in the

Golden Gloves tournament in Raleigh earlier in the year. The CPO would not only be Ken's trainer, but his sparring partner as well. And Ken began to work as hard as a boxer as he had in attacking his studies at yeoman school.

He would spend long hours in the evenings doing "road" work, except that in Ken's case the road work was, in reality, beach work. He ran for miles evening after evening along the sandy beaches of the Pacific outpost and tested his training with exhibition fights every Friday night in the base theater. There, Ken always had his own cheering section, the dozen sailors with whom he shared Quonset hut living quarters at Sumay.

Ken would be tested further in the ring in an inter-service match across the island in an area being used by the Army. He was matched up with a soldier in the same weight class and though it was a difficult fight, Ken won on a decision.

Ken discovered after the fight that the men in his Quonset hut had pooled their resources and had placed a bet of $1,000 that he would beat the Army boxer.

"I didn't know it until after the fight," Ken said. "And when I found out, I was mad as hell.

"If they had lost that $1,000, they would have hung me. That was a lot of money. We didn't make but about $100 a month, so ten or twelve guys bet what amounted to a month's pay each on me."

In a sense, Ken retired as a boxer on Guam, and the final bout made retirement from the ring seem a good idea. "I went against a man who was a Marine Corp welterweight champion," Ken said in 2011. "And he hit me pretty good in the testicles, a low blow, and I went down on one knee."

Ken had never been knocked out in his ring career, but this time he had come close. "The referee was standing over me and people were yelling a lot of things to me," he said. "But the only thing I heard was 'Get up! Get up!" He got up, and the Marine came on the attack once again, going for the knockout. He didn't get it, but there was little doubt that this loss had not been as close as the one in the Golden Gloves tournament back in Raleigh months earlier.

The next day, with Ken feeling soreness in every muscle and his face still puffy from the blows landed by the Marine, a stranger approached him. Ken remembers his name only as Lippincott.

"Ever think about turning pro?" Lippincott asked.

"You're talking to the guy who lost the fight," Ken reminded the stranger. "Don't you want to talk to the guy who beat me?"

"I saw the fight," Lippincott answered, "and I know that I can take a man who can take a punch like you and make a champion out of him."

"I'm not that man," said Ken. To borrow a well-known movie line, Ken never looked back on the incident, nor did he wonder if "I coulda been somebody."

For Ken, there would be other fights that would not be sanctioned and on which there would have been no bets. He worked nights now as a bartender in the NCO Club at Sumay, a place in which non-commissioned officers would go in the evenings to relax and let off a bit of steam, sometimes too much steam.

"I remember working this particular night when the club was filled with people," he said. Among the crowd was Barrett, a sailor from Denver and one of Ken's neighbors in the Quonset hut.

"Barrett had a big mouth," Ken said. "I knew that. And on this night, his mouth got the best of him. He started mouthing off to this big sailor, an Indian with a bad temper."

While tending the bar, Ken heard a commotion and looked up to see the Indian land a devastating blow into Barrett's midsection. "I thought he was going to kill Barrett," Ken said.

Ken leaped over the bar and hurried to the fight where Barrett stood pinned against a wall and clearly over-matched. Ken grabbed the big man by the yoke of his shirt, whirled him around and hit him landing a solid blow. Chairs and tables were being pushed aside like a scene from a movie.

Then the big man arose and moved toward Ken hitting him as though making a football tackle and driving Ken across the room with yet more tables and chairs bouncing around because of the physical nature of the confrontation. The Indian backed Ken past the bar over which Ken had recently leaped and close enough so that Ken could reach a whiskey bottle. Grasping the thick glass bottle by the neck, Ken shattered it over the big man's head ending the fight and leaving the big sailor to regain consciousness on the floor.

It had not been a happy return to the hut after the fight for Ken. He called out to Barrett the moment he entered the hut the night of the fight. Still nursing bruises from his part of the fight, Barrett had little to say, and Ken did most of the talking.

"You son of a bitch," an angry Ken said as he stood almost nose to nose with Barrett. "I'm probably going to have to fight that big son of a bitch again. It's not over. You can bet on that.

"If you ever do a thing like that again, Barrett, I'll just let him kill you."

For days, Ken feared the fight was not over. On a daily basis, he had to walk past where the big sailor worked and for days he expected to see him again, this time to threaten him well removed from handy whiskey bottles.

That confrontation never came.

Mister, Can You Spare an Airliner?

On December 12, 1948, Ken boarded yet another troop transport for a slow-boat trip back to the United States where he would have up to thirty days of leave time, then report for reassignment. He watched Guam slowly disappear over the horizon as the ship steamed away heading east for Seattle. For ten days it would churn its way through the Pacific and for the first five of those days Ken would be consumed with thoughts of getting home to Sue for Christmas, though that seemed unlikely at the time.

The ship was scheduled into the Port of Seattle on December 22, and under normal circumstances it would take much longer than the three days until Christmas for Ken to hitchhike his way diagonally across the United States to Wake Forest, North Carolina.

Still, he pondered the problem again and again and kept coming up with the same solution: the only way to be home no later than Christmas Day was to fly. But on a seaman's pay, flying in the traditional manner was too expensive.

As usual, Ken had an idea.

The first challenge, he realized, would be to contact an airline company representative in Seattle. How does one do that from a troop transport in the middle of the Pacific Ocean?

Ken visited the radio room on the troop transport and

there he began to ask questions of the radioman on duty. It was a yeoman-to-radioman conversation and, Ken believed, yeomen could solve problems.

"Do you think you can do a radio hookup with one of the airlines that flies out of Seattle?" Ken asked.

"I can try," the radio operator responded, and he went to work from the middle of the Pacific trying to contact one of the airline companies. Finally, there was a voice on the speaker, a sales representative for a Seattle-based airline company.

The radioman informed the sales rep that the call was coming from a troop transport, and then he turned to Ken.

"What do you want to know?" he asked Ken.

"Ask him if I could charter a plane?"

"Ask him what?!" the radio operator said, obviously surprised.

"Tell him that there are a bunch of sailors on board who need to get to the East Coast. Washington, New York, some place like that, as soon as we can once we dock."

The radioman was still stunned that a third-class yeoman would have such an aggressive plan. Still, he relayed the question to the crackling voice coming over the ship's radio.

"Are you asking about chartering a plane to the East Coast?" the voice asked, now not bothering to hide his own surprise at the audacity of the plan.

"Tell him that's exactly what I'm asking about," Ken instructed the radio operator.

"That's affirmative," the ship's radio operator said into the microphone before him, warming now to the challenge.

"Just a moment," the man responding in Seattle said.

There was only static growing louder and then soft again coming from the speaker and it continued so long that both men wondered if the voice would ever return through the interference in the connection. Time seemed to hang heavy now while Ken and the radioman waited. Finally, the radio was crackling once again.

"Our scheduling department says we can put on a plane

for a hundred people. Where would you like to go?"

The radio operator was now smiling as he witnessed a plan coming together. "Tell him we'd like to go to Washington, D.C., and then on to New York," Ken instructed him.

"Washington, D.C., and New York City, sir," the radioman said into his microphone.

"We can do that," the voice confirmed.

"Ask him how much it will cost," Ken instructed.

The radio operator relayed the question.

"We'd have to have $10,000 for a one-way flight from Seattle via Billings, Montana, and Minneapolis, Minnesota, and to Washington, D.C., and then on to New York," came the response.

"And he can take a hundred people?" Ken asked.

"That's what he said," the radio operator responded, then verified the number of passengers with the airline representative.

"Tell him I'm Yeoman Kenneth Simpson and I'll take it. Ask him to meet me at the dock when we arrive."

The drastic plan was in motion. If it came together, Ken would be in Wake Forest well before Christmas Eve. He would deplane in Washington, D.C., and depend upon Greyhound to deliver him to Wake Forest.

Now, all Ken had to do was to find ninety-nine other sailors wanting to make it home on the East Coast for Christmas. Each one would have to pay a mere $100 for the one-way flight. For the remainder of the trip, Ken told as many sailors as he could about the arrangements he had made and provided a signup sheet for those who wanted to reserve a seat on the charter. There were more than enough sailors willing to pay the $100 for the flight east.

"I could have signed up 200 before we got to Seattle if we'd had another plane available," Ken said.

When the ship docked in Seattle, the airline representative was there as planned finally locating Yeoman Kenneth Simpson in the crowd, and together the two waited as the sailors mustered to draw their pay. Ken and the airline representative stood at the exit point and collected $100 each from the 100 sailors who had signed up for the flight. The unlikely tour group then made its way to the airport where they boarded the unusual charter flight home for Christmas.

They all would be home for the holidays and most would remain at home as the New Year arrived. And so it was for Ken, and for a time he and Sue would be inseparable.

In the next year, Ken's travels around the world would become more adventuresome and his letter-writing relationship would continue with Sue. He would be assigned duties as a yeoman aboard an ocean-going refueling tanker, the *USS Mispailian*, which would deploy ahead of the Seventh Fleet in order to be available for refueling at remote locations. Among the destinations in the months just ahead in 1949 were Japan, Singapore and Hong Kong. Ken truly had become a world traveller.

But, if Ken thought his brawling days were over, he had one more coming his way, and it happened at sea on the tanker. A shipmate, who had been a Golden Gloves fighter in Washington state, discovered that Ken also had fought in the Golden Gloves ranks back home in North Carolina. And the shipmate wanted to test Ken.

"I'm going to whip your ass," he announced to Ken, then landed one devastating blow that knocked Ken to the deck.

"He knocked me flat on my back," Ken recalled. "So, I'm lying there trying to decide, do I get up or do I take the easy way out and just lay here? But the longer I lay there, the madder I got that he had sucker-punched me.

"I got up. That first blow was a tough one. But it made me angry too and I lit into the guy and I liked to have killed him.

"I'm not sure he got in another good blow after that first one." The antagonist looked at Ken. "I've had enough," he said. The fight was over.

"It takes a lot to admit that you've been beaten," Ken said in remembering the incident years later.

By mid-December, 1949, Ken's tour of duty was almost

over. But he was able to arrange one last leave of absence, and one more adventure as a Navy enlisted man, one more odyssey home to North Carolina when the *USS Mispailian* docked at Long Beach.

Ken began by bumming a ride to Edwards Air Force Base then getting to Dallas on a military hop, something he learned to arrange by typing his own orders as a yeoman. But getting to Dallas was the easy part that December and there was little military traffic available out of Dallas with destinations along the east coast of the United States. Then Ken discovered that a Navy fighter pilot would soon be in the air out of Dallas heading for Norfolk. What could be better?

When Ken asked the pilot if he could hitch a ride in the fighter plane, the pilot perhaps thought he was discouraging the addition of a passenger by reporting that he would have to be equipped with a parachute to ride in the second seat of a military fighter plane. Ken quickly checked a parachute out of the supply room and headed to the tarmac to climb into the second seat. He had strict orders to return the parachute as soon as he could.

"I don't remember what kind of fighter plane it was," Ken said in 2010, "but it was fast. It didn't take long for us to get to Norfolk."

On the ground in the Virginia tidewater country, Ken thanked the naval officer for the lift, took his parachute and headed off in search of the local Greyhound bus station and the trip to Wake Forest. Ken kept the parachute at home with him for about a week. When he started the trip back, he climbed aboard a bus to Norfolk and pushed the parachute into the overhead luggage rack. In Norfolk he caught a hop back to San Diego but was delayed by a Marine Corps guard on his way out the gate.

"What the hell are you doing with a parachute?" the Marine asked Ken.

"Beats the hell out of me," Ken answered. There was a more accurate answer, but Ken wasn't certain the gruff guard would be interested in the longer version.

"Well, you can't check in until you've turned that parachute in," the guard growled.

"Happy to," Ken answered, and hurried off to the supply center ending his odyssey with the parachute. He returned to the ship still tied up at Long Beach.

Though he and Sue had been regularly exchanging letters, they had never talked of marriage.

"I don't remember asking her to marry me," Ken said in 2010. "I think we just assumed that we would someday get married."

That someday came two months later, in February 1950.

Almost immediately after the wedding, Ken faced a potentially life-changing decision of another sort, to accept a Navy assignment to Washington, D.C., or accept a discharge from the military, in essence to remain in the Navy, as he had planned to do before marrying Sue, or test the civilian world as a new husband, a world of which he had never been a part as a married bread-winner.

"I probably would have stayed in," he said, "but my wife didn't want to be a military wife. So I took the discharge."

The newlyweds would find an apartment in Raleigh where she already was employed with an insurance agency with a salary of $135 a month. And Ken would begin preparing for life in the civilian world by enrolling in Hardbarger Business College in Raleigh. Ken drew ninety dollars a month on the GI Bill and supplemented his income only a month after the wedding by joining the Army Reserves, which was more convenient than attending Navy Reserve meetings in another part of town. He was given the rank of Sergeant First Class, the equivalent of his final Navy rank, and drew eight dollars per month as a reservist. The Simpsons were happy in their Raleigh apartment and the world was at peace.

But not for long.

On June 25, 1950, North Korean armed forces invaded

South Korea as a long-festering dispute over the divided country, a holdover from World War II, boiled over.

Back in Raleigh, Ken kept an eye on the fighting and tensions on the Korean Peninsula and as an Army Reservist understood that he could again be called to active duty and that the conflict could finally place him squarely into the middle of a shooting war.

Indeed, his call to active duty came in October 1950, but little changed in the lives of the newlyweds except that Ken now wore an Army uniform to work. He was assigned as assistant chief clerk at the induction station in Raleigh, the same center in which he had lied his way into the Navy almost a decade earlier. But, he continued his business school studies at Hardbarger and earned high grades academically.

Though he had to be guarded about his enthusiasm when he was with Sue, Ken was pleased that a call to active duty had come. "Another opportunity, another war. That's the way I looked at it," Ken said. "I thought it was great. Here I was working toward where I wanted to end up.

"I had to lie to my wife about it. She never wanted to be a military wife, and I kept telling her I had no choice, that they were forcing things on me over which I had no control."

His claim was only partially true. Perhaps complicating Sue's feelings on the matter was the fact that she was now pregnant with the couple's first child.

One of the "forced" issues Ken had discussed with his wife arose at the induction station in the spring of 1951 with the Korean Conflict heading toward the end of its first year. It began with the Air Force captain who was in command of the multi-branch recruiting station calling Ken into his office.

"Sergeant Simpson," the captain announced, "I've been looking over your service record."

Silently, Ken searched his memory, trying to determine what may now be amiss in his file. Signing up years ago when he was far too young had long since become a non-issue, he told himself. So, what could be wrong now?

"Unless I missed something in your record," the captain continued, "I think you may be eligible for a commission if you want one."

It was a development Ken had not expected.

"Yes, sir," Ken quickly responded smartly.

The captain reviewed the requirements.

World War II experience. "I had that, even if I was underage at the time," Ken said.

At least a high school diploma. "I had gotten that, too, even if it was through the GED program on Guam."

And an adequate aptitude test score of 110 or higher. "And test scores were never a problem."

"Do you think all of this is correct?" the captain asked.

"Yes, sir," Ken answered yet again.

"Are you interested?"

"Yes, sir," Ken responded enthusiastically.

"Good," the captain said. "I'll help you all I can. Let's get the paperwork ready and get it submitted and see what happens."

For Ken, the timing seemed perfect. "Everything was legal now and had been for years," he said. "And I was more mature. I was twenty-one years old."

When Ken broke the news to Sue that there was a strong possibility that his rank would change from that of an enlisted man to an officer, it was a good news-bad news event, good that as a commissioned officer his pay would substantially increase, but bad because already United States servicemen were dying in Southeast Asia.

Ken offered his bride his saddest face. "I have no choice," he told Sue.

Though saddened that her husband seemed to be getting closer once again to the military in every way now, Sue reluctantly agreed.

It seemed virtually overnight that his paperwork was

approved and he was called before a board of officers who were meeting at the induction center. The officers would review his application and make a decision. Near the middle of May 1951, the captain called Ken once more into his office at the induction center in Raleigh.

"I just wanted to be the first to congratulate you, Lieutenant Simpson," he said, smiling. The letter appointing Sergeant First Class Simpson to the rank of second lieutenant had arrived.

Second Lieutenant Simpson was to report to Third Army Headquarters at Fort McPherson, near Atlanta. Sue, now expecting the couple's first child, would remain behind in Raleigh and would continue working for the insurance agency. Ken would remain at the post known affectionately as Fort Mac for only two weeks before being sent on to his second assignment as an officer, this time to Fort Jackson near Columbia and in the middle of South Carolina's Sand Belt.

2nd Lieutenant Ken Simpson (1951)

He arrived at Fort Jackson on June 6. Though Ken saw no significance in the irony, he was jumping into a new phase of his military career on the anniversary of D-Day.

"I didn't know anything about the infantry," Ken said in 2010. "I didn't even know anything about the Army.

"But I knew it was hot. It was 106 degrees the day I reported to Fort Jackson."

It would not take long for Ken to prove to the rank and file at Fort Jackson that perhaps no one on the post knew less about the Army than he did. On his first day on the post, he merely followed along and observed a training company at work. When the sergeant in charge of the training asked Ken, "Can you take reveille in the morning?" there was no hesitation.

"Of course," Ken answered.

But as the sun rose at the beginning of another hot day in the sand hills region of South Carolina, the relationship between the sergeant and the new second lieutenant was no longer very cordial.

"Where were you, lieutenant?" the sergeant asked pointedly.

"Right here," Ken answered, though he was surprised at the testiness he detected in the non-com's voice.

"Where were you supposed to be?" the sergeant pressed.

"Well, right here, I guess," Ken answered. "You told me to be up for reveille."

"Lieutenant, reveille means that you're supposed to front the troops when they fall out in the morning, and report their readiness to company commanders."

"That's how dumb I was about the difference in the Army and the Navy," Ken said years later. "In the Army, reveille means a formation; in the Navy, it's the wakeup call. So, here I was, sitting in the office waiting for the music."

Ken was about to face the music in another way and the learning curve would be steep indeed.

At the start of his second week at Fort Jackson, Ken was assigned to teach incoming recruits how to maintain and fire the sixty-millimeter mortar. The officer who had been teaching the use of the weapon had been injured in an accident, and Ken was to be his replacement immediately.

"I've never even seen a sixty-millimeter mortar," Ken protested to a higher-ranking officer. "How the hell can I teach something I've never seen? This is a mistake."

"A mistake?" the officer responded. "It's no mistake and you're going to teach it."

Ken would appeal the order immediately, asking and receiving permission to speak to the regimental commander whose office was in the same building as the one to which Ken was assigned.

"All I had to do was walk down to the end of the hall and ask to see the regimental commander," Ken remembered.

He was called in quickly and just as quickly Ken saluted the colonel smartly and reported, "Lieutenant Simpson, sir."

"What can I do for you, lieutenant?" the high-ranking officer asked without looking up.

"I have a problem, sir. I have been ordered to teach the sixty mortar. How can I teach it if I've never even seen one?"

Now the commanding officer looked up slowly, his chin taunt, his eyes penetrating. "Do you see that little gold bar on your collar, lieutenant?" he asked softly.

"Yes, sir," Ken responded in his best military bearing.

"That signifies to me that you are an expert. That will be all, lieutenant."

It was not the response Ken had hoped to hear, nor did he think it prudent to try to push his case further. But if Ken was stunned at the developments, his neighbors in the off-post apartment complex where he and Sue had become residents must have been shocked. Ken went directly from the regimental commander's office to the weapon room and checked out a sixty-millimeter mortar complete with instruction manual. He drove home, set the mortar up on the apartment lawn, spread the manual before him and began the tedious task of learning which was the business end of the weapon and which was not.

"It was a tough way to go," Ken remembered in 2010. "I was twenty-one years old and I didn't know one end of a rifle from the other. And I had never been on a range."

But that was about to change. On the following Monday morning, there were 200 new soldiers on the range at Fort Jackson ready to begin learning from an "expert" the workings of the sixty-millimeter mortar. A weekend of study had made Ken marginally familiar with the weapon, but the manual had offered no instructions for teaching or how to set up a range for such instructions. But the critiques would be quick in coming.

Ken would learn in the days ahead that range protocol called for the proper positioning of the mortar, with ammunition set to the side, and soldiers at the ready to fire the projectiles at theoretical enemy positions. But there was no semblance of that on the first Monday morning when the post commander, a general, rolled up in a jeep.

The general looked about and then called Lieutenant Simpson to his side.

"Sir," Ken reported sharply as he saluted the man with the stars on his collar.

"Lieutenant, I just wanted to tell you that this is the most fucked up range I have ever seen," the commander growled.

"Sir, I couldn't agree more," Ken responded as the general climbed back into the jeep and sped away.

"I was making a complete ass of myself," Ken said as he remembered his introduction to the Army.

"As I look back now, after all these years, it seems a little hilarious. If I could sit back and look at it, it was like an Abbott and Costello act. But before it was over, I found out about every weapon they had in the infantry. I was an expert before it was over."

A week after the biting critique by the general in his visit to the range, all training officers were ordered to attend a new school for training trainers. "We were teaching and learning at the same time," Ken said.

Sue gave birth on October 2, 1951, at Fort Jackson to a son, the couple's first child. She named him Kenneth Walton Simpson Jr. He would be called Kenny. Ken, with his German shepherd dog at his side, visited his infant son and his mother in the post hospital, and when mother and son were discharged from the medical facility, Ken paid the eight dollars the stay had cost him.

Ken was now settling in as an Army officer and, indeed, became an expert at the sixty-millimeter mortar. For six months, he taught soldiers, many of whom were ticketed for Korea, how to use the weapon proficiently.

"Then I was sent to Fort Benning, Georgia, to learn once again what I already knew," Ken said.

And like the soldiers he was training, Ken too was Korea-bound for a white-hot war.

Annie Simpson (date unknown)

The Dead of Night

It was May 17, 1952, and Second Lieutenant Ken Simpson had just arrived in a remote valley just south of the famous 38th Parallel, the contentious line that separated South and North Korea. He had stowed his gear in a bunker that would be his home for as much as the next thirty days, if he lived that long. He would see action as an officer with the 223rd Infantry Regiment, Second Battalion. He would be assigned to E Company.

Precisely where he was at the moment and to what unit he was assigned seemed not important any longer. There was a war going on and this was the front line in that shooting war.

Everything else that Ken had known in his life seemed mere preparation for this moment. It was as though he had been born for this day, for this place and for this war. It now seemed that the twenty-three years he had lived had been little more than a dress rehearsal for this sliver of time. If he could have been so brave as a child as to have sat on a railroad track with a train bearing down on him, would the specter of death cause him to flinch now? When he had sat on the tracks all those years ago, he was stalking death in a juvenile, foolish way, he would admit years later. Now death was stalking Ken, and this was dead serious. If at the age of fourteen he had wanted to fight a war so much that he had lied his way into the military, would he now find the taste of battle to be repulsive?

Ken thought he understood all of that. He knew as well that confirmation or denial was at hand. Within less than twenty-four hours, he would have almost all the answers to the questions that had defined his life to this point. He would be in the middle of a firefight. Risking death would no longer be a game. There would be no way that, once the roar of battle had begun, he could figuratively leap from the tracks and live to taunt death another day. This truly would be a matter of life and death.

It would have been gallant to have been able to tell himself that he was fighting for freedom and American values against the encroachment of Communism, which was the stated reason any of the United States forces were engaged in the forbidding Korean countryside. For Ken, that lofty ideal would not have been the whole truth because the truth was that Ken was preparing to fight because Ken was, by almost any standard, a fighter at heart. Not only a fighter, but he was a fighting soldier at heart. If nothing else, his time in the Navy had taught Ken that.

"In the Navy, you never see the enemy eye to eye," he said. "It's always ship to ship. In Korea, I knew it would be different. I would be face to face with the enemy, and that's the way I wanted it."

As the sun dipped low on his first day in Korea, Ken was ready to face the foe. Quickly, he volunteered to join a night patrol. He was discouraged by higher-ranking officers, but he persisted. Sergeants, he was told, lead lower-grade enlisted men on dangerous night patrols, not officers. Most officers, he was reminded, remain behind the lines to plan and coordinate operations in the field. And among the officers, lieutenants were the platoon leaders, a role Ken would play for the thirteen months he would be in Korea.

None of that dissuaded Ken and he continued to press his case to accompany a squad from E Company on a patrol mission.

"To begin with, I don't want to be in charge," Ken protested. "I won't get in the sergeant's way. I just want the experience." As for an officer's role, he was, after all, an officer without specific duties who had not yet been assigned to a platoon. He was, indeed, an extra man in the unit. So, he would not be avoiding some other obligation. There were no planning maps or operational orders before him, and no platoon to call his own.

He argued his case again and again and finally was given permission to join the night patrol. Just beyond sundown, eight enlisted men and Second Lieutenant Ken Simpson walked out of camp and disappeared into the blackness of the night.

It was a night on which Ken would learn a fact of life that he had never anticipated. On most nights, this particular duty of patrolling the terrain that theoretically lay between U.S. forces and those of the Communists, whether North Korean or Chinese, was as safe as a shooting war could be. Night after night, Ken discovered, the Army patrol would venture into the darkness and near morning return once again with all men accounted for.

And morning after morning, they would report a quiet, uneventful night.

Ken had discovered how quiet and uneventful such missions had been for this squad. "I was told that they had been going on patrol, but instead of positioning themselves so that they might encounter the enemy, they would hole up in a bunker and radio in that the night's operation was underway," Ken said. Then, according to the information Ken had received, most merely slept the night away.

"It was a kind of unwritten ceasefire between them and us. Nobody will get killed. You leave me alone and I'll leave you alone."

But on this night, perhaps because a rookie second lieutenant was a part of the patrol, the procedure would change. The nine men pressed on through the night, finally stopping at the crest of a knoll. Silently, using only non-spoken commands, the sergeant ordered the nine men to establish positions around the crown of the knoll so the patrol could cover a full circle.

The nine had worked stealthily, and now lay peering into

the dark night, seeing nothing, hearing even less, the M1s the eight enlisted men carried at the ready. Ken's M2 carbine rested its weight in his left hand. His right hand was near the trigger, but not touching it. Ken felt a flutter of excitement, the same sort of excitement he remembered from watching trains roaring toward him in the dark of night. The nine waited. They spoke not a word. Even breathing now seemed noisy.

The meager light of the night was elusive, but near 1 a.m. Ken could see that at least two of the members of the patrol were asleep. He edged near the sergeant to point out the problem.

It wasn't something the sergeant was interested in correcting immediately, he responded to the second lieutenant. He and his men had been on patrol before, and this was the first for Ken. Speaking softly but pointedly, he assured the rookie second lieutenant that his men knew what they were doing.

Ken filed the incident away mentally for the moment then returned to his own efforts to keep an eye on the area ahead of him. Ken's eyes searched the dark shadows for any movement. He had never known such stillness.

Suddenly, from the other side of the circle opposite Ken's position, the night seemed to explode. Flashes of small arms fire ripped through the dark stillness and Ken opened fire from his position and in one frantic squeeze of the trigger on his carbine emptied the thirty-round magazine in the direction from which the flashes of fired weapons had come.

As quickly as the night air had been ripped apart with gunfire, it now grew silent. Deathly silent. The smell of smoke and battle was thick in the air and the stillness of the night returned, though with an ominous feel now.

"The enemy patrol had walked right on top of us," Ken remembered.

No one was sleeping now, and the nine men had come through unscathed and now their undivided attention was on every shadow, and even the slightest movement in the night.

Now came the oppressive uncertainty. "We had to wait,"

Ken said. "We didn't even know what we were waiting for."

Was this a solitary enemy patrol that had ventured far on this dark night? Or, was there a larger force that perhaps had heard the firefight from a distance and even now was moving in the direction from which the night had exploded? And had Ken's patrol's position been pinpointed? What could they expect now in a night that seemed even darker? Perhaps a mortar attack?

Nine men spoke not a word and they peered into the darkness hoping that if the enemy was coming, they would see the approach before it was too late.

For Ken, there was time for deep thought. "I thought about how quickly it had happened," he said in 2010. "I had felt no fear, but probably nobody felt fear because there wasn't time to, it was so fast. But I was shocked, in a way, that I had been in action so soon."

The uneasy patrol remained in position for most of another nervous five hours until first light.

Now as they looked down in the faint glow of the approaching day from the knoll on which they had taken up their position, they could see three motionless bodies, enemy soldiers who had been caught in the fusillade of the early morning. Nine sets of eyes scanned the terrain around the fallen soldiers, looking for signs that these men were not alone. There was no movement, no telltale signs that elements of the enemy patrol had lingered to fight yet again. Ken's patrol would use the lingering darkness as cover and in the half light of a morning in Korea now, the nine men would carefully withdraw from the knoll on which they had spent this eventful night. Once away from the scene of battle, the nine made their way back to camp where the sergeant briefed his platoon leader on the confrontation with the enemy.

"How many dead?" the platoon leader asked.

"Three, sir," the sergeant reported.

"Where are they?" the officer asked.

"They are where they fell."

"We want the bodies brought in," the officer said. "We

want to take a look. We might be able to figure out what outfit they're with. That could be helpful."

Cautiously, the men assigned to the patrol made their way back to the knoll now in the full light of day. Carefully they moved toward the three victims of the battle in the night. They recovered each of the three bodies and moved them to the camp.

"I don't know whether they were Korean or Chinese," Ken said years later. "What I do know is they had walked a long way. They had calves in their legs the size of small trees. They wore what looked like fatigues and they had what looked like sneakers on their feet.

"Whether any intelligence was gleaned from the bodies, I don't know."

In the aftermath of the confrontation with the Communist troops, a Bronze Star medal was pinned on the sergeant who led the patrol. For years afterward, Ken would see that commendation as an injustice.

"He didn't do anything," Ken said in 2010. "The sergeant's actions were nothing more than my actions or the actions of any of the members of the patrol.

"But no one asked me anything about it. I knew that if there was any credit to be handed out, none of it was going to come my way."

Blood on Hill 449

Within a month, Ken was promoted to the rank of first lieutenant, and already quietly, and behind his back, the men closest to him in the company had chosen a nickname for the eager young officer. Gung-Ho Simpson seemed to perfectly fit.

Had he known, Ken perhaps would have complained, though only mildly. If the rank and file soldier needed any proof that Ken, indeed, was gung-ho, it came only a month into Ken's first tour of duty on line in Korea. High-ranking officers were seeking to establish an elite group of fighters, perhaps squad size or slightly larger, who could take on especially difficult and dangerous assignments with some assurance of success. And they were looking for one lieutenant to head up the special unit and that lieutenant would report directly to the battalion commander, Major McCrory.

Ken was quick to volunteer for the assignment, and just as quickly his offer to take charge of such a group of fighting men was accepted. He would learn later that he had been the only lieutenant to volunteer. "I thought it was great," Ken remembered. "It's something I wanted to do."

In turn, in order to build the small, skilled fighting force, Ken also looked for volunteers from the ranks of enlisted men up through and including sergeants. And he would lead them in an intensive training program.

"I made a deal with the soldiers," Ken said. "Anyone could volunteer for the program. But if at any time during the training – and I told them it would be intense – they wanted to quit, there would be no questions asked."

Ken began with thirty-four soldiers. By the time he had put them through the training and felt comfortable with their readiness for the battlefield, it was a much smaller group. "In the end, I had thirteen men and a medic left," he said. "And that was fine."

Though small, the group already had pride in its ability to fight and in order to further stand out in the company, they decided to adopt their own name. They would be known as McCrory's Rogues in honor of their battalion commander.

Major McCrory did not bother to hide his enthusiasm for his new elite squad, and he hoped to put it into action at the first opportunity, which was not long in coming.

"The decision was made to attack Hill 449," Ken recalled. "It was what we knew as a 'limited objective' because it was the little hill in front of the big hill we needed to control."

And McCrory's Rogues would have a key role in the operation. Ken's special unit was to move to a position high above Hill 449 and to be ready to seal off the area so that when Fox Company launched the attack from the front, reinforcements for the Communist troops could not get through from their rear.

Like some of the football plays Ken remembered from years earlier at Wake Forest High School, the plan worked better on paper than it would in reality.

Fox Company, only about 150 strong on this day, had scheduled the attack for June 17, 1952, and Ken, now a seasoned warrior with thirty days under his belt in the barrenness of the Korean Peninsula, would lead his elite unit. His orders were to take his men through the gate in the barbed wire barricade and then move across what was truly a no-man's land to the ridge behind Hill 449.

"But the guides couldn't find the gate in the dark, so we were late jumping off in the attack," Ken said, "My men and I had to go *through* the barbed wire." Simpson's main objective was to depart the main line of resistance (MLR) through the barbed wire five hours before the company was to attack. Moving through the area without detection would be slow and deliberate. Indeed, it would be so slow that when the company attack began, Ken's men were less than halfway to their objective. But the lag in time became an advantage that would be critical in the hours ahead; it placed Ken's outfit in a perfect position to take action against the machine gun nest that had relentlessly hammered American forces from the ridge overlooking Hill 449. The information Ken had gathered during a reconnaissance patrol a week earlier into the KumWaw Valley now became invaluable because Ken understood perfectly the lay of the forbidding terrain and he knew precisely how to use that knowledge.

Cautiously, the fourteen crawled through the night, moving quietly, pausing seldom in this ground-level advance through the treacherous valley.

Near daylight, machine gun fire was crackling from the hillside above and word came by radio that the commander of Fox Company had been killed, shot through the head, and that Lieutenant Morris was now in charge.

"That's what forces being attacked try to do, they try to pick off the man who is directing the attack," Ken said. "And this time, the first man killed was the company commander."

The death of the commander was, Ken said to himself, a particularly devastating blow because the death of the leader had briefly left the entire operation in doubt. Still, with the scene growing clearer with the sunrise, Ken could assess the situation for himself and the fact was that an enemy machine gun nest on the ridge behind Hill 449 was keeping U.S. soldiers pinned down and causing havoc with the overall operation.

He also knew that his outfit could become the wild card in this deadly chess match. "Nobody knew where we were," Ken said. "Lieutenant Morris, who was now in command, didn't know at the time where we were and the North Koreans had no idea where we were as daylight came. But I knew exactly where we were, and I knew that we could do some good."

Ken reached for the phone being carried by a member of his outfit and he keyed it.

"Lieutenant Morris," Ken said into his radio. "Simpson here. I can see where the machine gun fire is coming from and if you want me to, I think my men can get up there behind them and take them out."

"Go!" Lieutenant Morris virtually yelled in response. "Do anything you can do to take care of it, for God's sake. We're getting nailed."

Ken split his outfit into two teams of seven men each. Half would approach the ridge from the left flank using what Ken called the "wilderness" as cover, and the other half would ascend on the right.

They moved quickly now with heavier vegetation around them shielding them from the Communist gunners, and Ken's half of the elite group was the first to reach a point well above the machine gun nest and he knew that the other half of his outfit was approaching from the other side, as well, and would soon be in position to offer backup.

Now, Ken and his six teammates moved out onto the ridge and finally were looking down on the machine gun nest that still was busy pumping lead into the valley below where most of Fox Company now was dug in against the withering fire. As the Rogues moved into position, they were in almost as much danger from the "friendly fire" coming from across the valley as from the North Koreans who had not yet discovered their presence.

But they soon would be discovered by the Communist forces. As Ken rose and began to move his carbine into position, one of the North Korean soldiers wheeled quickly and pointed his own burp gun in Ken's direction. Quickly, Ken squeezed the trigger on his weapon, but nothing happened.

"I will never know why he didn't shoot me with that burp gun," Ken said in 2010. "My own gun had jammed and would not fire and I thought more than once I was dead."

Instead of a fusillade from the burp gun, Ken watched a hand grenade tossed by another North Korean bouncing his way. It exploded only a few feet away lifting Ken into the air and sending him tumbling down the hill. A bullet-proof vest had protected Ken's upper body, but from his waist down, he had taken dozens of slivers of shrapnel. And now he was tumbling from the initial explosion, and then rolling under his own power in his effort to escape further assault by the enemy soldiers' grenades.

"I found out that there's just something about me that attracts hand grenades," Ken said. "Every time I stopped rolling, there was another grenade bouncing toward me. I didn't know whether they were their grenades or ours; everybody was throwing them. I'd roll some more to get away from them and they were always exploding just above me. I'd stop again and there'd be another grenade. Each time I rolled away just as they went off."

Quickly, Ken tried to regroup by first determining how badly he was injured, and whether he had come through with his equipment intact. But something was missing. He had carried his grandmother's .38 revolver in a shoulder holster on his vest. The holster had remained in place, but it no longer held the revolver. His grandmother's weapon had been lost on the tumble down the Korean hillside. "It's probably still lying there somewhere on that hillside," Ken guessed.

Ken was injured but he began trying to find a way to go back up the hill where six of his men in his half of the Rogues still held their ground though all six had been wounded. But above them, as soon as the dust of the original assault had eased if only a bit, the other seven members of the squad who had climbed into position from the other direction opened fire. This time, when the noise and dust had subsided, the machine gun nest had been eliminated and the position belonged to the Americans.

Despite the victory, Ken knew that the advantage would be short-lived. Enemy reinforcements were sure to arrive at any moment. But, he reasoned, by the time they arrived, his team would be gone.

It seemed a logical plan to Ken, but halfway down the hill as his once-split team began to reassemble into a single unit, he discovered that four of the original fourteen men were missing.

"I had a choice to make," Ken remembered. "I could get out and leave my men, or go back and find them."

"Sergeant," he said to the highest ranking NCO, "you take these men and get out of here. I'm going back to find the others."

"No, you're not," the sergeant challenged his boss. "You're not going alone. If you're going, we're going."

"You're going to get us all killed," one of the team members grumbled.

"Malone," Ken growled, "you can take your ass and go anywhere you want to go. We're going back to get the guys we left on the hill."

Though wounded and in pain, Ken and his men began to work their way once again up the hill. They didn't get far. With North Korean reinforcements certainly underway, the four missing men suddenly came with a rush down the hill. They had lingered behind when the firefight had ended to collect souvenirs from the dead North Koreans scattered along the ridge.

The delay in leaving the ridge and the reason for that delay angered Ken. He quickly and angrily verbally lashed out at the four and with urgency continued his rush to meager safety closer to other American units.

In all, eleven of the fourteen members of the unit who had been involved in the fighting had suffered wounds. But none was dead and all were able to assist in finding their way back to safety.

But it would not be easy.

"As soon as we got off the mountain, we walked right into an enemy mine field," Ken said. "It was daylight and we could see the mines that were intended for patrols moving at night. We could get through them, but we had to be careful. We had to take our time."

Finally clear of the mine field, a yawning ditch straight

ahead seemed welcoming. It was large enough for all fourteen team members to climb into and offered some protection from enemy artillery.

For the first time, Ken had a chance to contact company headquarters by radio. It seemed a surprise that the fourteen McCrory Rogues were checking in and all had survived the battle.

"What can we do to help?" came the strange question from the control point.

"We have eleven wounded out here in this ditch," Ken replied pointedly. "Get some help to get us out of here."

In short order an armored carrier came roaring in, but there was room to extract only twelve of the fourteen. Ken and the sergeant, who had led the other half of the split unit up the hill, would await a return trip. And just as quickly, the armored carrier was gone leaving the two men in the ditch.

Not only had the armored carrier rescued most of the men, it also had tipped their position off to the enemy and now the lieutenant and the sergeant came under artillery attack.

"I can't believe after what we've been through today that I'm going to lose my life to artillery," the sergeant said. Indeed, the shells were well-placed and coming closer and closer. Each explosion rocked the ground where the two lay huddled against the earth, unable to mount an escape or anything else.

"Dirt was flying and pretty soon the two of us were covered," Ken said.

Finally, the barrage subsided and the world seemed quiet for a long time. Then came a welcome noise as the armored carrier swooped in yet again, quickly rescued the two men and at least temporarily moved them out of harm's way.

Only when Ken and the sergeant were safely delivered to an area behind the American lines did Ken fully understand the magnitude of the battle and the price the Americans and South Koreans had paid in the assault of Hill 449. As he looked about, Ken could see what looked like a small army, with all the soldiers on hospital litters. There were so many that the row upon row of wounded and dying covered an area half the size of a football field.

One solitary doctor made his way through the carnage. His was a daunting task because many of the injuries were so overwhelming. The soldier who lay moaning on the litter near Ken waited his turn to briefly have the attention of the only field doctor. The soldier's abdomen had been taped together to keep his intestines in place.

Like ten other men in his squad, Ken was evacuated to a M*A*S*H unit. There Ken was quickly wheeled into a surgical unit and placed on an operating table. He looked up into the faces of two surgeons who were examining all the points of entry below his waist where shrapnel from the grenade had pitted Ken's body.

"This is a waste of time," one of the doctors said. "We'd do more harm digging it out than it would cause just leaving it in."

So, Ken would have souvenirs of the conquest of the ridge behind Hill 449 to take with him through the rest of his life.

Overall, the brief stay in the military hospital was not a pleasant respite for Ken.

"In a military hospital, they treat you like a second-class citizen," he said. "You fight your ass off and jerks running around the hospital speak to you in a language you just don't care to hear at that point.

"I instructed my men if they got any treatment like that, just to tell them to go to hell."

When Ken himself tried that approach, a medic reminded him that "you don't have any rank in here, lieutenant."

"I realized that the best thing I could do was to get out of that hospital," Ken said. And when a doctor, a captain, made the rounds, Ken informed him that he felt well enough to return to his unit.

"I think it would be best if you went to Japan," said the captain, referring to a rehabilitation center which was usually a precursor to being shipped back to the United States and perhaps out of the military for medical reasons.

"I'm not going to Japan," Ken announced to the doctor.

"Whatever you say," the doctor responded, and was gone, continuing his rounds.

Soon after the visit from the doctor, a lieutenant came by to check Ken's chart as well and stood beside his bed studying what had been written on the medical reports.

"The captain said I could go," Ken told the lieutenant, stretching the truth.

The lieutenant flipped the pages on the clipboard, and then looked again. "There's nothing here that says he has released you."

"Well, let me put it this way, lieutenant," Ken said, virtually biting the words as he spoke them. "I'm going back to my unit with your approval or without it. Makes no difference to me."

"I don't give a damn where you go, lieutenant," the visiting lieutenant said, then slammed the clipboard containing Ken's records down and left.

Ken quickly pulled his fatigues on over sore, painful wounds, claimed his rifle and left the military hospital. Now he was on the dusty streets and the man who knew something of hitch-hiking in the United States began trying to find a way back to his unit at the front more than forty-five miles to the north.

He was able to flag down a two-and-a-half-ton truck for part of the trip, and then briefly became a passenger in a succession of other military vehicles for the rest of the journey. Among the first people he encountered when he arrived at the control point was the doctor who had sent him to the M*A*S*H unit from the front line.

"What the hell are you doing here?" Dr. Brooks asked.

"I didn't like my accommodations," Ken answered. "They were a bunch of bastards."

For more than two weeks, Ken would be assigned to Dr. Brooks' tent so the physician could more closely monitor Ken's recovery from his injuries, something of the kind of attention Ken might have received had he accepted the assignment to Japan while he recovered.

Injured or not, Ken was back and he had returned to his unit just in time to see the three members of his elite squad who had not been wounded, including Malone who had not wanted to return to rescue the wounded, receive Silver Stars for their bravery from division commander General Joseph P. Cleland.

When Ken read Malone's commendation, he was devastated. Malone had been awarded the prestigious military medal for returning to the ridge and rescuing four fellow soldiers who had been wounded. Indeed, it was precisely what Ken had done on that fateful day.

"I realized that they wanted to pin the Silver Star on someone," Ken said in 2010. "So, they gave another soldier, one who wanted to run, credit for what I had done and had pinned the medal on his chest.

"They thought that no one would ever know. They thought I'd be on my way to Japan, and then back to the States, and no one at battalion headquarters would ever see me again."

The presentation became a problem for the Army, and for Ken.

"General Cleland himself came down and pinned the silver stars," the battalion commander reminded Ken.

"Tell General Cleland he made a mistake," Ken responded.

"You can't do that."

"Then don't do anything," Ken replied.

Still, Ken said, the Army sought to make amends. The solution was to write up yet another commendation for Ken, but the details were fabrications based not at all on what had transpired on the ridge across from Hill 449.

When Ken learned of the plan to recommend him for the Silver Star, he went to the unit's orderly room and asked the lieutenant there if such an effort was being made. The lieutenant handed Ken a draft of the recommendation that outlined fabricated details of what he was given credit for accomplishing in battle.

"It was a good story," Ken remembered. "It had only one

problem; it wasn't true. Someone had made up the whole thing."

Ken read the document. Then without saying a word, began ripping the paper into small slivers and dropping it shred by shred into a handy trash bin.

"I would appreciate it, lieutenant, if you didn't do anything about this," Ken said softly. Then he walked away.

In more than one way, Ken was a marked man. Among the soldiers on the line, he was now known as something of a pariah. "Well, word got around that I had taken fourteen men out on patrol and eleven of them had gotten shot up," he said. He understood the reaction of enlisted men who might once again come under his command.

Indeed, when Ken, still recovering from his wounds and still under the watchful eye of Doctor Brooks, took command of the First Platoon of Easy Company. He faced a platoon of reluctant soldiers, most of whom already had expressed interest in serving under platoon leaders other than Ken. McCrory's Rogues would be no more, he told the men, but the training still would be difficult and intense.

"Now, I understand that most of you men would like to transfer to some other platoon," he continued. "I don't have any problem with that. But you can't do it for thirty days. For thirty days, your ass is mine, and after thirty days if you still want to transfer out, I'll do all I can to help you."

True to his promise, the training Ken brought to the men was intense. At the end of thirty days, Ken once again brought up the subject of commitment to the goals of his platoon. "I told them the thirty days were up and any of them who wanted to could ask for a transfer and I'd do what I could to help that happen," Ken said.

No one sought a move to another platoon. All of the soldiers volunteered with their silence to remain under Ken's command.

"That's when I learned something important about loyalty,"

Ken said. "After thirty days of training, I felt a deep sense of loyalty to all the men and, surprisingly, the feeling apparently was mutual. Nobody wanted out."

Ken (in helmet) surrounded by some members of his platoon, Mitchell (left) and Majur (right) with (kneeling L-R) Campbell, Staples and Bertram.

The Relationship

First Lieutenant Ken Simpson was an American fighting man in the truest sense of the word. Certainly by the time of the Korean War, he had come to admire other men who displayed courage in battle. At the same time, he fully understood that not all of those whose lives were daily in jeopardy faced that reality with the same reckless abandon as he. "I didn't really worry about what happened to me," he said. "So, maybe that's the reason I looked at battle and other things in life the way I did." Yet he was not quick to judge the men whose raw courage did not match his own.

He was more inclined to judge more harshly the officers who held ranks above that of first lieutenant, and his existence in Korea with higher ranking men was occasionally less than cordial. But, Ken's relationship with Colonel William Locke, the commander of the Second Infantry Battalion, was both a case-in-point and an exception.

In his best-selling book, *About Face*, the late Colonel David H. Hackworth, once one of the United States' most decorated fighters, painted Colonel Locke as a man with whom one should not trifle. "The man was mean as a snake and looked like one, too," Colonel Hackworth wrote.

"He was thin, almost bald, with a long face and thin, tight lips he mashed together like Humphrey Bogart. He chewed tobacco, had a stain from it on his cheek, and his teeth were ground down like an old horse's." Hackworth wrote that Colonel Locke ran his unit on "pure fear."

It was Colonel Locke's use of the fear factor that first brought him face to face with First Lieutenant Simpson.

Ken and his platoon had taken their regular rotation off the front lines south of the 38th Parallel in Korea and were moved well back of the battle zone to the small town of Nasan. Ken's own living quarters for his break from combat was a railroad boxcar. And the men of his platoon also were accommodated in similar boxcars. As he applied a fresh coat of paint to brighten the inside of the old boxcar in which he lived, Ken heard a call from beyond the open door.

"Lieutenant Simpson!" the voice Ken did not know called out. For a moment, Ken delayed.

"Lieutenant Simpson!" the strange voice repeated, this time more insistently.

Ken finally put his paint brush down and stepped from the boxcar. He was stunned that the call had come from a man whose helmet bore the silver leaf of a colonel. With the colonel was Ken's company commander, Captain Futrell. Since he had been busy painting his living quarters, Ken could not have passed inspection himself, but still he saluted smartly.

"Here we were, thirty miles from headquarters, and here were the battalion commander and the company commander looking for me inside an old boxcar," Ken said years later. "These two officers were the last people I expected to see."

Sternly, Captain Futrell introduced Ken to Colonel William Locke, an unhappy looking man who conveyed the unmistakable impression through his mannerisms and his voice that he was a no-nonsense military man.

"Lieutenant Simpson," Colonel Locke said pointedly to the paint-smeared first lieutenant. "Where are your men?"

"Taking a little break, sir," Ken answered, trying to anticipate where this visit would lead.

"Fall them out. I want to take a look at them right now,"

the higher-ranking colonel demanded.

Now Ken had a problem. He knew his men were scattered about the area. He suspected that one or two of his soldiers could be found at a known house of pleasure in town and only a short walk from the makeshift billets where they were being housed. Others, he was certain, would be in an area drinking establishment, and already some of his squad members were scurrying about trying to round up the men who took their orders from Ken.

Finally, his men were appearing from all directions, some half-dressed, others half drunk, none in possession of his weapon.

Colonel Locke looked over the ragged assemblage and grew angrier by the moment.

"Lieutenant Simpson, do you know what I'm going to do to you?" he asked loudly.

"No, sir," Ken answered, still mustering as much military bearing as possible under the awkward circumstances in which he found himself.

"I'm going to give you a dishonorable discharge and ride you out of town on a fucking rail," the colonel growled.

"Yes, sir," Ken responded.

"What do you have to say about that?" Colonel Locke growled.

"Nothing, sir," Ken answered.

"Is that all you can say, 'Nothing' and 'Yes, sir?'"

"Yes, sir," Ken repeated as he now fought to control his own temper.

"And why is that, lieutenant? Why is it you have nothing to say to defend yourself?"

"Because, sir, you are in no mood to hear what I might have to say."

The remark did not serve to improve Colonel Locke's disposition. But the colonel wasn't through.

"Don't your men have weapons?" Colonel Locke pressed Ken even more.

"Yes, sir," he answered yet again.

"Well, lieutenant, where are they?"

"We'll have to go get them, sir," Ken said, his voice now surprisingly even.

"Call the names on the roster," the colonel now ordered, seeming to change directions in his verbal attack upon Ken and his platoon.

The platoon sergeant, in his strongest military voice, began the roll call. When he came to "Barnett," two different voices answered.

There, the platoon sergeant stopped his roster recitation.

"Do it again," the colonel ordered.

"Barnett," the sergeant repeated loudly.

This time, no one answered.

From the direction of the nearby town, one final soldier came running and took his place with Ken's platoon. Now Colonel Locke moved and stood in front of the late arrival.

"Soldier," he said gruffly. "What's your name?"

"Barnett, sir," he responded.

"Where the hell have you been, Barnett?" Colonel Locke roared.

"I've been over in the village like everybody else," Barnett answered. Earlier in the day, Barnett had been released from the hospital. A member of Ken's McCrory's Rogues, Barnett had been one of the eleven soldiers who had been wounded on the ridge behind Hill 449 and had that morning been deemed once again fit enough to rejoin his platoon. The colonel perhaps could not have known that.

Colonel Locke now looked Barnett over and his expression indicated that Barnett's appearance at the moment did not please the commander. Still he turned away from the enlisted man and now Colonel Locke turned his attention once again to Ken.

"Lieutenant, I can't believe this could get any worse, but we shall see," the colonel grumbled. "I want to inspect the guard posts."

Ken, who had six native-born South Koreans who had

been assigned to his platoon, now summoned the interpreter and the four men, the colonel, the company commander, Ken and the interpreter, went striding off smartly toward the guard posts. There the colonel looked things over, his mood improving not at all. And when the colonel came and stood in front of a smiling Korean soldier, his mood darkened even more.

"Tell this Korean soldier to wipe that smile off his face," Colonel Locke ordered the interpreter. He waited while the interpreter translated.

The South Korean continued to smile.

"Soldier," the colonel then stormed to the interpreter, "tell him again to wipe that smile off his face and tell him the same way I'm telling you."

And again the interpreter relayed the message, seemingly with no more enthusiasm than he delivered it the first time. And the South Korean soldier in question continued to smile.

When the interpreter turned for further instructions from Colonel Locke he could only see the officer's fist coming at his face and the blow was sufficient to send the interpreter sprawling on his back. He arose, dusted himself off and kept his distance from the angry colonel.

"This is a disgrace, lieutenant. A damned disgrace," Colonel Locke growled. "But just to show you I'm a fair man, you have from right now until sunrise to do something about this."

Now the colonel turned to Ken and asked, "Where are we gonna sleep?"

"I have cots available for both of you," Ken replied.

"I don't want anybody else's bed; I want my bed," Colonel Locke said, the fire still in his voice.

"Yes, sir," Ken responded. Ken had guests for the night; both the colonel and the captain spent the night in the freshly painted boxcar.

Ken said little to his platoon. There was no need; every man, except for Barnett, had heard almost the entire exchange between Ken and the colonel and most had witnessed the blow that knocked the interpreter to the ground. Every man knew where he stood, and where they stood with the colonel was not the sort of place soldiers like to spend their time away from combat.

The sun was only peeking above the eastern horizon, and when Ken appeared before Colonel Locke, he no longer was paint-smeared. The shoes he wore gleamed as they always did when he wasn't involved in battlefield maneuvers, or in the domestic chore of painting. Once again, Ken saluted smartly as he came and stood before the man who on this day had the power to end his military career and who, in fact, had said he would do just that, and with dishonor.

"Lieutenant, fall out the troops," Colonel Locke demanded, though not with the fire-breathing attitude of a day earlier. Still, he seemed angry.

Ken gave the order and the platoon fell out in perfect formation.

Colonel Locke moved silently up and down the line, stopped before every soldier and, saying nothing, looked him over from head to foot. Every soldier in Ken's platoon looked straight ahead and never flinched, nor even blinked throughout the inspection.

Now, the colonel came again and stood before Ken. "Lieutenant, last night I would not have given you a quarter for the lot of them," Colonel Locke said, no longer displaying the fire of a day earlier. "But today, these men look like they've just stepped off the parade field at West Point. They really look sharp, like fighting men ought to.

"Lieutenant, do you have an explanation for why that happened?"

"Yes, sir," Ken said, though not bothering yet to explain.

"Well, then, lieutenant, what is the explanation?"

"Sir, these are some of the best soldiers with whom I have ever served. Every one of them is a great soldier. If there is a difference between this platoon and other platoons under your command, it is that when these men work, they work very hard.

When they fight, they fight with everything they have. And when these men play, they play just as hard.

"And I, sir, will not take that away from them. They are a credit to the United States Army, sir."

The colonel merely smiled.

The two higher ranking officers then climbed into their waiting jeep, told Ken that "we will be back," and sped away. Ken was left to wonder if the comment that they would return was a threat or a promise.

He didn't have to wait long. A week later, Colonel Locke indeed did return, this time no longer the roaring lion he had seemed in his first visit.

"Well, lieutenant, I have looked into your background during the past week," the battalion commander announced. "And the conclusion I have come to in your case is that any son of a bitch who will take a grenade, and then trade a shipment to Japan to go back to the front lines must be crazy. I think you're crazy, lieutenant, but I know that sometimes that's what it takes.

"I've changed my mind about you," Colonel Locke said. Then he leaned in closer to Ken and spoke softly, as though his words were meant only for the two of them. "You can forget that discharge crap," he virtually whispered.

The two men, the young lieutenant and the old soldier, smiled and it was clear that there now was respect between the two fighters.

"Lieutenant, are you any good at making coffee?" Colonel Locke asked.

"Yes, sir," Ken answered enthusiastically.

"Then may I join you for a cup of coffee?"

"Yes, sir."

Ken invited the colonel into his freshly painted boxcar home and quickly began to brew coffee in an aluminum pot he had brought from Japan and that he kept just for that purpose. When the aroma of the boiled coffee filled the boxcar, Ken poured the first cup for the colonel and then filled his own cup.

Colonel Locke drank cautiously of the piping hot liquid at first and then, as the coffee cooled slightly, quickly finished off the cup.

"That, lieutenant, is a good cup of coffee. I could use a cup like that a lot more often."

"The pot's always on, sir, and you're always welcome," Ken answered cordially.

"Before I go, you could do me another favor," the commander said.

"Anything I can do, sir," Ken responded.

"Will you do me the honor of giving me a critique of my staff, everybody you have come in touch with since you've been in Korea?"

It was an assignment which Ken saw as a mine field all its own. Still, he saw it also as an opportunity as well. Though he hesitated for a moment, he finally told the colonel that "all I can do, sir, is to give you what I think, and I might be wrong. But I will do that."

For most of another thirty minutes, Ken talked usually in unflattering terms about some of the officers Colonel Locke had inherited with the battalion command and others who had joined his staff since his arrival. All and all, the critiques were pointed. By the time Ken had ended his assignment, the colonel was smiling.

"As I said, sir," Ken reminded Colonel Locke, "these are just my opinions and they don't mean anything to anybody else."

With that, Colonel Locke slapped his leg and laughed loudly. "Well, they mean something to me. You've just confirmed what I had been thinking," the commander said happily. "I thought those fat sons of bitches have got to be worthless."

The colonel once again thanked Ken for the coffee and the critique, and then said his goodbyes. "Lieutenant, I won't be bothering you anymore," the colonel promised. And he climbed down from the boxcar, into the jeep and was gone.

Ken would see Colonel Locke frequently in the weeks ahead and he would join Ken for coffee on the front line. But never again did Ken become the target of one of the loud tirades for which the colonel was famous.

"We never had another cross word between us. Oh, he fired me several times," Ken said, "But he'd always re-hire me when he did that. I never took it very seriously when he fired me.

"He became my buddy. To me, he was God-sent. Every time I got in trouble, I'd call him and he'd get me out of trouble," Ken still remembered in his own golden years. It indeed was a friendship that came in handy in Ken's case and had a direct impact upon the remaining time Ken would be in Korea.

When Ken's next rotation to the front came about, a new captain arrived from the United States and moved into the squad tent assigned to all the company officers. The captain was impressed that he out-ranked all the company officers with whom he would share living quarters, while Ken was generally unimpressed with the captain.

"When a new man shows up, he doesn't get much respect when he's never been in combat, and the captain never had," Ken said. "I'd been in combat on three different occasions for a month each time, so I didn't have much regard for the new captain until he had been in action himself. And I certainly wasn't impressed by his captain's bars."

The only action the captain would see, however, came in the living quarters he shared with other officers including Ken. As he had been doing for weeks, Ken regularly stoked the fire in the pot-bellied stove and would place his coffee pot in place to brew fresh, hot drink in a winter in which temperatures just beyond the flap of the tent frequently reached thirty degrees below zero.

Finally, the captain had apparently had enough of the bubbling coffee on the fire. "I want you to get that coffee pot out of here," he ordered Ken. "This isn't a mess hall."

Ken simply ignored the officer whose rank was only slightly higher than Ken's own. The captain would be away briefly, and when he returned, he wanted the coffee pot gone, he warned

Ken.

Once again Ken ignored the captain as though nothing had ever been said.

It was a short thirty minutes, and when the captain returned, the coffee pot still rested on the pot-bellied stove, its contents contentedly bubbling away giving the atmosphere in the tent a warm caffeine aroma.

"I told you, lieutenant," the captain said, biting his words, "that I wanted that coffee pot out of here."

Now Ken slowly rose from his cot and walked toward the captain until he was almost nose to nose. "Captain," he said pointedly though softly, "there's only one way that coffee pot's going out of here, and that's over my body."

The captain turned and left the tent. Now Ken had another problem with a captain, one that seemed to indicate that a word once again with Colonel Locke might be prudent.

When he had discussed the matter with Ken, the battalion commander instructed Ken to return to his quarters and wait. It was a short wait. Within half an hour, Colonel Locke appeared in the company area and ordered the captain to fall the company out. When the captain next fronted the troops, it was he who knew the legendary wrath of the colonel.

"Captain," the commander said as he stood before the new man in the outfit, "I don't want you in this company, I want you out of my sight and I don't ever want to see you again. My recommendation is that you report to regimental headquarters as soon as possible and ask them if there's anywhere they can use a man like you."

The captain turned and walked briskly away. But it was not the last Colonel Locke would see of the officer. Within hours, Colonel Louis W. Truman, the regimental commander and a cousin of President Harry S. Truman, was in touch with Colonel Locke informing him that he could not dismiss a captain out of hand as he had done.

The colonel discussed the development with Ken. "I can't

fire the guy," he informed Ken, "so what can I do?"

"Colonel, I can take care of myself. You don't have to do anything," Ken responded.

Colonel Locke seemed not to have heard Ken's remark, so lost was he in his own thoughts. "Well, how'd you like to be the headquarters commandant?" he asked Ken. "The slot's open, as you know. It calls for a captain, but you're a first lieutenant and we can take care of the promotion later."

Quickly, Ken took the new assignment. Within a week, the captain was en route back to the United States on emergency leave. Ken never saw him again.

No Name Ridge

During the time Ken's home was the railroad boxcar in the area far removed from the front lines in mid-1952, a regular visitor was an eight-year-old South Korean orphan who came to be known as Mighty Joe. Despite his remarkable youth, Mighty Joe was bi-lingual and fluent in both Korean and English, and he had developed a friendship with Lieutenant Simpson and other soldiers in the platoon. Ken, who considered Mighty Joe a more valuable interpreter than most of the others who were available, hired him as his houseboy and as such he became a point of controversy between Ken and Captain Futrell.

"Mighty Joe would wake me up in the morning," said Ken who almost sixty years later still kept a black and white photo of the young Korean boy. "He would polish my shoes and take care of my clothes in addition to serving me very capably as an interpreter from time to time."

And Mighty Joe also became a pawn in what Ken saw as an unwarranted attack by Captain Futrell, the company commander.

"For some reason, the captain decided that he didn't like me and that he was going to become a thorn in my side," Ken said. He began, Ken recalled, by trying unsuccessfully to link Ken to "the whores" who made a living in the nearby village and included soldiers among their most rewarding clientele. "He said that he had information that I was shutting up the 'whores' before he could get to them to question them.

"It wasn't true, but he was upset that none of the ladies would confirm the dumb charges he had drummed up."

What was fact, though, was Mighty Joe. Seizing upon any opportunity to take action against Ken, Captain Futrell ordered Ken to remove Mighty Joe as his houseboy. "The young Korean boy may not be a houseboy because he is too young," the captain told Ken.

"The hell he can't be," Ken said to the captain not bothering now to hide his anger. "As an officer, I am entitled to one houseboy, and Mighty Joe's it."

"Get rid of the kid," the captain ordered Ken.

"And if I don't, what're you going to do? Fight about it?"

The captain now was silent, and Ken took the silence as a challenge.

"If it's a fight you want," Ken challenged the captain, "then it'll be a fight. You've got … oh … about thirty pounds on me and you may win the fight. But I can tell you one thing: when it's over, you're going to know you've been in a fight."

The captain hesitated for a moment as though considering the challenge, then turned and walked away.

Witnessed by all the company officers, the confrontation that on the surface centered on Mighty Joe was over, but Ken was certain he had not heard the last from Captain Futrell. It had been such a challenge that Ken soon was sharing his side of the story with Colonel Locke.

"Colonel, I really need to get out of here," he finally told his friend and now confidant, Colonel Locke.

"Lieutenant, I've got a captain handling supply over in Wanju and I need to make a change there. So I've got that opening in supply if you'd like to move to that."

"Colonel, I don't know a thing about supply," Ken responded.

"You don't need to know anything about it. Just treat it like it was your platoon."

"I'll take it," Ken said.

Ken left the next morning for Wanju to take over battalion supply duties, and with him went Mighty Joe. For two months, Ken worked as battalion supply officer before returning once again to the front. Before returning to the fight, Ken made arrangements for Mighty Joe. He would leave him in the care of a major who served as the battalion's mail officer. "I wanted him to be where he would be safe, and Wanju was about as safe as any place in South Korea at the time," Ken said.

(Ken would never again see his little friend, Mighty Joe, though he would search for him in later years in the United States where Ken believed the youngster would have wound up when the fighting along the 38th Parallel had come to an end. During his search, Ken read of a South Korean whose story paralleled that of Mighty Joe and who was living in Chicago. When he contacted the man by telephone, the South Korean had no memory of having been with Ken during the war.

Ken and Mighty Joe, Korea (1952)

"I sent him a copy of the picture I had," Ken said years later, "and I hoped it would jog his memory. But I never heard again from the man in Chicago and I have come to believe that man is not Mighty Joe.")

With Mighty Joe in the care of a major in Wanju, Ken returned for another tour on the front lines. And already, the annoying Captain Futrell was missing. When Ken asked about the man who would have fired Mighty Joe, Ken learned that Captain Futrell had suffered shrapnel on a reconnaissance of the front line and was shipped off to the hospital.

Though Ken's tour in Korea was growing short, even more

disagreements with higher-ranking officers lay ahead.

As the S4-supply officer at Wanju, Ken had been responsible for all of the material, including trucks, jeeps and personnel carriers, being used by the battalion.

"When the supply officer changed, there was paperwork that had to be done," Ken said. "One of the documents I had to sign when I became supply officer was one that made me responsible for all the vehicles and supplies for the battalion.

"Now they were scattered all over the place and it wasn't very convenient to account directly for every individual one. So, I went ahead and signed the paper."

When it came time for Ken to move back to the front, he expected the same sort of transfer with the officer who would replace him.

But the Fifth Regimental combat team that was taking over supply duties refused to sign for rolling stock it could not see. "I told them I didn't have it in my hands," Ken said, "and that it was spread over 200 miles.

"Anyway, I was going back to the front, so I said, 'To hell with it,' and I left."

But the problem followed Ken. He had been at the front and already in combat yet again when Colonel Locke called to ask Ken what he was going to do about the unsigned transfer papers. Ken explained the problem to Colonel Locke and was instructed to get in his jeep and go back to Wanju and resolve the problem.

Ken took a jeep (one of the vehicles for which he was responsible) and a case of whiskey and drove the thirty miles back to Wanju "to straighten it out."

Straightening it out would be difficult, Ken knew. The inventory contained more than vehicles. And some of the vehicles that had been listed on the inventory no longer were in operation. Many had been cannibalized in efforts to keep similar vehicles operating in the war zone.

"The only thing I knew to do," he said, "was to try to

trade whiskey for signatures." The plan worked so well that in only a few days, Ken had for his purposes accounted for everything on the inventory list except one item; a movie projector was officially missing though Ken knew it could be found at battalion headquarters.

By the end of November, 1952, the supply red tape was but a memory and winter had closed its icy grip along the 38th Parallel. The ground already was frozen to the texture of old brick and the wintry wind, laden with tiny flecks of icy snow, tore at exposed flesh as though it were sandpaper.

"Korea seems like the coldest place on earth in winter," Ken remembers, an almost imperceptible shudder running across his shoulders at the thought.

But it was warm in the bunker of Colonel William Locke, the battalion commander, and was soon to get a lot hotter. Ken had been called in with other officers to discuss the possibility of infiltrating the North Korean line and taking prisoners who perhaps could be sources of valuable intelligence. The objective, yet without plans, was shared with Ken who viewed the possibility of success as, at best, remote.

"What it comes down to, Lieutenant Simpson, is that I want you and your men to find a way to infiltrate along No Name Ridge. They've been hitting us pretty good with fire from that ridge," the colonel said.

Ken pondered the assignment only briefly.

"Well, colonel, that's a ridiculous order," Ken said bluntly.

It was not what Colonel Locke wanted to hear. Instantly, the anger for which Colonel Locke was known welled within him and he finally grasped a telephone and slammed it against a wall and watched it drop to the floor in pieces.

"Lieutenant," he said heatedly to Ken. "I want you to clarify what you're talking about."

Ken did not back down. "To begin with," he said, "no American forces that I know of have ever been on No Name Ridge, so what we know about the ridge is limited. But more importantly, the enemy must be at close to regiment strength in that area. And you want me and eight of my men to challenge that?"

There was silence now. The room seemed a powder keg. Then Ken was the first to speak again.

"Colonel, I will do it," Ken said somberly. "I just want you to know that the odds are very much against a squad having much success along No Name Ridge. But we will do everything we can to carry out the mission."

There was silence in the bunker for a moment before Ken spoke again.

"I tell you what, colonel," he said. "Give me three men and we'll go after some prisoners."

"When will you come back?" Colonel Locke asked.

"When I get a prisoner."

"You may not get a prisoner, lieutenant," the commander said.

"Then I won't be coming back," Ken responded.

"What if you get captured and you become the prisoner instead of some North Korean becoming your prisoner?"

"Then it's my ass, colonel," Ken answered.

"Lieutenant, it doesn't work that way."

Ken agreed to accept what he considered a most difficult mission. And at last, Colonel Locke was mollified. For Ken, it seemed his death warrant had just been signed.

On the appointed day in late November 1952, Ken would take seven men on the patrol mission that had been ordered by his battalion commander, and he hoped to return with at least two prisoners who could be interrogated. Among the seven men who would be assigned to Ken's patrol out of E Company on this day was new arrival Private William Novajosky about whom Ken knew almost nothing.

Ken knew, of course, this could be a dangerous mission. His eight-man patrol would be in enemy territory the entire time and out-numbered many times over if they were detected. And their objective was what Ken considered a normally worthless bit of Korean real estate just south of the 38th Parallel. It had become clear that enemy soldiers were now dug in there and in a perfect position to continually create difficulty with American forces in the area.

Ken was certain that no U.S. soldiers had ever stood atop No Name Ridge. Now, he would try to do just that. The eight moved stealthily through the night with No Name Ridge as their destination, and toward whatever destiny awaited them.

Pvt. William Novajosky, Korea (1952)

When the eight arrived in the area of No Name Ridge where the enemy soldiers were thought to be dug in, Ken visually surveyed the lay of the land as best he could from his limited vantage point. He decided to leave five of the eight patrol members behind at the base of a cliff that was the final obstacle to overcome before perhaps facing the enemy. From that position, Ken theorized, the five could provide cover and reinforcements if needed. Ken, Private Novajosky and a South Korean soldier, who spoke broken English and might be of help in case prisoners indeed were taken, approached the cliff of about twelve feet that had to be scaled.

Ken sent Novajosky, armed with a pump shotgun, and the South Korean, who carried a carbine, up first, and when Novajosky silently waved him up, Ken, armed with the M2 he carried through the Korean War, also climbed to the top of the cliff while the five remaining squad members took cover. Now on No Name Ridge, the three crouched behind a rock that might have provided cover for one soldier, but was far too small for three to use as a shield. Without speaking, the three Americans watched three North Koreans scanning the valley below in the cover of the rock wall and darkness. During the long night, while Ken watched, more Communist soldiers made their way along the ridge to reinforce the three Ken and his men had seen there.

Ken's patrol's mission was still to take prisoners if possible and he quickly decided that to wait as even more reinforcements arrived for the Communist soldiers would make such an objective impossible once everyone was in place. Already, more enemy soldiers had joined the original three back of the rock wall. Soon, there would perhaps be more. Even the coming of the day's first light would work against Ken and his men now. Silently Ken passed his plan along to Novajosky and the South Korean with him. On his signal, the three began rolling hand grenades toward the enemy soldiers.

"The problem is," Ken said in 2010, "it takes eight seconds for a grenade to explode, and that was too much time.

"Eight seconds is long enough for the enemy to react," he said. And the enemy, reacting quickly, began tossing their own grenades along the ridge and toward the edge of the cliff where the two Americans and the South Korean seemed very vulnerable.

"They were going off all around us," Ken said. "I know the five soldiers we had left at the base of the cliff didn't know what was happening on top. It was just us. So, for practical purposes, I had lost my squad." Clearly now, the reinforcement capabilities of the five men below had been rendered useless for the moment.

"It was a stupid thing," he said, still angry about the developments on No Name Ridge even more than a half century later. "I should have just shot those sons of bitches right there. It would have been so easy. But I was still trying to carry out my mission. Colonel Locke wanted prisoners and I was trying to do that."

Now, though, the confrontation had turned bleak for the Americans. Hand grenades being thrown by the North Koreans that weren't exploding around the three were raining down into the valley back of the cliff and exploding among the five remaining squad members. "Finally one got too close and the three of us were blown in three different directions," Ken said. "I got blown back off the cliff and most of it hit me in the ass."

Once Ken was lifted into the air by the explosion, he went tumbling back down the cliff. The South Korean who had ascended the ridge soon reappeared to rejoin the patrol after being blown off the ridge as well and making his way back. But Novajosky was missing and Ken presumed he had remained on the ridge and was perhaps mortally injured. One of the five who had waited below, a second South Korean soldier, had also been hit by one of the grenades tumbling from the top of the ridge and had suffered a grotesque leg injury.

Now Ken ordered the four uninjured soldiers to help the injured South Korean and together find a way to return to the rallying point Ken had designated on the way to No Name Ridge. Though injured himself, he would climb once again to the top of the cliff to find Novajosky and he designated the South Korean who had been on the ridge to provide cover in the event he came under fire in his search.

"I knew I had to go back," Ken said as he scanned his memory years later. "I was certain I was going back to get killed, but I had to go. The odds were just too great against me that there would be no way I'd come out of this alive." Despite his pain and his foreboding, Ken began his own lonely search mission.

With the South Korean lingering behind and the remainder of his patrol presumably moving once again to the rallying point, Ken began searching for Novajosky.

Still moving cautiously through the half-light of early morning, Ken from time to time called out to Novajosky despite the presence of enemy soldiers in the area. No response came and Ken still searched. He finally stepped over a log and realized that a soldier was lying sheltered against the fallen tree. He looked more closely.

"I had gotten lucky," Ken said. He found his squad member in the relative safety of a large tree trunk.

"Novajosky!" he said barely above an excited whisper when he recognized his companion from the cliff.

"Yeah, lieutenant, it's me," Novajosky replied calmly and softly. "But I can't see. I think the grenade blinded me."

"That's OK, private. I'm going to get you out of here. Just hold onto me and we'll get out." The two moved once more down the hill. The South Korean who was to provide cover also moved along with them. The rallying point was several hundred yards away and beside a creek that ran along No Name Ridge. There, they expected to meet up yet again with the five other patrol members including the South Korean who had suffered the traumatic leg injury in the hail of grenades.

It had taken close to an hour to reach the rallying point with Ken leading the blinded Novajosky every step of the way, but the other five were nowhere to be seen.

Ken once again had no choice, he felt. He had to return yet again to No Name Ridge in search of five members of his squad. He left Novajosky and the South Korean well hidden at the rallying point and began yet another long, dangerous trek, this time alone.

Little by little, he made his way once again to the distant side of No Name Ridge, to the place where tumbling grenades had rained down on much of his patrol as the North Koreans had blown him up for the second time since he had been in battle. There he found the five squad members still huddled together.

"I was about as mad as I've ever been," he said. "Here they were, sitting there waiting to be captured or killed. I could have shot them myself on the spot. I called them every name in the book."

Now Ken began leading the five, including the badly injured soldier, once again through the night and down No Name Ridge. He had grasped the badly injured South Korean by the neck of his bullet-proof vest and was himself dragging him hopefully to safety.

"It's the only way I could get it done," said Ken who ignored his own wounds in his effort to rescue the badly injured South Korean squad member. "In the movies, they make it look easy. They just put the injured soldier on their back and walk away. In real life, it's not that easy. I had to drag this poor guy most of the way back to the rallying point."

The dragging and the frozen, bumpy ground brought great pain to the South Korean, but Ken kept moving despite the occasional cry of anguish from the injured soldier. To have stopped would have meant death, he reasoned. To have left the five where they were also would have meant certain death or a long confinement in one of North Korea's notorious prisons. It was a scenario that troubled Ken even into his golden years.

Indeed, Ken had been disappointed more than once at the conduct of some American soldiers in the wake of fighting.

But now, following the exit from No Name Ridge, all eight patrol members were together again and Ken led the way finally away from the lower reaches of the mountain and to an area beside a stream that flowed between the hills. There, the eight found refuge in the growing light of the day in an area where vegetation had not yet been obliterated by battle or by winter.

Now, the snow came heavily and was blanketing the valley, and the South Korean's pain from his mangled leg was growing more intense. Ken sought to calm him, hoping his moans would not attract the attention of North Koreans who must certainly be in the area.

Finally, in the distance and near the base of the mountain, but on the opposite side of the stream from which the Americans huddled hidden in the wintry surroundings, Ken could see through the whiteness of the snowstorm an enemy patrol, their weapons at the ready. They apparently were looking for the Americans the way people in North Carolina might have hunted rabbits, hoping to flush them from the dense undergrowth turned brittle by the winter.

The North Korean patrol was drawing closer, and surely the moaning of the South Korean would attract attention, Ken reasoned. He held the wounded soldier in a bear hug about his neck and began stuffing snow into the mouth of his seriously injured patrol member so that the sounds of pain at least would be muffled if they could be heard at all.

Remarkably, however, the North Koreans never crossed the stream to search the opposite bank and Ken's patrol remained in place there in their life-saving cover for several hours after the enemy soldiers had disappeared in their quest to hunt down the Americans.

Already, Ken was second-guessing his decision process as he thought back to the advantage Novajosky, the South Korean, and he had in the first moments after scaling the cliff. There was time, he lamented, when the North Koreans had not yet discovered the trio at their backs and near the small rock at the edge of the cliff. In Ken's mind, he had missed a golden opportunity to eliminate more than a few North Korean soldiers and the thought would haunt Ken even into his ninth decade.

The sun was moving higher in the sky on a new day in battle-scarred Korea, the snow had finally subsided, and Ken's patrol finally was on the move again, this time to an area that seemed safe enough that radio contact with the rear could once again be established.

Now the radio was crackling with questions from the control point area. How had the assignment gone? Were there prisoners? How well fortified was No Name Ridge? But Ken was in no mood yet to share the details of the long night.

"Well, what can we do for you?" came the voice finally from the rear on the radio.

"We don't need anything from you except for litters down here to move the wounded out," he responded pointedly.

"How many wounded?" he was asked.

"Two," he responded.

Ken had not counted himself among the wounded. It was the nature of the man. "There were many times I was disappointed in my own behavior," he said of his battle experiences more than a half century later. "Like all good soldiers, I always thought I could have done more.

"But the thing I'm proud of is that I never lost a man, I never went off and left one of my men, and I always wanted to lead men instead of sending men."

Once Novajosky and the South Korean had been taken away to get medical attention, Ken made his way to battalion headquarters to make his report to Colonel Locke. He had returned without prisoners, but with seven squad members still alive, and therein was the miracle.

At the end of his briefing for Colonel Locke, his commander had one other order. He demanded that Ken immediately seek medical attention for his own wounds.

Ken took Colonel Locke's recommendation as an order and made his way to the medics. But he did not linger long in the relative safety of the medical facility before once again returning to his company.

"I was a sight," Ken said. "For several weeks, the backs of my legs and my ass were blue from all the shrapnel I had taken from the grenades."

Friendly Fire

Snow fell through the night, through all of the following day and into the evening of the second day so that it filled the trenches back of the imposing strands of barbed wire that had been positioned to impede the possible advance of Communist troops against the American positions south of the 38th Parallel in central Korea. Now in the half-light of the evening, Ken, zipped snugly into his winter wear, waded alone through the drifts that were from time to time waist-deep. He found the places where the rolls of razor-sharp concertina wire had been spliced together and with gloved hands pulled it apart strand by strand. Now he swung the loose ends of the wire to one side well back from the line creating a gaping hole in the defenses the wire had represented.

Privately conceived and personally carried out, the break in the razor wire fortification was to Ken a matter of drawing a line in the sand which, in this case, turned out to be snow. Even if it mattered to no one else, it was important to Ken that a challenge be made.

And Ken had good reason. What he had witnessed had made him angry, and he would work to find a way to exact revenge. When the North Koreans had killed an American soldier in a recent battle, they had booby-trapped his body and left it lying in an area where it could clearly be seen by the men with whom he had fought.

"We couldn't go near it without getting even more soldiers killed," Ken said bitterly. "So, it just lay there and rotted."

And now, by drawing the concertina wire back, Ken was trying to find a way to avenge what he considered inhumane treatment of an American service man.

"I was trying to give the enemy an opening to come into our territory," he remembered. "I had been fighting on their turf for a long time. I wanted a chance to fight on my turf, where I had all my machine guns in place, and I wanted to do everything I could to invite them in. I was trying to make it easy for them. We would have had quite a welcome for them if they were to accept the invitation."

But what he got was not an all-out frontal attack by the Communist troops seeking to take advantage of the opening in the defenses. What Ken got instead was love of a sort. From somewhere deep in the frozen, battle-battered wilderness, from loud speakers set up by North Koreans, came a sound that Ken and thousands of United States servicemen knew well – a recording of the Glenn Miller Orchestra playing "In the Mood." On another day, it might have been one of those "mad minutes" with which both sides were familiar, a minute in which one side or the other sought to demonstrate its frightful fire power by firing at once virtually everything in its arsenal. But this time, it wasn't a "mad minute" but music from home. This wasn't only a shooting war; it was a psychological war as well, and this too was an attack. And the psychological grenades were the music and the voices Americans loved so much. Occasionally, from deep behind enemy lines from time to time came the sensual voice of Jo Stafford singing one of the songs that in another war had won her the honorary title of "G.I. Jo." The soft, easy-listening sounds of not only Miller, but other big bands of the 1940s and the early 1950s filled with love and romance, would continue as night shrouded the snow-covered front and together the weather and the music would create a deceptive feeling of tranquility.

Ken would not permit his mood to grow mellow.

"It was part of their strategy," Ken said. "They wanted to make us lonesome for home and hopefully take some of the fight out of us."

Taking the fight out of First Lieutenant Ken Simpson wasn't a high probability. Even as he listened to the soft music drifting up the valley and past the frozen no-man's land, Ken was in a fighting mood. His manpower-short platoon had been assigned a 400-yard stretch of the front lines. Although Ken had opened the barbed wire barrier hoping to invite the North Koreans in to their deaths, his platoon's assignment was to see that there indeed was no infiltration from the Communists that would cost additional American lives. Now Ken walked along the positions his men had taken in setting up their lonely sentinels and fretted that spreading so few men over 400 yards left the defense frighteningly thin.

Ken knew that the vulnerability was as serious psychologically as strategically. Only two weeks earlier, while making a similar inspection of the line he and his platoon were charged with holding, Ken had found that four members of his platoon had left their positions in the bitter cold and were holed up in a nearby bunker drinking hot chocolate. He had threatened to shoot the lot of them if he ever again discovered such a lapse.

The result was that his men in recent days had seemed especially alert and intent in seeing that no incursions occurred on their watch. Still, he walked down the line, speaking over the continuing music to each man who was dug in and enduring the bone-chilling Korean winter weather.

Not far from the end of the line, however, he spoke to a member of his squad, one of six South Koreans under Ken's command, who did not respond to his greeting. He moved closer to the soldier. Ice glistened on the soldier's helmet as he leaned against a support. Ken wondered if, indeed, the soldier had been killed by a sharpshooter. Closer now, Ken could hear him breathing steadily, the breathing of a man asleep.

Better that he was dead, Ken thought as he felt the anger

welling up within. With one hand on the soldier's belt and another on his collar, Ken hurled the startled soldier into the nearby snow-filled defensive trench, and then went sliding on the snow and ice into the trench with him. In an instant Ken had drawn his bayonet from its sheath and, grasping the frightened soldier once again by the collar, placed the blade of the long, lethal knife to the man's throat. Wide awake now, the soldier looked up at Ken with terrified eyes. "Clearly, he understood that he was about to die," Ken remembered.

"You're going to get us all killed," Ken said as succinctly as he could, and he hoped the South Korean understood what he was saying but, more importantly, the significance of his outrage. "If I ever catch you sleeping on duty again, I will kill you myself."

He loosened his grip on the petrified soldier, sheathed his bayonet and climbed once again from the trench. "Now get back to your station," he ordered.

A few days later, a member of Ken's platoon brought up the incident.

"Lieutenant, what did you do to the South Korean?" the soldier asked.

"Why do you ask?" Ken questioned him.

"Because the guy used to sleep all the time. Now we never see him sleeping, day or night."

Ken was particularly sensitive to such breaches of security as he had been trying to avoid by the frightening episode with the South Korean. When North Korean soldiers earlier had successfully infiltrated and killed two American soldiers, the breach was charged to the First Platoon, which Ken commanded. But Ken protested the effort to place the blame at the feet of his soldiers who, on this occasion, had gallantly held their end of the line together and repulsed efforts by the Communists to breach the line in their area. "The breach had come in the line where Third Platoon had been positioned," Ken said, seeking to set the record straight even decades later.

"I would have prayed to have them try to come in on my end. My men were ready for them."

More than once, before Ken's time on the front lines would be completed, friendly fire tragedies would leave him in shock.

One of those came on a bitterly cold night typical of Korea in the dead of winter when Ken led an eight-man squad out along a dangerous ridge to relieve an eight-man squad that had been on line for three hours in the numbing Korean weather. Carefully, he worked his way through the darkness with the eight men aware that there always was danger when more than one friendly patrol was in the same area because men in harm's way always react to unexpected movement in the night. Frequently, theirs is a shoot-first mentality.

Finally, however, Ken's group had safely connected with the squad it was to replace.

"When you do a replacement like that, you take in the same number of soldiers that you intend to replace," Ken said. "It often is so dark during the replacement that recognizing the faces of the men is difficult at best. So, you count heads and I had eight heads with me and I expected to go back with eight, which is what I did."

The eight newly arrived soldiers then took their places once again in a circle, replicating the defensive posture of the squad they were replacing, and there they would remain on alert in every direction for up to three hours until they too were relieved by yet another eight-man squad.

But tragically, though it was an eight-for-eight swap, one soldier with the original patrol had fallen asleep in the night and had slept through the exchange. Finally, the soldier awakened from his slumber apparently thinking he was with his own patrol and that, therefore, his position was well known.

It was a fatal assumption. Just as he stood up, one of the members of the new squad opened fire killing the soldier instantly.

"In looking back, it was almost certain to happen," Ken said. "Soldiers on patrol are trigger-happy anyway. And when they see someone in the darkness that should not have been there, it isn't unusual for them to fire quickly. You don't often ask questions in combat."

Obviously, Ken said, the eight squad members had assumed they were the only American soldiers in the area and anyone else would be considered to be an enemy soldier. Even being dressed in what appeared to be standard American combat issue was viewed skeptically because the North Koreans occasionally would use such disguises in seeking to infiltrate American positions with what were known as "line-crossers."

Now with an apparently dead soldier lying a few dozen yards away, the squad leader sergeant radioed in that a "line-crosser" had been killed.

As soon as he heard the report, Ken felt a nauseating feeling of dread.

Now he radioed that he was returning to the squad still in position along the knoll where he had left them. When he arrived, he quickly hurried to where the dead soldier lay.

"They hadn't even turned him over," Ken remembers. So, Ken grasped the man by the shoulder of his jacket, rolled him onto his back and looked down into the face of the dead man. "I could tell he was dressed too well to be North Korean," Ken said. "He was even dressed too well to be a line-crosser because he had *everything* an American soldier carried in Korea.

"I called back to the company to confirm that we had shot a line-crosser, but that they ought to take a close look when they pick him up. I told them to check his clothes and his identification very closely."

Tragically, the casualty was indeed an American soldier who had found a deadly place to fall asleep.

"It was a tragic mistake," Ken said in 2010. "We found out that when the original patrol went out, there were eight men and a medic. When I took the eight replacements out and came back with eight, one of the eight was the medic. They should have reported nine men out."

If Ken was overly cautious when it came to such lapses, it was because he too often in Korea had been a witness to tragedy, particularly that which the military for generations has referred to with the oxymoronic phrase, "friendly fire."

In fact, he had taken one such tragedy personally.

When a lone engineer was assigned to disarm enemy explosives in a mine field spread before a new line occupied by American forces, the company commander sent word down the line to make the dangerous operation as safe as possible. It was Ken's last day on the line in Korea, but he wasn't dropping his mental guard yet. He took the message to members of his platoon one at a time, hoping to make sure that each man, including the South Koreans assigned to his command, understood that the man who would be in the field was friend, not foe.

"Don't shoot the guy in the mine field," Ken told his platoon members individually again and again as he moved along. "He's one of us."

At midnight, his relief lieutenant arrived precisely on time and Ken retreated to his bunker and bundled himself into his cot against the cold Korean night.

Near six the next morning, Ken was suddenly awakened by a shaking. He looked up into the eyes of a platoon sergeant.

"Lieutenant," the sergeant said as Ken sat up wide awake now. "I've got bad news. One of the South Koreans shot the engineer."

Ken was stunned at the news. And he felt a nauseating flash of anger. "As soon as what had happened registered in my mind," Ken said, "I wanted to kill the South Korean."

The lone soldier assigned the already hazardous duty of making the area of the mine field safe for soldiers involved in coming operations had entered the field at first light. One of the South Koreans who had been in Ken's platoon assumed that the engineer was indeed a Communist soldier and had taken him down with one shot. He then tossed a hand grenade meant to finish off the man trying to defuse the mine field to protect fellow American soldiers. Careful not to trigger any of the mines in their haste, medics had hurried to the engineer and carried him away on a litter. He still was clinging to life despite the devastating "friendly fire" assault.

"I never heard whether he made it or not," Ken said years later. "I just know he was in really bad shape when they got him out of there."

Nor did Ken ever know what eventually happened to the South Korean soldier who had pulled the trigger. Soon after the friendly fire incident, representatives of the South Korean army arrived and took the soldier away.

On a daily basis at the front in a shooting war, most soldiers are constantly reminded how fragile life frequently is. Most know that the next breath may be his last, the next blink of an eye the final one, the next step the end of the journey. And the manner in which soldiers deal with such reality is almost as varied as the warriors themselves.

If there ever was a case-in-point in that regard, it came on November 29, 1952, as Ken and the company commander, a first lieutenant, discussed the problem of machine gun placement as they stood bundled in the cold in the trenches.

A shot in the distance rang out, and a small twig from a tree behind Ken and the fellow first lieutenant snapped and fell to the ground almost instantaneously. A North Korean sniper had one of the two lieutenants in his sights and narrowly missed. The shot went between the two officers whose heads had been no more than eighteen inches apart as they had stood beginning to discuss possible strategy.

The company commander grew ashen. His hands shook so that the shaking was unmistakable.

Both officers quickly made themselves less of a target by ducking out of the sight line from which the shot had come and Ken, hoping to help his fellow officer regain his composure, continued his planning almost as though nothing had happened.

"Frankly, I thought it was damned funny," Ken said. "Patrols, both ours and theirs, always wanted to take out officers because they are the men who direct everybody on the battlefield. Without an officer, a patrol or a company is without a leader at least temporarily.

"And in this case, the sniper had taken his shot and hadn't succeeded. That was okay with me."

Missing no more than a beat, Ken continued his discussion with his shaken company officer. "As I was saying, we'll place the machine guns in strategic locations," Ken suggested, his voice strong and steady. He looked at the lieutenant in command who nodded in agreement, though he remained shaken and silent.

(Years later, Ken tried to locate the former company commander and found him living in New Hampshire. The first lieutenant's wife answered the phone when Ken called. Ken introduced himself and was greeted with a reaction he did not expect. "My husband said that Lieutenant Simpson would not think I was a very good soldier," she said.

"Not true at all," Ken had answered speaking directly to the woman. "I thought your husband was a great soldier. He did his job better than I could have done it."

Ken's opinion of his fellow lieutenant, the company commander, never changed with the passing of time. "I had a higher opinion of him than he had of me," he said. "I'm sure of that. I was being honest when I told his wife that he was a great soldier. I thought he was quite a leader and was perfect for operating the company. But, that doesn't mean that he would have been good up front with a gun. I think I was pretty capable up front with a gun, but I wouldn't have been as good as this lieutenant in the control point. I thought he was great at what he did. You have to have the right people in the right places if you're going to be successful." It was a philosophy Ken would use years later in the business world.)

In war, principally because of the constant specter of death, there has always been the inclination to avoid friendships because the friend you have today may be en route back to the United States tomorrow in a flag-draped coffin. Sudden death, of course, is commonplace in wars such as that in which Ken found himself in Korea.

But for Ken, there was an exception to the rule. Lieutenant Barry M. Rumbley was a Methodist chaplain "and even today I consider him one of the best friends I have ever had," Ken said in 2010.

"He took a liking to me because I would always fall my men out to hear him preach. And we just hit it off. We respected each other."

And when Lieutenant Rumbley came to Ken with a problem, that mutual respect was obvious even if the roles were reversed. Ken was being asked to bring perspective to the dilemma facing the chaplain.

"I have a bit of a problem," the chaplain from Kentucky began.

"What's the problem?" Ken asked.

"Well, the commanding general has decided he wants to award the Silver Star to the Catholic chaplain," Lieutenant Rumbley said. "But he apparently thinks it would only be fair to award one to me as well as the representative of the Protestant faithful."

"Why the Silver Star?" Ken asked. "The Silver Star's for bravery in battle and, usually, chaplains don't see that kind of action. I can't imagine why the general would choose the Silver Star."

"Well, lieutenant, that is precisely my problem. I don't even know how to feel about it. I didn't do anything to deserve the Silver Star. And I'm a man of God. So, do I accept it or do I reject it?"

Ken was silent for a time while he contemplated the moral issue.

Quickly, Ken sorted out the problem before him in his

own mind, though he too was in obvious conflict. He had earlier watched while this same general had pinned Silver Stars on three of Ken's squad members who, in Ken's opinion, also had not been truly deserving.

"Here's what I think it comes down to," Ken finally counseled the parson. "I think you need to decide if you will stay in the military when this war's over, or if you will return to civilian life and find a church somewhere to pastor."

"And what difference would that make?" Lieutenant Rumbley asked.

"If you're going to stay in, then I think you ought to accept the Silver Star," Ken advised the chaplain. "If you don't accept it, and you stay in, you're going to be just another chaplain in the military and you'll finally just get swept under the carpet.

"But a chaplain with a Silver Star, that's something different. Having that will give you more of a forum for doing the Lord's work. So, maybe the Lord has a hand in this. He wants you to be heard as a military chaplain."

After Korea, the two close friends lost touch for a number of years, until Ken began searching for the preacher as he would later search for Sergeant Novajosky. He would finally locate the chaplain's widow living in Kentucky, and when he asked her if her husband had received the Silver Star, he regretted the question almost as quickly as it was asked.

"Maybe I kind of spilled the beans," Ken said years later.

Mrs. Rumbley confirmed that her husband, indeed, was the recipient of the Silver Star and that he remained in the military following the Korean War. He rose to the rank of major before he died in 1970.

So, Who Was Billy Mitchell?

By the time of the Korean War, Colonel Louis W. Truman had been a military man for a quarter century. A West Pointer, he had been a first-hand witness to the Japanese attack on Pearl Harbor on December 7, 1941, and later saw action in the European Theater in World War II including along the Siegfried Line, the Bulge and the Ardennes.

Colonel Truman's and Lieutenant Simpson's paths crossed in Korea. From the beginning, Ken had seen Colonel Truman as a man impressed with his own identity, not only in name but also in rank.

"Every West Point cadet that I worked with thought he was a superior soldier," Ken said, still sticking to his appraisal of such officers in 2010. "They're the famous few. Most of them are looking for glory and trying to build reputations to ensure success in the future."

Ken's assessment was in no way altered when Colonel Truman came along.

Perhaps because he had entered the military himself in 1926 as an enlisted man, Colonel Truman regularly intimidated low-ranking enlisted men, a fact that angered Ken. "He had a habit of inspecting the troops, and when he'd go down the line, he would take a soldier's weapon away from him.

"In time of war, you aren't supposed to give your weapon to *anybody*. But when there's a colonel standing there with that insignia on his helmet and you know he's the commander, lower-ranking enlisted men are naturally intimidated," Ken said.

"I kept telling my men that Colonel Truman would do this and when it happened, they should hit him in the head and refuse to be disarmed. Colonel to private was not a fair exchange. And I hated that the colonel would do a thing like that. An enlisted man could have flattened him under those circumstances and gotten away with it.

"But it never happened. None of the enlisted men would flatten a colonel for demanding their gun. But someone should have."

Indeed, Ken would have bigger problems in his dealings with Colonel Truman. As the headquarter commandant appointed to the job by his friend, Colonel Locke, Ken was the man to whom Colonel Truman turned when he inspected the 2nd Battalion headquarters. Together, Colonel Truman and Ken toured some of the facilities that were available to both officers and enlisted men at the headquarters placed well back of the fighting which was taking place still just south of the 38th Parallel.

Again and again, Colonel Truman pointed out facilities that, in his opinion, needed upgrading.

"I want cement showers," he said to Ken, who was making a list. "The mess halls here are awful. I want acceptable mess halls for officers and men. I want fabric dressing on all windows. I want the place to look a lot better than it does now."

Colonel Truman left it to Ken how all of that would be accomplished.

Ken searched for ways to obtain concrete and other building material, supplies not normally provided for military use in war zones and in areas supporting war efforts. Finally, he realized that the only thing he had available in great quantities that would be of interest to civilian South Koreans who could find ways of providing the needed material were C-Rations, pre-prepared canned meals made available to soldiers when better fare was not otherwise available. And C-Rations, he assumed, would be a hit in the world beyond the post.

And he was right.

The desirability of C-Rations among the local civilian population clearly established, Ken instructed his interpreter to make arrangements to exchange the military food fare for the material needed to renovate and build the projects Colonel Truman had ordered.

Within days, Ken was being questioned by an officer from the Criminal Investigation Division who wanted to know if Ken had approved the transaction of trading C-Rations for supply materials. The interpreter already had been questioned and the trail seemed to lead to Ken.

"I approved the transaction," Ken confirmed.

"It's black market, lieutenant," the unsympathetic CID officer charged.

"It's trading!" Ken said, raising his voice.

Ken would later take consolation in the fact that C-Rations had gotten the supplies needed to bring the military post up to Colonel Truman's standards. But it would cost Ken militarily. He would be charged with involvement in the black market and would face a court-martial.

Even there, Ken would not go quietly. It was a military trial that lasted most of two days, and for most of the two days Ken's lawyer paraded before the military court a list of character witnesses, people who knew Ken best and with whom he had worked. To a man, they defended Ken's character and his reputation and some pointed out that Ken's combat record was without equal. "They have affirmed the fact that Lieutenant Simpson is a dedicated and capable lieutenant," the lawyer told the military court.

The lawyer was content to permit the glowing assessments of his client to speak for themselves and Ken was advised again and again to remain silent which, of course, was not the lieutenant's nature. He insisted upon facing the court and answering questions, much to the dismay of military lawyers on both sides.

So, against their better judgment, lawyers called Ken to the stand.

"Lieutenant," began one of the prosecuting attorneys when his turn to question Ken came. "You're charged with trading C-Rations in the general population for various things."

"Yes, sir," Ken answered grimly.

"What things?"

"Concrete mix, curtains, paint, and various other building supplies."

"Did you do it?"

"Yes, sir," Ken responded.

"Did you know you were involved in the black market?"

"So I've been told," Ken said, not bothering to soften the sarcasm in his voice.

"And why do you not think you should be held accountable?"

It was the opening Ken had hoped for. He could not persuade the soldiers under his command to hit the colonel when he demanded their weapons, but he could do it verbally now. And he was ready to take his shot.

"Because, sir, you've got the wrong man," Ken answered slowly and distinctly.

"Then, if not you, lieutenant, who should be on trial here?"

"Colonel Truman," he said clearly so that all in the room could hear.

There was a hush in the military courtroom.

"Colonel Truman, lieutenant? The regimental commander?" There was incredulity in the military lawyer's voice.

"Yes, sir. Colonel Truman. Colonel Truman ordered me to see that we have concrete showers, that I do something to make the mess halls a lot nicer, and he wanted curtains on all the windows," Ken said, warming to the occasion.

"Colonel Truman knew that the Army doesn't manufacture that stuff. But he wanted me to get it somewhere. And I think he knew that the only way I could get it in Korea was on the street."

Ken stopped talking. Still, the courtroom was hushed.

When the sitting officers rendered their verdict, it amounted to the mildest of slaps on the wrists – a $250 fine, the fine suspended, no reduction in rank and no prison time to serve.

When the proceedings had come to an end, Ken was given a written transcript of the court-martial proceedings and ruling. In all, the paperwork was about an inch thick. He walked out of the building reading what was written on the first page, mere confirmation that there would be no penalty. He smiled and crumpled the court papers and tossed them into a trash receptacle just outside the tent in which the trial had taken place.

Even in 2010, Ken still regretted that he had discarded the only confirmation he has ever seen of the court action. It exists nowhere today in his records.

Whether Colonel Truman ever was told of the testimony Ken presented to the military court is uncertain. The colonel's career continued unfettered by small details and after the Korean War had ended he became the commander as a three-star general of Third Army, the force once commanded by George S. Patton.

In the first half of 1953, Ken was closing in on the number of points he needed for rotation back to the United States and his departure date was drawing near.

As Ken was gathering his belongings and preparing to begin his journey back to the United States, a fellow lieutenant, Richard Weden, the company executive officer, stopped by to wish Ken well.

"I've got something I want to ask you," Weden said in the course of the short conversation.

"And what would that be?" Ken asked.

"Well," Weden said, "I was wondering if I could have your helmet."

It was a request Ken had not anticipated, and it caught him by surprise.

"Lieutenant, why in the world would you want my helmet?"

Because, lieutenant, you're the luckiest son of a bitch I ever saw. I thought maybe I could use some of that luck."

Ken tossed his helmet to Weden. Perhaps the luck of the helmet had remained. Ken would learn years later that Weden indeed had survived the battles in Korea and had died in Massachusetts in 1970.

On the day Ken would finally depart the Asian Peninsula, he packed his bags and drove a jeep to the control point. There the regimental commander, Colonel Herman Kaesser, and his entire staff has assembled and as Ken's jeep pulled up to the control point, Ken was ordered to report to the regimental commander. This time, Colonel Kaesser saluted Ken. And the command staff stood at attention honoring a fighting man. Among those gathered for the surprise ceremony was his chaplain friend, Lieutenant Barry Rumbley.

The commander read aloud a commendation for the awarding of the Bronze Star. William Novajosky, now a sergeant and his vision clear after the blinding grenade explosion, had recommended the man who returned alone to the battlefield to rescue him be awarded the medal for bravery, and the Army had agreed.

The ceremony had caught Ken by surprise, partially because he never felt he had performed heroically.

"There's so little to be pround of in war," he said. "You always have the feeling that you could have done more. The only asset I had when it came to war was that I was just about fearless. I think Novajosky was the same way.

"To be honest being a hero is an accident. If you face a situation and don't do anything about it, nobody ever knows about that but you. If you do something about it, they call you a hero and the whole thing just happened. It's just an accident because nobody goes out planning on becoming a hero."

Days after the ceremony in Korea honoring Ken, a short article appearing back home in the *Raleigh News & Observer*, read:

First Lt. Kenneth Simpson of Raleigh recently was awarded the Bronze Star for heroic service near Sohui-ryong, Korea, last November 29-30. Although painfully wounded when attempting to take an enemy outpost as head of a combat patrol and in the teeth of heavy enemy fire, Simpson disregarded his own personal safety to look for a missing patrol member and return him to safety.

The news release had contained much of the commendation read by the regimental commander as he stood before Lieutenant Simpson.

Handing the commendation to an aide, Colonel Kaesser then took the clasp off the medal and pinned it to Ken's uniform. As he pushed the tines through the cloth of the uniform, the commander smiled.

"Lieutenant," he said, "I'm sorry about the court-martial. The only thing that it means is that you and Billy Mitchell now have something in common."

1st. Lt. Simpson: 'He was fearless'

Ken wondered for years if his regimental commander had noticed the blank look on his face when he heard that remark. At the time, he had never heard the legend of Billy Mitchell, the pioneering general known as the father of modern air power, who once was court-martialed for what was considered the heresy of insisting that airplanes could be used to bomb ships at sea.

Sergeant Novajosky was not in attendance at the ceremony that he inspired and Ken never saw him again. But for years, he searched phone books, especially those in the area of Scranton, Pennsylvania, Novajosky's hometown. Fifty-three years and two weeks after Ken received the Bronze Star, he finally found Novajosky's sister. She told him that the sergeant had died in Hawaii on February 1, 1978 at the age of forty-seven. He is buried in the National Memorial Cemetery of the Pacific, a graveyard known less formally in Hawaii as the Punchbowl.

(Novajosky had remained in the military and saw combat in Vietnam where he was awarded both the Bronze Star as a member of Company C, 1st Battalion, 27th Infantry, and the Silver Star in action with Company B, 3rd Battalion, 22nd Infantry.)

Three days after Ken departed Korea for the last time, Chaplain Rumbley wrote a letter to Sue who was waiting for Ken's return back in Raleigh, North Carolina. Many years later, Ken gave his youngest son, Sam, a $500 reward for locating the letter from the chaplain. The chaplain wrote:

Dear Mrs. Simpson,

On the 6th *of May your husband climbed aboard a jeep bound for the U.S.A. In about 36 days you can start looking for him – He will probably go by boat & land at New York.*

I have known him since I came in August & consider him one of my best friends – He is the bravest & best Lt. we had & I know you are proud of him. He was fearless when he faced the enemy & has a great deal on the ball.

He is well & was happy at the thought of going home. I gave him orders to write you also.

Sincerely,
F.M. Rumbley

The hand-written letter remains among Ken's treasured keepsakes.

"It is my most prized possession," he said. "It's the only thing I've got that says I was worth a damn to anybody."

Home on the Rails

Lieutenant Rumbley, the Methodist chaplain, would have perhaps been right had this been any other soldier going home from Korea. The trip might have taken more than a month. But this wasn't just any other war-weary soldier. This was Lieutenant Ken Simpson, a master at improvising. Indeed, as the chaplain had mentioned in his letter to Ken's wife Sue, Ken was booked on a ship bound for New York with yet another transit of the Panama Canal.

"I wanted to shorten the trip," Ken said in 2010. "So, I traded my .45 pistol for passage to Seattle instead of New York, and even with the trip across the country, that cut five to ten days off the trip."

By the time Ken had reached Fort Jackson near Columbia, South Carolina, the post to which he was assigned as a returning combat soldier and the place where his career as an Army officer had begun, word had reached Ken through the military grapevine that some of the soldiers in his former platoon had died when North Koreans breached the line that he had worked so hard to hold on each of his tours of duty at the front.

"I don't really know what happened," he said, "but the word I got was that a North Korean patrol caught one of our patrols coming back in. They just sort of latched onto the back end of the patrol and followed it right into our position."

On June 20, 1953, Ken was discharged from the Army and headed home to Wake Forest with Sue to join his growing son Kenny, a babe in arms.

Though Ken didn't know it at the time, there still would be soldiering to be done, but Ken's life had just made a dramatic turn. It would be years before, in looking back, he would come to appreciate how dramatic the change for him had been. He would return to his wife and son and to Wake Forest and he knew that North Carolina winters would seem tropical compared to the bitterly cold winter he had spent fighting in Korea.

As much as one can, Ken would be resuming the life he had known before he had been called to active duty not long after hostilities had broken out in Korea. Not only would Sue and Kenny be waiting, he also was reunited with one of his childhood friends, Alan Goldston. Alan's father, the proprietor of a local sawmill, had been president of the Wake Forest Rotary Club and had been instrumental in arranging for new uniforms to be purchased for the high school team.

Ken (right) and lifetime friend Alan Goldston (2004)

Like Ken, Alan also had been a military man and had seen action, but not in Korea, as a Marine. He was savagely bayonetted by an allegedly drunken American Marine while stationed at Camp Pendleton, California, and would carry the scars of that misfortune with him for the rest of his life. In the months after both old friends had returned from military service, Alan lived in the same block as the Simpsons in Raleigh and a friendship continued that would last until Alan died in 2009.

There was another motivation for Ken. He knew that although he had been a successful military man by rising from the rank of enlisted man to that of officer, he still needed a stronger academic presence on his resume. He enrolled once again at Hardbarger Business School.

Sue continued to work for the insurance company in Raleigh, and Ken applied himself in his studies. While he had been, at best, a mediocre student in high school, he now viewed academics from an adult perspective and quickly was at the top of his class.

Ken would view his matriculation at Hardbarger as a surprising extension of the same sort of inspiration that made him years earlier aspire to become a yeoman in the Navy. By the time he returned to civilian life and resumed his studies, Ken already was a whiz at taking and transcribing shorthand using the Gregg system, and was among the fastest typists in his class. He hoped down the road to begin his business career as a secretary.

But in September, the Simpsons' lives began to move in another direction, one that had not been expected. Though he had been back in school only briefly, Ken learned that the Atlantic Coast Line Railroad had made contact with the placement center at Hardbarger. The railroad had an opening for a male secretary. "And I was the only male in the school with any training as a secretary," he said.

Ken was offered the job and quickly accepted.

Given the option of going to work for the Atlantic Coast Line Railroad in either Rocky Mount or Wilmington, North Carolina, Ken chose Rocky Mount where he would work in the office of John Wilson, the ACL agent there.

"It was a tiny office," Ken remembered. "In all, it was only about sixteen feet by sixteen feet and not a lot of work to do." And for a year, Ken was the only male secretary working for the

Atlantic Coast Line in Rocky Mount. It was a remarkable change of pace for the man who spent more than a year leading platoons in Korea and who twice had been blown up by hand grenades. It was a job that would not last. The male secretary position in Rocky Mount was abolished in 1954, after only a year, and Ken was offered and accepted a job with the railroad that would require a move to Philadelphia.

Even though he was battle hardened, Ken was a handsome young man in the early 1950s who had married his high school sweetheart. On a summer day in 1959, when Ken was working in the railway agency office in Philadelphia, his life made another sharp turn. He looked up to see "the most beautiful woman I had ever seen" walk into his office and into his life.

"Wow!" he said to himself and under his breath when he first saw her. "Here comes a home wrecker." Though twenty-one years would pass before it happened, Ruth, the beauty, would become Ken's second wife.

Ken also still had military blood coursing through his veins and he signed up once again in the Army Reserves, this time with a transportation company that offered little in the way of challenges for Ken. "It was just a way of making dog money," Ken said. "It was easy" and it added to his total time in uniform.

Within a year of his move to Philadelphia, Ken would be in yet another war. But this one would be a corporate battle between railroad companies serving the United States' east coast from New York to Florida, the Atlantic Coast Line for which Ken worked and the Seaboard Air Line Railroad, the competition.

Despite its name, Seaboard owned no airplanes. The "Air" in its name referred to the company's contention that the quickest route from one city to another by rail was theoretically a straight line which it called "air lines." And Seaboard based much of its aggressive relationship with travelers on that theory.

Atlantic Coast Line, on the other hand, had no intention of ceding the region to Seaboard and would instead bet its future on providing unparalleled customer service. Ken would be in the front lines of that war from his new base of operations in Philadelphia.

"The whole thrust was to get passengers to routinely choose Atlantic Coast Lines," Ken said. To do that, Ken began by becoming acquainted with ticket agents all over Pennsylvania, and particularly in Philadelphia.

"As they say now, it was our intention to grow the business," he said.

Ken discovered that if he took extra steps, he could more successfully lure new customers and keep them coming back. "So, not only did we book passengers onto Atlantic Coast Line Railroad, we also booked their hotels, reserved cars for them and took care of their travel needs in a lot of ways," he said.

For Ken, it was an eye-opening experience because for the first time in his life, he was paid on a salary-plus-commission basis. "I found out about commissions," he said, "and I learned that can lead to considerable money."

At one time, Ken was bringing in more business, and thus cashing larger commission checks, than the rest of the Philadelphia sales staff combined. And the railroad also was learning something about commissions, as well. It eventually poured the commission funds into a single account and divided it evenly among its sales force, a move that cut into Ken's income significantly.

Ken could use the money. In 1956, Sue was pregnant once again and on January 4, 1957, the family grew to four with the arrival of a baby daughter who would be named Larke.

Though he no longer was paid based solely on the business he generated, Ken had become a star with the passengers, so that ACL assigned him to regularly accompany the run out of New York's Penn Station to Jacksonville, Florida.

"It was a bit of a nondescript job," Ken said. "My job was to take care of the passengers on the train, to make sure they were comfortable and to do everything I could to make train travel an enjoyable experience.

"The conductor's job on a train is to run the train. My job on the train was to run the passenger end of it."

And Ken's work was not always simple and straightforward.

When Ken was scheduled out of New York, his routine was to travel into the city the evening before the scheduled departure and spend the night in a nearby hotel. He would then walk across the street and into Penn Station to board the Atlantic Coast Line train soon to depart for Florida.

It became routine, except for one run in 1959.

The train had just pulled out of Penn Station when word came that among the passengers on this day were the Duke and Duchess of Windsor and their entourage heading for a holiday in Palm Beach, Florida. The former King Edward VIII and his American-born wife Wallis Simpson were less than impressed with their accommodations and were expressing their dissatisfaction.

He hurried to the car in which the couple who prior to World War II had been at the center of a controversial romance that at one point threatened the very structure of the British Empire. There, he introduced himself to the Duke and the Duchess.

"The Duke said very little," Ken said, "and the Duchess did all the talking. She said that they were unhappy that their accommodations were so spare that there was not enough room to have his valet and her maid at their sides on the run to Florida."

"There really is little I can do about that at this point," Ken told the Duchess, adding that he would try to improve their accommodations when the train arrived in Washington. In the meantime, he would move the valet and the maid into their own compartments in the car in which the Duke and Duchess were traveling.

By the time the train reached Washington, Ken arranged for a special car to be added to the train for the famous couple's eventual return trip to New York City. And when the Duke and Duchess visited the dining car that evening as the train continued its run south, Ken had made his way to the dining car where he also had planned to dine and relax for a bit.

Their dinner completed, the Duke arose to pay for the meals on which he and the Duchess had dined. He was told that payment had been made in advance. When the Duke asked who had paid for the dinner, the steward pointed to the distant end of the car where Ken sat. As a thank-you, the Duke bowed deeply to Ken, and smiling, Ken nodded his head to the former King of England.

The question of whether Ken remained a fighting man, in the physical sense, was tested during his seven years at Atlantic Coast Line's Philadelphia headquarters. On most days, Ken would seek out a non-metered parking place on the street about ten blocks from his office. Near Christmas, Ken had done some gift shopping on his way into the city for a railroad meeting and found a parking space not far from his office.

He almost had completed the walk to his office when he realized that he had left his car unlocked and a scooter he had purchased for Kenny and a sweater meant for himself had been left where it could be easily seen. And now he remembered that two men had been loitering nearby when he had pulled to the curb. Now he rushed back to his car. The doors on the sidewalk side were standing open and the two gifts where gone.

Quickly, Ken got into his car and began driving slowly through neighboring streets looking for the two men before finally spotting one of them who was carrying a box under his arm that looked like the box that contained the scooter for Kenny. Stopping the car at the curb, Ken leaped out, rushed to the man and jerked the box from his arm.

"Where's my sweater, you son of a bitch?" Ken yelled at the startled man as he ripped the box containing the scooter from his arms. The man answered only with his actions.

Quickly, the man drew a switch-blade knife from his pocket and with a click that produced the large, gleaming blade began advancing toward Ken.

Ken put the box down on the sidewalk and prepared for the attack.

"Bring it on," he challenged the man. "I'm about to take that switch-blade away from you and ram it up your ass."

Before the man could advance further, a policeman who had been nearby arrived and ordered the man to put down the knife then listened as Ken offered his version of what he considered a theft. The man was arrested and when he was booked at the station, police discovered that he had a long record of arrests and assaults.

The police kept the scooter as evidence, though it was returned to Ken just in time for Christmas. The sweater, perhaps in the possession of the second man who had been nearby when Ken had parked, was never recovered.

If Ken had a routine in New York for getting ready for the New York-to-Florida run, he also was a creature of habit on the southern end of the trip. At the end of every run he made out of Penn Station, his home on the end of the line was the Mayflower Hotel in Jacksonville, Florida. There he became a dining room regular and became a first-name acquaintance of Billie Gimblet, the woman who was the manager of the hotel's dining facilities.

It was a conversation with Billie that would once again bring significant changes in Ken's life.

"Ken, I think I know a little something about people," she said as he enjoyed dinner at the hotel one night, "and I think I know something about you. I think you are a born salesman."

The possibility surprised Ken. "Billie, I've never even thought about being a salesman. Oh, I do a little selling for the railroad, I guess, because I try to get people to choose our line when they're traveling up and down the East Coast. But really a salesman? I don't think so."

"I'm telling you, Ken, maybe you don't know it but you're just waiting for it to happen. I'd like for you to meet my brother."

Billie would arrange the meeting between Ken and her

brother, Jim Norman, who was the vice president and marketing director for Norcross Greeting Cards. Jim would join Ken for breakfast at the Mayflower at the end of another trip a few weeks later, and he would introduce Ken to a new world of possibilities.

The two made small talk and then discussed the work Ken was doing for Atlantic Coast Line Railroad, the travel, the interaction with passengers that had been his way of life for most of eight years at that point.

The toast was getting cold and the coffee had run low and Jim was about to say goodbye. "You've got a good job with the railroad, Ken," he said. "But if you ever decide to change jobs, you need to give me a call."

For six months Ken thought about breakfast with Jim, and when he was a guest at the Mayflower he regularly suggested that Billie say hello for him. He also thought about what it might be like being a salesman. He had done well with railroad commissions until the line decided to split the commissions evenly with most of the people in the agencies. Commissions, he knew, could be lucrative and he presumed that working in the greeting card industry would be a draw against commission. By the second year, Ken said, "I was in clover."

And there was another factor that had become clear to Ken after eight years of railroad work. "The only way to get the really good promotions in those days on the railroad," he said, "was when somebody died or they retired. Once you made it into management, you pretty much had a job for life, but getting to that level was difficult."

Ken placed a call to Jim Norman.

A Change in the Cards

Ken's first impression of Jim Norman was a lasting one. He was slightly taller than Ken and, Ken thought, had a rare quiet dignity about him. He had the distinguished look of a gentleman and he spoke softly. Jim Norman seemed a man who had never known an angry moment.

Ken, on the other hand, had spent all of his life to this point in a world in which speaking softly offered no reward and conducting oneself in a gentlemanly manner was to be desired only in polite company. Ken had been a fighter and his had been a world of battles, individual and military, physical and emotional, and of brushes with death whether by roaring trains or whistling artillery. And here before him stood a man who seemed of a different, more orderly world, whose fights had come quietly in the pursuit of business, and Jim's demeanor captivated Ken.

Jim had spoken softly for a time giving Ken a glimpse of the world of greeting cards, of happy birthdays, anniversaries, congratulations, get well wishes, and of condolences and the like. And when the conversation had gone on long enough, Jim had invited Ken into his world.

"I decided right away that if this guy can be a success selling greeting cards, then I can, too," Ken remembered. "I took the job more because I was impressed with Jim Norman than for any other reason."

Ken also had one more reason to seek a profession with more potential than that offered by the railroad, and to work hard at achieving success in that profession. On March 10, 1962, Sue had given birth in New Jersey to the family's third child, Sam.

Though he didn't know it at the time, Ken made one of the most important phone calls of his life when he dialed Jim Norman's phone number at Norcross Greeting Card offices at 244 Madison Avenue in New York City.

"I'm ready to change jobs," Ken told Jim after introducing himself once again and mentioning Jim's sister, Billie, to make sure the memory connection had been made. From Jim's point of view, the hiring of Ken was merely academic. Jim suggested Ken meet with Paul Franzen, the company's district manager in Philadelphia. Ken's office was at Broad and Walnut and Paul's nearby at 13th and Market in the city, and a luncheon meeting was arranged.

Over Philly steak and cheese, the two men talked about Ken's work with the railroad. Ken would officially be a hire of Jim's, but Ken's training would be in the hands of Paul in Philadelphia where Ken would spend his first six months as a greeting card salesman.

Thus Ken entered the printed world of flowers and butterflies and gay ribbons and golden sunsets. But the fighter in Ken would not go quietly away. Indeed, a subsequent move to Jacksonville, Florida, where his post-training greeting card career would begin, offered Ken a far more intriguing outlet for the soldiering he still felt within. Ken would apply to become a member of the Army Reserve as a part of the Jacksonville-based 13th Special Forces unit, an outfit with challenges far greater than he had known with the Army company to which he had been attached as a reservist in Philadelphia.

If Jim Norman had questions and wise counsel for Ken, there would be questions of a different sort from the board of officers who would interview this new greeting card salesman to determine his worthiness to become an Army Ranger. "They literally would determine whether they wanted you or not," Ken said.

The possibility that Ken would not win acceptance was remote because his military record, especially in Korea, revealed that Ken was a soldier who possessed rare attributes and a unique dedication as a fighting man. His already was the heart and the soul of a Ranger.

Special Forces, the official military collective name for the Rangers, were yet to be tested in combat in a new kind of war then bubbling from a United States point of view in Southeast Asia. In that war in Vietnam, Special Forces would become legendary as "Green Berets" and would even be celebrated for years in song, including The Ballad of the Green Berets written by Robin Moore and Staff Sergeant Barry Sadler, himself a Green Beret. In a ratings war, the ballad performed by Sadler remained atop Billboard's charts for five weeks in 1966 in an era dominated by the Beatles and surfer music. As a wildly popular crossover, the musical tribute to soldiers fighting an unpopular war also hit No. 1 on Billboard's easy listening ratings and No. 2 in its country survey.

One of the primary missions for the Special Forces was the skilled practice of "unconventional warfare." Established in 1952, the Special Forces were marginally active if unheralded in Korea. In the years after the shooting war along the 38th Parallel had ended, the force of elite soldiers became a high priority in both training and mission by the Army. These were the men, according to the Special Force mission, who would swoop in to rescue hostages, who would specialize in clandestine operations and whose reconnaissance skills would be second to none. Above all, they would be fighting men, the elite of the armed forces.

In retrospect, it must have been the sort of unit that Ken's commander had in mind in Korea with the development of McCrory's Rogues and it seems likely that Major McCrory had been merely a man ahead of his time in that regard.

The Ranger style of fighting had been in Korea and still was the kind of soldiering for which Ken felt he had been best suited. But now, the self-appraisal came with a caveat: the man who was for a time perhaps America's youngest fighting man since the Civil War was now among the elders in a military world in which even the art of waging war had undergone a striking metamorphosis.

Militarily speaking, Ken was an old man of thirty-three.

With Ken's acceptance to join the Special Forces late in 1962 came a long-deferred promotion from first lieutenant to captain, a necessary step when it was determined that Ken would command the 13th's twelve-man A Team, a slot that called for the double bars of a captain. For Ken, the promotion had been far too long in coming.

Indeed, Colonel Locke had offered to "take care" of the promotion to captain when in 1952 in Korea he had offered Ken the post of company commander which, as with this Reserve assignment, also required the rank of captain. "It was just a matter of choice," Ken said in 2010. "In Korea I had wanted to be where the action was. On the front in that war with a carbine in my hands, I found something I was good at and that I wanted to do. It was just two steps above being a master sergeant. The rank of captain just wasn't very important to me in Korea."

But now the promotion to captain was significant to Ken for at least two reasons: he had remained "in grade" as a first lieutenant far longer than most silver bar officers, and Ken eventually would benefit from the modest difference in retirement pay between that of first lieutenant and captain. Though the age at which Ken could collect his military pension seemed far away in 1962, he knew that retirement from the military itself was growing closer by the day.

It was only the beginning of the card salesman's evolution from fighting soldier to a new kind of warrior in the Army Reserves. Because his role in the transportation company in

Philadelphia had been passive at best, Ken now would find out if he could successfully wear two hats, one in the business world as a greeting card salesman and the other as a Special Forces officer. The two worlds were almost as diametrically opposite as one could imagine. And though only a reservist, his new military training would become so intensive that Ken also would lead his A Team through Jump Master School with the 6th Special Forces Group at Fort Bragg, North Carolina, would undergo training in the Ranger School at Dahlonega, Georgia, and would parachute into jungles as part of the Jungle Warfare School at Fort Gulick in Panama.

America was preparing for a new kind of war, and Captain Ken Simpson was becoming a part of an important new approach to dealing with world tension. "As a side benefit," he said, "during that period I was probably in the best physical condition of my life except for the time I spent in Korea."

So it was in February 1963 that Captain Ken Simpson took his place on a C-123 Provider at the Fort Benning jump school, a transport from which he would make his first parachute jump from an airplane. He heard the engines of the big troop plane power up and felt the craft lumbering and lurching down the runway before finally lifting slowly into the Georgia air.

This was a training exercise, but this was different from most training exercises Ken had known over almost twenty years of active and reserve military service. "If you're on a range for weapons training, you get to try again if you miss your target," he said. "But you don't get practice jumps from a plane. There are no practice jumps. Every jump you make is for keeps. You don't get a do-over very often. If something goes wrong, you can't simply begin again."

On this day, as the team commander, it was Ken's lot to jump first and when the C-123 had climbed to about 2,000 feet over the jump zone, Ken was moved to the exit door by the training staff.

"But they wouldn't let me jump," he remembered. "They just put me in the door and kept me there while the plane circled the field. They wanted to find out if it bothered me." As Ken watched the world below him seem to move and turn with each motion of the big aircraft and watched the countryside far below seeming to rush past the toes of his boots as he looked down, he could feel as well the relentless blast of wind on his goggled face.

He was aware of a slight pain in his knee as a shrapnel souvenir from Hill 449 in Korea troubled him, and he ignored the reminder of another war. What would have been a dizzying vantage point for some soldiers was merely a place to stand for Ken. "It didn't bother me," he said.

Finally, he was falling toward the earth below and the trip back to the ground was, as such events are measured, routine. And suddenly he was down. He looked up at a line of other parachutists, the other members of A Team, with some of their chutes just then blossoming on opening.

"My first jump," he said, "but it hadn't been particularly thrilling. It was just something that was required with the job." Ken had limped away from his maiden jump, but the uneven gait was the result of the old shrapnel wound and not the landing. The offending twisted sliver of shrapnel would work its way out of his knee during Ken's training and would not prevent him from completing the required three jumps for graduation in jump school.

In all, Ken would bail out of airplanes exactly fifty times in the course of his Special Forces training and not all his jumps fell into the routine category.

"I jumped into fences and trees," he said, and for a time he was known as the only man ever to crawl back *into* a C-130 Hercules military transport plane in flight.

"The 101st Airborne Jump Master School was a hard ass school," Ken said. And it was to that "hard ass" school he and his team were assigned for training in August 1964 and it was there that Ken perhaps made history by aborting his own jump even after the first step from the plane.

"Unlike earlier jump training," he said, "at Fort Campbell

you were always jumping with packs that weighed close to 100 pounds. When you go, you fall out; you don't really jump, and the hardest part is carrying that bag off the field when you land."

But changing one's mind on a jump is not taught in any jump school. As both the team commander and jump master, Ken was scheduled to be the first to exit the plane.

"The jump master's supposed to count down the jump," he explained. "It's 'Stand up!', 'Hook up!', 'Move to the door!' and then the jump master's final command should be 'Go!', which is often forgotten or not heard." The hasty exit is designed to keep the small force of paratroopers relatively close together when they reach the ground so that the movement of the airplane over the jump zone does not scatter the soldiers too widely.

"I counted down the jump and all of the commands went fine, except I forgot 'Go!'. I realized this as I was about to leave and I tried to stop."

Ken crawled back onto the plane long enough to shout "GO!", then continued his jump. It had taken eight seconds for Ken to crawl back into the plane to correct his omission. Had it taken nine seconds, he would have failed the course.

To this day, Ken carries a physical reminder of another jump that went wrong, and almost fatally so. On another training jump, he became ensnared by the retrieving line trailing out of the body of the plane and lived to tell about it.

"I had just jumped, and as I put my arms around the equipment pack and my reserve chute in front of me, I apparently gathered up the retrieving line as well," he said. The line was trapped under Ken's left arm as he held his reserve parachute to his chest, and with Ken going one way and the plane the other on the parachute run, the retracting line quickly spun Ken violently head over heels.

"I knew, of course, that something had gone wrong; I just didn't know what had gone wrong," Ken said. "Besides, when anything goes wrong when you're jumping, it's already too late to fix it."

Ken could only partially "fix it" by keeping his cool in spite of the danger he was in. Ken was momentarily out of control as he tumbled through the sky, his static line opened his parachute automatically and he began to feel the first of the burning, painful sensation from the back of his upper arm. He floated to the ground and freed himself from his chute. Then he zipped open his jacket for a quick look to determine the extent of the injury. Much of the muscle under his upper arm had been ripped away apparently by the retrieving line.

Calmly, Ken once again zipped his jacket closed. "Not much I could do about it at the moment," he said, which was much the sentiment of doctors who later inspected the ravaged upper arm.

"They just said there were no broken bones and that it would pretty much get better by itself and that there was nothing left to be rebuilt," Ken said.

The oldest man in the school had survived a nightmare of a parachute jump.

But nothing compared to what had been expected to be a normal parachute jump into the jungles of Panama, if leaping from an airplane during a rainstorm into that tropical wilderness in the darkness of the midnight hours can ever be considered normal.

"A sergeant on the plane thought my equipment pack needed a little attention," Ken remembers. "I shouldn't have let him touch it, especially after I thought I smelled alcohol on his breath, but I did." It could have been a fatal mistake had the non-com been interested in Ken's parachute instead. When Ken led his team once again off the plane over the heart of the jungle near one in the morning, his equipment pack suddenly broke away, no longer tethered to his body, and disappeared into the darkness and the jungle canopy below. Ken floated down without the pack that had contained the things he would need to help him survive including his sleeping bag, food and tools.

"It was never found," he said in 2010. "Really, there wasn't much need looking for it in the jungle."

Ken's trial and that of his team was only beginning.

"To begin with," he recalled in 2010, "my men were so scattered in the jungle that it took me hours to round them up. They were everywhere."

Near sunup, Ken's twelve-man team was suddenly surrounded and bathed in flood lights so that the jungle scene looked and seemed surreal. They were told in English with a heavy Latin dialect to climb into a two and a half-ton truck for a ride to what they thought would be their base camp during the training session, an area considered a safe haven in a combat zone. A tarp was pulled over the bed of the truck covering Ken's team for its bumpy ride into the camp. They drove into the compound and pulled back the tarp and now Ken's team faced the blinding, penetrating glow of flood lights aimed directly into the bed of the truck. Suddenly, a sickening thought rushed through Ken's mind.

"We were prisoners!" he said. "We'd been tricked into prison. I was shocked. I realized that some son of a bitch had screwed me."

There seemed to be not a single American presence among the captors. All of them spoke Spanish and several of them, who would do most of the talking, spoke only broken English. Ken deduced that they were troops from a South American country. The fact forces foreign to the American Ranger candidates were at least temporarily in charge made the exercise in jungle survival even more realistic.

It was all a part, though intense, of the grand design in the making of a Green Beret. Now Ken realized that the sergeant's tampering with his equipment pack in the plane before his jump also was perhaps part of his own test. It became clear that not all the men would pass the test and those who failed would be washed out of the Ranger program. Despite this loss of his equipment, Ken would not be one of those considered not to be Ranger material.

"They stripped us naked and put us in a dungeon for twenty-four hours," Ken said. The team then was subjected to an intense form of both physical and mental testing. "We had to sit naked on the floor of this dungeon which had been a large, old septic tank." A metal roof protected the "prisoners" from the blazing tropical sun by day, but the heat from the roof also heightened the repulsive odor from the residue of material for which the tank originally had been used. "It was so bad you almost couldn't breathe," Ken said.

"It was a miserable way to train."

By day, the team was subjected to the mental part of the training. Still unclothed, eleven of the twelve, including Ken, were required to sit on the filthy concrete floor while the only black soldier on the team was given a chair, an apparent effort to tear the team apart. Together, they were exposed to the battering of a propaganda assault unlike any they had ever known.

"They were telling us why America wasn't worth a crap," Ken recalled. "They had a lot of nasty things to say about our leaders in Washington and in the military, and said again and again that a lot of Americans would be turning to the enemy. The enemy was our only salvation, they said."

Ken received special attention as the group's leader. He was subjected to still more potentially demoralizing talk about America and was finally given a promise of better treatment if he would become, in essence, a turncoat. Still angry that all of this had been visited upon his team without warning, Ken resisted until the end.

Finally, freedom came for the A Team, but the test was not yet over. There was one test remaining, a ten-mile escape and evasion test and it would begin when Ken's team was left in the jungle terrain ten miles from home. The test would be whether they could find their way back without assistance or transportation. In fact, there would be efforts to recapture the group as they worked their way through the jungle.

Ken considered the challenge, then suggested that the team work its way along trails that obviously had been frequently traveled and would not offer the dangers lurking in the jungle's natural world, or of getting lost.

"Doesn't sound like a good idea to me," one member of Ken's team grumbled. Most of the men wanted to go directly through the jungle and Ken accepted the will of the majority. Twelve men walked into the thick, tropical world and seemed to disappear into the thick vegetation of the Panamanian jungle.

The journey had been underway into the dark night for several hours when Ken called a first lieutenant who was in charge of plotting the direction the group should be going. It was a dark, overcast night with no stars visible, and no moon. "In fact, it was so dark you could barely see your hand in front of your face," Ken said. "We were blind."

But he took comfort in the fact that the lieutenant was known as an expert when it came to direction orientation.

"Do you know where we are?" he asked his fellow officer.

"I don't have the foggiest idea, captain," he responded.

"Well, what do you know for sure?" Ken pressed.

"Captain, in this darkness, I don't know a thing. What do you think?"

Ken was silent for a moment. Before he could come up with a plan, there was the flickering of a flashlight behind them.

"We're in luck," Ken thought, assuming that here approaching from the rear was a unit that knew where it was going.

"Glad to see you," Ken said to Sergeant Robert (Bob) McCort, his counterpart with the newly arrived team which also had been freed from the jungle warfare training and had followed the A Team into the jungle.

"We're lost, too," Sergeant McCort reported. It was figuratively and literally a case of the blind leading the blind. Now, there would be two dozen men searching for a way out in the dark night. Ken became the man in charge and he turned his thoughts once more to the problem at hand. Now Ken had a plan. This time, he would not consider the democratic majority.

"I think that if we keep walking until we hit the French

Canal, then turn left, we'll wind up where we're supposed to be," he suggested. Twenty-four weary soldiers began once again working their way through the forbidding jungle. They finally walked into the small river known to American soldiers as the French Canal on a night so dark that almost none of the soldiers realized they had reached the landmark until they became aware they had stepped into moving water and not stagnant swamp. In fact, the soldiers had reached the river on a moonless night in which the darkness far away from known settlements was so deep that it became necessary for the soldiers to hold onto each other so that their ranks would not be scattered in the lightless night.

Turning left, the group soon ran into more problems.

"There was swamp everywhere," Ken said. Still, the twenty-four waded in stepping on brushy growth when possible for footing and sometimes wading in waist-deep water.

"I warned everybody about swallowing too much of that swamp water," Ken said. "But I didn't want to tell any of them what bad shape we were in."

It occurred to Ken, and certainly to the other men in the group that the swamp is home to a wild array of creatures, some of them capable of and known for life-threatening attacks.

"Certainly I understood that," he said, "but you have to ignore thoughts like that. I just kept telling myself that there's room enough in the swamp for all of us."

Sometime after midnight, the two teams walked out of the swamp. They were within mere yards of their home base.

"They wanted to see how we would handle ourselves in the jungle," Ken said. "What you have to remember is that in Panama, there are mountains and valleys and swamps in their jungle. Getting through the swamp was not an easy thing, but I also didn't want my men walking off a cliff. Some of the cliffs there are so covered in growth that you can walk off one before you know it. This was a very dangerous trip."

Not all of Ken's team would be considered Ranger material,

though most would. And some of them would use their skills in Vietnam.

It was a war Ken would finally miss.

"If I wasn't ashamed of leaving home again, I probably would have been in Vietnam," he said. "But from the beginning, I thought it was a war we couldn't win, the wildest war we were ever involved in."

Ken retired from the Special Forces and from the military on March 1, 1968. He had spent twenty-three years as a fighting man.

(Ken has maintained a life-long friendship with Bob McCort, who continues to live in Jacksonville, Florida.)

The Transformation

Billie Gimblet, the food service manager at the Mayflower Hotel in Jacksonville, had suggested that Ken consider sales as a post-military profession. The wisdom of that advice was still uncertain in the summer of 1961. On the surface, it seemed an unlikely possibility. As a military man, Ken had spent his career in uniform not particularly interested in pleasing the people around him, including higher ranking officers. Now, he would be in the business of selling feel-good moments to people who would be browsing in the card sections of places of business served by the Norcross Greeting Card Company.

Even the personalities in the upper reaches of the company offered stark contrasts to some of those Ken had known in the military. If Colonel Locke had been a snarling, disagreeable, in-your-face superior officer, Jim Norman was an exact opposite, soft-spoken, gentlemanly, and quiet though he could be a Mr. Hyde when he had too much to drink. If Colonel Truman commanded blind loyalty, Norcross founder Arthur Norcross was at the distant end of the spectrum. His own family played key roles in the conduct of Norcross business including the selection of greeting card designs, and Arthur Norcross himself considered employees to be virtually members of his extended family. That relationship permeated the company in both word and deed. When Norcross employees were called away to military duty, it was customary for Mr. Norcross to keep in close touch through the exchange of letters and – of course – greeting cards. And he invited wives or brothers and sisters of employees in the military to fill the vacated positions until military obligations had been served. Arthur Norcross did not demand loyalty; he inspired it.

Ken's take-no-prisoners approach as a soldier through the last dozen and a half years would not change. He simply would no longer wear a helmet and meet resistance with an M2 carbine. Ken's new profession as a greeting card salesman that began with Ken simply working the card racks for one of Paul Franzen's accounts, the John Wannamaker stores in Philadelphia, soon would produce a warrior of a different sort.

In the spring of 1962, Ken moved his growing family from the Philadelphia suburb of Haddon Heights, New Jersey, back to Wake Forest, North Carolina. It was uncertain where Ken would be assigned following his six months of training and Sue had the infant Sam to demand her attention.

"I was worried about expenses at the time," Ken said, "and Wake Forest didn't cost anything." Sue and the three children would have a place to live with Sue's mother and her grandmother until Kenny finished the school year and Ken had found a new home for them all wherever his new location took him.

What Ken did not know in those early months was that from the moment Ken had signed on with Norcross to begin six months of training under Paul Franzen in Philadelphia at Wannamaker's and at Pomeroy's in Levittown, Jim Norman had picked Ken to work the company's weak Jacksonville, Florida, market. The Philadelphia experience had amounted to a different sort of boot camp for Ken who could have spent his half a year under Paul's tutelage merely making sure the right envelopes were with the right cards in display cases in stores to which he was assigned. He did that, of course, but he also watched the idiosyncrasies of potential customers, noted the lifestyles of browsers at various locations and studied what was hot in greeting cards and what was not without realizing at the time that all of that had a name – demographics. He would become an expert at demographics and also spend time listening closely to both compliments and complaints from store managers.

From the very beginning of his greeting card sales career, therefore, Ken stood out, mostly because of early assumptions he made. Among those assumptions was the conclusion that most salesmen are more likely to cultivate a business they already have rather than working to find new accounts, and he decided that the fear of being intimidated and the dread of rejection was at the root of this approach. Ken decided that he would not take it personally when he was told "no," and that he certainly would not be intimidated. Norcross was the big winner. While still in training, Ken made pitches to the Philadelphia Navy Yard and the Army's Frankfort Arsenal and successfully landed both accounts taking the business away from Hallmark in each case. The two accounts became very large contributors to the Norcross sales volume.

But to land the two big accounts, Ken also relied upon his understanding through experience of the way the military operates. And he decided upon what the Army would call a covert method for getting the audience he would need to make his pitch on behalf of Norcross. Since a trainee, which he was at the time, would have little chance at success at the Navy Yard and Frankfort Arsenal, Ken decided to introduce himself as a visitor from Norcross's home office on Madison Avenue in New York City. If he could sell that approach, perhaps it would not matter that he had no title of salesman or district or regional sales manager, nor did he even have business cards to offer. He wanted to give the impression that he was his boss' boss, someone important enough to be shown through the office door and to the desks of decision-makers. In the end, he would tell them, a local salesman would be assigned to the account and would assist in the presentation.

The plan worked.

At the end of Ken's six months of work with Paul Franzen, Jim Norman and his wife met Ken at a Travelodge Motel in Jacksonville, Florida, and loaded him down with Norcross Greeting Card samples and cases which he would use to launch his work in Jacksonville. Even then, Jim Norman recognized the eagerness in the company's newest salesman and he cautioned Ken to look after the meager business Norcross already had established in Northeast Florida before looking for new business.

"Don't you think we ought to look after the business we already have here before we go looking for more?" Jim suggested.

"If we had any business to look after, it would be a big help," Ken had replied almost sarcastically.

The most significant account already established in the Florida city was the card section of the May-Cohen's department store, a part of the massive May national chain, in downtown Jacksonville. And Ken would certainly serve that location. But one of his first moves was to go across the busy street from May-Cohen's to discuss installing Norcross as the principal greeting card concessionaire in Ivey's, which arguably was destined to become May-Cohen's biggest competitor in the local upscale merchandising business.

Though Jim Norman had advised Ken to shepherd business that already had been established, Jim already had laid the groundwork for possibly adding Ivey's to the Norcross client list in Jacksonville. Ken was advised to contact Irving Jackson, the manager of the Ivey's store then being built near the May-Cohen's downtown. While construction was underway, Jackson's office was in the Florida Bank Building where Ken called on him.

From the beginning, the Ivey's approach was a test even though Jim had done the preliminary work. Hallmark, Mr. Jackson said, would control 60 percent of the card concession with the remaining forty percent going to Norcross. Ken knew the unfavorable split was, nevertheless, a foot in the door. He also knew that Jim Norman had negotiated a sixty-forty split that favored Norcross.

"May I use your phone?" Ken asked Mr. Jackson. He dialed the number at which he could reach Jim Norman, briefly explained the split with Hallmark that Mr. Jackson had just laid out, and then handed the phone to Mr. Jackson. Jim then explained that John Fielder, Executive Vice President of all Ivey's stores, had assigned control to Norcross.

It was at the moment not good news for Mr. Jackson who, with resignation, told Ken that it had been his preference to keep Hallmark in control of his card department.

"In six months, Mr. Jackson, you will be delighted that you have Norcross in charge," Ken predicted cheerfully. Ken's prophesy came true; Ken eventually took over 100 percent of the store's card business and Ivey's remained under Ken's direction with both Norcross and later Gibson until the chain was sold to Dillard's in 1990.

Despite Jim's counsel, Ken had hit the ground in Jacksonville fired with enthusiasm for the challenge of creating his own territory. Ken would prove to be in his element in his new work and his new location. On the surface, the prospects in Jacksonville seemed to be outstanding and the financial carrot for Ken would be a potentially lucrative agreement and included a commission of up to fifteen percent in addition to a monthly draw against commission.

"It was a high commission rate, but there was no business in Jacksonville," Ken said. "Fifteen percent of almost nothing is still almost nothing. That was okay with me. All I had to do was to establish some business and pretty soon I'd be making a lot of money."

It would take persuasion to find one key businessman willing to give him a chance before Ken could change the way the greeting card business worked in Northeast Florida. That one key businessman would be John Greenall, the owner of the Jacksonville area drug stores including Lakewood Pharmacy, Greenall's No. 1

store.

At first, John seemed less than enthusiastic about turning over his card section to what amounted to a green greeting card second lieutenant. But, neither John nor anyone else had ever dealt with a greeting card salesman such as Ken.

John already had considered a modest renovation of his greeting card display for Lakewood and now used that plan, though not yet formalized, as a reason to delay giving Ken and Norcross the green light in one of his stores.

"I'd need to sell the old displays," John said defensively, "so you could bring in new ones. And that might take some time."

"How much are they worth?" Ken quickly asked.

"Oh, $350, I suppose," John answered.

Ken didn't have $350, but he knew where he could get it. He mortgaged his personal life insurance policy, used the money to buy John's old greeting card fixtures, and then hauled them to the dump.

John had his new fixtures and $350 and Ken had an important toehold in North Florida. "It was the best store he had," Ken remembered. "It was a great drug store, but it was not a great card store when I got it." Yet, in the final quarter of 1962, the only Lakewood Pharmacy in Duvall County featuring Norcross cards saw a substantial increase in sales from the card racks and more than doubled Lakewood's anticipated revenue stream from the concession in that one test location. At the end of the first year, sales from greeting cards alone would be up for Greenall because of Ken and Norcross by more than $10,000.

In Ken's case, there was an even more significant development. By the end of the year, John had become an important reference, though unofficially so, for Ken's growing business. Regularly now, managers of other stores in the area with modest or under-performing greeting card sections began calling John Greenall to ask about Ken and his operation.

"Almost all of them had the same question: 'Is this guy for real?'" Ken said.

"I can tell you this," John said as the calls and the questions came in, "you can forget about that part of your business if you give it to this man. He'll set it up and run it and all you have to do is take in the money."

John Greenall was more than talk. Before 1962 had run its course, he had turned over all four of his Jacksonville area drug stores to Ken and the positive impact upon income was almost immediate.

"I was doubling what they were getting before," Ken said.

It was an impressive start. Word was spreading and both American Greetings and Hallmark had learned that the Jacksonville area was no longer their exclusive territory to share. Now they had to deal with Norcross and, more specifically, Ken Simpson. Within months of putting the new fixtures and a new method of operation in at Lakewood, Ken was adding more locations for Norcross. Through Jim back in the Madison Avenue home office, Norcross was now installing new fixtures in all of the newly acquired locations. The coffee shop in the Prudential Building, one of John Greenall's locations which had belonged to the giant Hallmark, was next to make the move to Norcross and Ken in something of a coup. It was a key and highly profitable location with an upscale clientele.

In short order, Ken was adding the final two Greenall locations, Service Drugs and Mandarin Drugs, to his list of clients as well. For the new greeting card salesman, life was good.

Ken wasn't doing it with new fixtures alone; he also was introducing new features to the business that to the buying public were not as obvious as shiny new fixtures in the card department. He offered a petite widow who worked at a gift wrapping job at May-Cohen's in Jacksonville one dollar an hour to look in on card sections in Lakewood Pharmacy once a week. It was the same amount she was being paid in the downtown department store. She took the part-time job.

"So, we took control of maintaining the card sections,"

Ken said. "We didn't have to rely on perhaps a stock boy who might or might not have much interest in keeping everything neat and attractive. Store managers quickly found out that they didn't have to pull an employee off another job any longer to straighten up the card racks. In fact, they didn't have to worry about the card section at all."

Store owners, such as John Greenall, loved the concept. Within months, Ken hired two more housewives part-time at one dollar an hour, paying all three out of his own pocket, to keep other Norcross card sections in pristine condition. In the years immediately ahead even more women would be added to the part-time rolls and Norcross began sharing equally with Ken in the costs of that service as well.

Ken had resorted to the part-time help because of a lesson he had learned in Wannamaker's in Philadelphia and at Pomeroy's in Levittown. "I found out that when you keep the card display straight and attractive, you wind up selling more," he said.

It was a concept that store owners and managers could understand. But at first, store owners were less certain about yet another innovation Ken brought to the business. With the display racks for cards fully stocked, the storage drawers were, by Ken's design, empty which meant that the host business had less money invested in inventory. In the future, Ken would again implement this program while working for Gibson Greeting Cards, and Gibson would adopt the system throughout its empire and it would become known as the "Everything Up" program. In a sense, "Everything Up" would revolutionize the way Norcross and its imitators did business and in the distant future would sweep through the industry. It seemed a small adjustment, but over time "Everything Up" would revolutionize the business for the greeting card industry nationwide.

If Ken faced a major challenge day in and day out from the well-entrenched Hallmark system, early in his time in Jacksonville he began to face a strong approach by American Greetings as well. American was offering better terms than either Norcross or Hallmark by paying the cost of shipping and also instituted a program of returns and credits on seasonal cards. But once again, Ken didn't roll over.

"If you're not happy with Norcross and the profit we are making for you, which should always be more than three percent (average shipping costs in the 1960s), I will pay the freight out of my pocket."

Then Ken matched American by instituting a season return policy by offering his customers credits and a re-billing program.

In less than six months, Ken's approach to his new job would be vindicated. He had honored Jim Norman's cautious charge to take care of the customers he had inherited, but he had gone much beyond that point in whirlwind fashion. And it was all typically Ken Simpson.

"I never changed my attitude," he said in looking back to those important early months in the greeting card business. "In all of my life, all of my jobs conflicted with logic. But no job was ever too little or too big, and every job I ever took, I could find ways to make it work.

"I suppose it was a God-given thing. Anybody can see what is; it's seeing what could be that makes all the difference in the world.

"Through it all, I had the enjoyment of just being me."

That Simpson style had attracted attention not only of rival card companies because of its rapid successes, but also, of course, from Norcross. Back on Madison Avenue, Arthur Norcross himself was keenly aware that the Jacksonville, Florida, area had quickly become a major producer for his company and he discussed the developments there with Jim Norman.

"What you need to do," Mr. Norcross told Jim, "is to go out and find some more Ken Simpsons."

"I didn't find Ken Simpson," Jim responded truthfully. "My sister did."

The Florida Years

Jim Norman himself had launched his career with Norcross in Jacksonville and therefore had a paternalistic feeling about the territory in which he had played a pioneering role. If he had been concerned that Norcross customers who predated Ken Simpson might not get the care and attention he felt they deserved, time would work to allay his fears. Ken had inherited the May-Cohen's account that when Ken arrived in Jacksonville was bringing in about $14,000 a year to the downtown department store. It had been and would remain one of the area's most profitable Norcross clients. Indeed, the May-Cohen's profile would only improve. With Ken establishing his own business footprint and his own personality in Northeast Florida, May-Cohen's would bring in more than $30,000 annually in greeting card sales.

Ken had only just begun.

"I had known since I ended my six months of training that I had made a good move," Ken said. In fact, as a trainee, Ken had been Norcross' top salesman in the Philadelphia area and his zeal for the job had only been confirmed in his first months in charge of his own district in Northeast Florida. And he had been paid the princely sum of $10,000 by the end of 1962, $2,000 more than he had earned in his last year as a railroad employee of eight years.

Ken began to spread his business wings. He went after the account of the office supply company, Chestnut's, and broke Hallmark's long relationship with that firm. In the process, a friendship that would last for years was formed with Mrs. Chestnut, the widow who ran the company, and her son, Joe Dunlap, a former Eastern Air Line pilot. It was Mrs. Chestnut who had made the initial contact with Ken.

"She called and said she had a couple of $100 Christmas orders and wondered if that would be enough money," Ken remembers. "It was pretty big money to me at the time, and I handled the order for Mrs. Chestnut."

Within two months, Ken and Norcross had taken charge of the greeting card end of Chestnut's business and had completely redesigned the section. Norcross' presence in Chestnut's had become permanent and so had his friendship with the family.

Ken then landed a major toy store in the university town of Gainesville, and continued to expand his territory by placing Norcross in stores in Daytona Beach, New Smyrna Beach, Deland, Ocala and Tallahassee.

Then he turned his attention to a bold experiment as a test for what he perceived about the buying public. He contacted Sam Getzen who operated the book store at the University of Florida in Gainesville seeking at first a small part of his floor space.

"Give me three fixtures," he challenged Sam, "and I will sell more cards than you can sell in the whole department."

Clearly, Sam was skeptical, but he could not pass up the challenge. Ken filled his three fixtures with something close to a specialized line of cards. "Look, who comes into a college book store? Students. Teenagers. Young adults.

"So, there were almost no cards wishing speedy recoveries from surgeries or illness, no retirement cards, almost no condolence cards. It was simple logic. You put in the things that students buy and they don't buy the same cards that their grandparents buy. It took just three months and Sam was convinced," Ken said. Hallmark was out and the book store account belonged to Ken and Norcross. The card section continued to perform at a high level with Ken believing in his own informal demographic studies.

The storm warnings were not yet hoisted for the major greeting card companies in Northeast Florida, but day by day, Ken was improving the Norcross foothold in the region. In 1963, Atkinson's Pharmacies was the strongest private chain on the drug store scene in the Jacksonville area when Ken began calling on them. Atkinson's was no easy sell, even for Ken, but the quality of the management at the top made the chain desirable for Ken. It would take him two years, however, to persuade owners Frank and Frances Atkinson to switch their card sections to Ken. The private chain was a dominate player in Jacksonville when Ken set his sights on it. Ken's interest in the Atkinsons' operation came as the pharmacy business nationwide was undergoing fundamental changes based primarily on the switch from family-owned operations to chain establishments.

Atkinson's Pharmacies was a bit of both, family-owned and yet a chain operation with stores in the Jacksonville area positioned well in key locations demographically. Ken had made inroads with Frank Atkinson, a tough, no-nonsense man. "He had a good name, did a good business, and paid his bills," Ken said. He also was a shrewd entrepreneur, and in 1968 when twin brothers Harold and Howard Osteen came to inquire about purchasing some of the Atkinson's operations, Frank Atkinson was willing to listen.

He eventually sold all but one of his stores to the brothers with whom Ken already was doing business in other North Florida area drug stores which they owned.

For most of five years, as Ken spread his growing influence throughout Northeast Florida, he continued to deal with the Osteen operation and to remain a supplier for Frank Atkinson in the pharmacies he had retained under the Atkinson banner.

"Frank Atkinson knew the drug store business inside out," Ken said, "and when he told me that Eckerd was going to expand in the Jacksonville area, I listened." Among the properties on which the growing drug store giant had set its sights was the group of stores Atkinson had sold to the Osteen brothers.

"It's going to happen," Frank Atkinson warned Ken, "and if you're going to stay in those stores, you're going to have to do the best selling job you've ever done to Harry Roberts, and he's tough. But, you've got to sell him or lose the stores."

Emboldened now with a growing list of successes and more optimistic than ever, Ken decided that he not only wanted to keep the locations that would go to the national chain, but he set his sights on expanding his greeting card reach even more significantly in North Florida. The Eckerd chain was growing rapidly and was becoming a major business presence in North Florida and Ken wanted Norcross cards available to Eckerd customers.

Warned by Frank Atkinson that Harry Roberts was a tough negotiator, Ken knew this conquest would not be easy. Clearly Ken would have to deal with Roberts, the president of Eckerd who answered only to Jack Eckerd, the chain's owner and founder. The challenge for Ken would be in getting Roberts' attention, if only briefly, and his first attempts in the form of telephone messages seemed to have been repeatedly ignored.

Ken did not give up. He found his opening in the pages of a newspaper and a story that Eckerd had scheduled a grand opening for a new store in Tarpon Springs. Ken knew that Roberts, along with Jack Eckerd, had a policy of attending all grand openings. This time, Ken also would be there.

Ken had done his homework and knew that Roberts was a no-nonsense kind of man. He was a former Marine Corps colonel who looked every bit the Leatherneck. And when on the day of the grand opening Ken approached Roberts in the new drug store, the man still had the bearing of a strong military man.

"Mr. Roberts," Ken greeted him. "I'm Ken Simpson with Norcross Greeting Cards."

Ken waited for a response. There was none, only the stern look this man had obviously used in his career as a Marine Corps officer. The silence in effect became the man's response.

If this was an attempt at intimidation from Roberts, it wasn't working on Ken, just as First Lieutenant Simpson had been more amused than intimidated the day Colonel Locke had shattered the phone against the bunker wall in anger.

"I need just five minutes of your time," Ken said, breaking through the stony silence.

Now, apparently using a bit of drama to make a point to Ken, Roberts looked at his wrist watch and noted the minute. "You have five minutes," he said, and Ken knew that he had not a second more than five minutes to make his pitch on behalf of Norcross.

"I have Norcross cards in the drug stores you are purchasing in Jacksonville," Ken began bluntly. "I can give you a card section second to none and I will do it in a way that's different for the industry and for Eckerd, and before you throw me out, I want to make sure you know what you're throwing out."

Ken paused, gauging whether he still had the man's attention. Roberts' gaze into Ken's face had not changed, and Ken felt the seconds ticking away in his timed five minutes.

"I know American Greetings," Ken continued, "and the big difference between Norcross and American is who pays for the labor and accepts the responsibility for the success of the card department. In the case of American, they criticize and you pay for the corrections. Working with my company, you do the criticizing and I pay for the well-being of the card department. I have people who service your department every week at my expense. Your job primarily is taking in the money. I would like for you to observe my operation before you terminate it."

"I'll be in touch," Roberts responded. Ken made sure Roberts knew how to reach him by handing him his business card. Ken thanked the Eckerd president and turned and walked out of the shiny, new store.

Roberts kept his promise. Three weeks later, he was on the phone to Ken from the lunch counter at his Five Points location in Jacksonville.

"Roberts here," he said gruffly when Ken had picked up

the phone. "Been thinking about what you said at the Tarpon Springs opening, and I've got a couple of questions."

"Where are you?"

"The Five-Points store," Roberts answered.

"I'll be there within the hour," Ken said and hurried to his automobile. Arriving at Five-Points, Ken found Roberts quickly. "What are your questions?" Ken asked.

"Do you really think you can do better with my card department than I'm doing?" Roberts asked pointedly.

"No doubt about that," Ken answered quickly.

"Tell me how your operation will work," Roberts responded.

"My people will do everything to make the operation a success at my expense," Ken said. "They do the servicing, the reordering, and the stocking of the card racks. The testimony from your people to your supervisors will tell you that this is a big improvement on the way you operate your card departments."

"And what will that cost me?" Harry Roberts pressed.

"Nothing," Ken said. "Not a thing. That's just part of the Norcross service. We will pay the people who keep the card section looking good and we'll always be on top of things. And if your managers want something done a different way, all they have to do is tell us about it."

"I'm leaving your operation in the stores you already have until further notice. Time will tell," Roberts said, apparently not yet fully convinced but willing for the moment to accept Ken at face value.

Ken's relationship with Roberts was off on the right foot. "He approved of me for whatever reason," Ken said. "The key from that point was that we were as successful as I knew we would be. After the meeting at Five-Points, we got all of the new Eckerd stores in Jacksonville. And a short time later we got all the stores in Gainesville, Palatka and Daytona Beach.

"It was what they would call today a 'home run,'" Ken said.

Ken had a very good 1968 and bought his second new Porsche, which happened to be the automobile make preferred as well by Harry Roberts.

"For a long time, when we had a meeting with Eckerd Drugs, I'd always try to park my Porsche as close to his as I could," Ken said with a grin. "Just a little thing to amuse myself."

Roberts even came to be pleasantly amused at the manner in which Ken kept records of card inventory in various locations. Roberts was accustomed to American Greeting representatives arriving with long, unfolding IBM printouts to which they constantly referred; Ken, on the other hand, merely leafed through a small black notebook in which he kept track of his operations in the various stores whose accounts he held. Ken thought his method was the more advanced one.

In an era well before the boom of the dot-com era and the age of expansive houses called McMansions, it was boom time for Ken. From his modest salary of $10,000 in his first years with Norcross his compensation rose steadily and impressively to $40,000 "all on Eckerd, existing business such as May-Cohen's, and on new business," he said.

"And we were making friends wherever we went."

Ken had become a star in the Norcross Company and an intimidating force for his contemporaries with other greeting card companies, particularly American and Hallmark. By 1967 the times had begun changing for Arthur Norcross' company.

Most importantly, Arthur Norcross' health was no longer reliable. Cancer had taken its toll and the Norcross founder died in 1968 at the age of 72. His death signaled the beginning of the long road also to the death of the company he had nurtured through the heart of the 20th Century. Mary Calvo, Mr. Norcross' long-time assistant, moved to the head of the company as its president and in 1974 presided over the sale of Norcross to William Mannion whose father-in-law, John Dorance, was the CEO of Campbell's Soup. The company would then dissolve into a relationship with Rust Craft Company and the once-proud family business was finally sold ignominiously at auction, with American Greetings buying most of what was left, in 1981, a year in which Ken was named Regional Manager of the Year by Gibson Greeting Cards.

Despite the upheaval at Norcross in the days long before Ken would land in the Gibson company, Ken continued to work his territories and make friends, among them Ron Campbell. Ron worked with his mother and father at the Happy House Shop in the Bellaire Shopping Center in Daytona Beach, one of the companies whose account Ken had landed soon after arriving in Florida. The Campbell's Happy House itself was a survivor, one of the last of a chain of retail outlets under the Happy House name, a chain that had failed to thrive. Homer Campbell was a hard-nosed business man who had prospered with the A&P grocery chain in Pittsburgh before moving to the warmth of Florida. Mr. Campbell was a man who took little at face value and could be convinced only with proof. And when Ken was able to back up his promises to Happy House with increased greeting card sales, the elder Campbell was happy.

When Homer Campbell died in 1967, the victim of a long-standing respiratory illness, not long after Ken had taken over the account, Happy House was left to Ron and Homer Campbell's widow, Catherine, who also had health problems that led to a stroke.

Mrs. Campbell was not particularly happy when on January 2, 1968, Ken hired her son away for a brighter future and for more money than he had been earning in the family business. Ken expected Ron to take primary responsibility for half of the business profile Ken had created in North Florida including all of the accounts in Gainesville, Tallahassee, Ocala, Palatka and Daytona Beach. With Ron leaving the family business, his wife, Billie, moved in to take his place at Happy House. But Ron's departure, coming as it had with the lucrative Valentine Day card bonanza on the horizon, threatened to split mother and son, and Billie's presence in the family shop did nothing to smooth the transition. Ken ordered Ron home.

"You've got a job with me, so don't worry about that," Ken advised Ron. "What you need to do now is go home and straighten this situation out with your wife and your mother. Find a way to make them happy, and then come back. Your job will be here when you get that taken care of."

It was the kind of business relationship with which Ron had not been familiar. Yet, through Valentine's Day, Ron remained so much in conflict between the job with Ken and the family business that he confided with his wife that he would probably withdraw from the Norcross card staff.

"If you do, I will divorce you," Ron's wife warned him.

"I never knew if she really meant that or not," Ron said in 2011, "but I wasn't willing to take a chance." He helped get Happy House through the lovers' holiday, made peace with his mother, and returned to Ken's staff to tend his accounts. By Easter that spring, his mother had sold the business and retired.

Ron's employment with Ken lasted thirty years, far longer than most marriages but not the one between Ron and Billie. The friendship between Ken and Ron still was intact in 2011 more than forty years after their first meeting. When Ron retired from Gibson Greeting Cards in 1997, he had worked only briefly for anyone other than Ken. In most of the years together, Ron was Ken's Director of Operations and was a logistics expert and a man who was perhaps the foremost expert in the nation at installing card sections in large chain accounts against remarkably tight deadlines.

Though markedly different in the talents they brought to their professions – Ken was the idea man, Ron the man who made the ideas work – they shared interesting memories of youth.

Like Ken, Ron had volunteered for the military and became a merchant marine on D-Day, June 6, 1944, at the age of only sixteen.

"My second voyage as a merchant marine was into the Strait of Gibraltar, going from the Atlantic into the Mediterranean. When the Germans found out I was coming, they surrendered as we sailed through the strait," Ron exaggerated.

Ron celebrated his seventeenth birthday in the port of Odessa, Russia.

"A few weeks later, we were sailing out of San Francisco bound for Asia. As we crossed the International Dateline, the Japanese heard I was coming and they gave up too," he laughed.

Also like Ken, education was not a high priority in Ron's teen years. Ken won his high school diploma through the GED program on Guam. Ron would finally graduate from high school through the adult education program at the same Florida high school from which his three sons graduated.

The Simpson-Campbell combination would dominate for a time a large part of the national greeting card business for much of the final quarter of the twentieth century.

In the late 1960s, however, there were other concerns that would get the attention of both Ken and Ron.

After the death of Arthur Norcross, Ken's own sphere of influence began to shift in the company, thanks to his obsessive drive to succeed as a salesman. Jim Norman was still in place on Madison Avenue and he chose Ken to assume responsibility for Norcross sales from Baltimore south to Florida, a geographical area Ken managed from Jacksonville, Florida.

Despite his increased responsibility, Ken, however, would not be around for the final rites for the Norcross Greeting Card Company. As expected, everything changed under Mannion who exhibited, in Ken's estimation, none of the humanity of the late Arthur Norcross.

To create his brain trust for his newly acquired company, Mannion turned to Hallmark and the fact that Ken led the company in sales and had been doing so for years now apparently meant little to the new regime. Still, the chatter figuratively around the company water cooler was that "we can't wait for the new bosses to meet Ken Simpson."

There were those left over from the old company who thought such a meeting would favor Ken. Ken understood that wasn't likely. "They were the bosses and they could do what they wanted," he said.

Among the first moves by the new leadership was to call a national sales meeting in January 1975 in the new company offices in West Chester, Pennsylvania. All the sales staff from around the country was required to attend, including Ken who was by then the best-known and most successful salesman in the stable.

Two former Hallmark men would run the meeting, and one of them, Tom Blades, as the new vice president for sales, was Ken's new boss. The other was Al Vikowski. Blades and Vikowski called Ken for a private hotel room meeting soon after he arrived for the national meeting.

Blades came straight to the point.

"We want your resignation," he said, stunning Ken.

"You're in charge, so you don't have to have my resignation to fire me," Ken responded.

"Then we will fire you," Blades said.

"What are the terms?" Ken pressed.

"There are no terms. You're fired," Blades said pointedly.

"That's where we part company," Ken said. "There will be terms one way or the other. I've been with this company thirteen years now; that means at least thirteen weeks of pay."

Ken would succeed in getting thirteen weeks of salary from the new company, but his first order of business was to find out when the next flight could get him back to Jacksonville. Before Ken could gather his bags and check out of the hotel, the sales meeting involving the remaining staff from across the country was called to order and Blades stepped to the microphone.

"We just fired Ken Simpson," he announced. "So if any of you think we won't make changes, you'd better reconsider. No one is untouchable."

Privately, Ron Campbell would seek answers to the question of why Norcross' most productive salesman had been brought to an end.

"It is an integrity issue," Ron was told.

"I don't know what your idea of integrity is," Ron bristled in response, "but the Ken Simpson I know is not short on integrity."

If the warm, family approach had not died with Arthur Norcross, it now unquestionably was dead.

"The growth of the Northern Florida market was the greatest success Norcross ever had," Ken said, still defending himself long after retirement, "and they fired me."

The new company officials had made an example of their most productive resource. The company's days were numbered and the departure of Ken did nothing to change that except, importantly, to accelerate it. The great flaw in reasoning by Blades and Vikowski was that the accounts Ken had created belonged to Norcross. It became clear within days that the owner of those accounts was Ken when with one phone call Ken cancelled eight accounts and moved them to American Greetings, the new company for which Ken had just gone to work.

If there was to be *quid pro quo* for Ken, it would be years in coming. Ken, of course, would land on his feet after being fired and within two years would become one of the leading sales managers for Gibson Greeting Cards. It was in that capacity that Ken would take a phone call from company headquarters informing him that Tom Blades was being considered for a position with Gibson.

"Do you know him?" Ken was asked.

"I sure do," he had responded. "And I know you'd better stay as far away from him as you can."

Blades never became a Gibson employee.

Horses, of Course

If the new movers and shakers at the helm of Norcross thought that the firing would be the last they heard of Ken Simpson, they were wrong. Even before he arrived at the Philadelphia airport for his return flight to Jacksonville, Ken placed a call from a pay phone to Dale Wolff, a former fellow Norcross employee then associated with American Greetings, expressing his interest in continuing his sales career under another umbrella, perhaps that of American.

Wolff was excited about the possibility and was quick to act taking the news of Ken's interest in American to the highest levels of the company. The response came even more rapidly than Ken expected. By the time Ken arrived at home in Jacksonville, Dale had left a message that Ken should call again as soon as possible. When he placed the return call to Dale, Ken was told that Morry Weiss, Vice President of Sales, Marketing and Creative Services, wanted to meet with Ken in Miami where Weiss maintained an apartment. Ken would be there within the week, they agreed, and in the course of a pleasant visit with Weiss, Ken was told that American intended to offer him a job.

"I don't know what we're going to do with you, Ken," Weiss finally said, "but we're going to hire you." Weiss offered Ken a starting salary of $17,000 a year plus a $4,000 bonus to join the American ranks. It was far less than Ken had been earning, mostly through commissions, in his final year at Norcross, but it wasn't a matter of considering one or the other; the Norcross income had come to an end except for a severance amount yet to be determined.

For thirteen years, Ken had been one of American's biggest headaches. Now, at least, the big headache could be removed. Theoretically, with Ken in the fold, competition for greeting card sales would become a pain for other companies on behalf of American. For Weiss, it was a hire that would do nothing to derail his ascension at American Greetings. Two years later, he would be appointed president and chief operating officer and eventually would reach the top of the ladder as American's chief executive officer and chairman. (A capable executive in his own right, Weiss also was well-placed in other ways. He was the son-in-law of Irving Stone who, at the time, was American's chief executive officer and Stone also had controlling interest in the company through his stock holdings.)

In the short run, it also was a hire that did almost nothing for Ken except to for a time provide him with an income, albeit a reduced one. On paper, it seemed a shrewd move by Weiss and American. In reality, Weiss' words in his conversation with Ken became prophetic: American didn't know what it was going to do with Ken. In the clear retrospect of looking back more than forty years, Ken said, the relationship had little opportunity to work well.

"The concept was flawed from the start," Ken said. "The people I had been taking business from for years were all of a sudden supposed to become buddy-buddy with me. It just doesn't work that way.

"I got along good with the regional manager in Atlanta, though. But, I had the feeling that he was more interested in keeping me out of the business from the American point of view than getting me into it.

"It became clear that most of the people at American were just anti-Simpson and potentially what I could do for the company was of no consideration."

Ken's marketing strength, which he had honed over the previous thirteen years, never became a trump card for American. Certainly in Florida if not most of the rest of the country, Ken had set a new standard for the marketing of greeting cards, a standard based upon service to the retailer. Harry Roberts of Eckerd had liked Ken's marketing approach so much that he turned over forty stores, twenty of them in Dade County, to Ken long ago in a major coup for Norcross. It was so much a major move that American Greetings launched its own merchandising service program. Owners and managers of other stores and shops across North Florida had, like Roberts, also become believers in the Simpson style. There were dramatic sales increases at almost every shop Ken touched that would have confirmed the validity of his marketing plan.

But, Ken would learn that American had a long-standing opposing view of his introduction of merchandiser service to the greeting card accounts. Before Ken became one of them, if only briefly, some American executives said that Ken's marketing style had set the greeting card industry back twenty-five years. It was a view that was particularly prominent among sales representatives who had felt the sting of clients lost to Ken. On the other hand, beneficiaries of his marketing techniques would say that Ken had advanced the business by at least a quarter century.

Interestingly, none of the major card companies other than Norcross moved quickly to the new marketing approach that had been so successful for Ken. But Ken would stick to his plan and, though American would finally grudgingly buy into a watered-down version of his program, Ken still was preaching its virtues long after he retired.

"It's something I'm still very proud of," he said. "All of a sudden, the plan to serve the retailers in a new and different sort of way moved from the hiring of one part-time woman to two and then to three at the beginning. Then you look around and something like a thousand jobs like that had been created around the country. It is satisfying now to realize that we were putting people to work. It was a new job with a new job description, and the workforce was readily available. They were mostly housewives who didn't want to work full time but who were interested in earning a little money by looking after card sections in stores."

With Ken on the way out, Norcross had its own problems. No sooner had his hiring by American Greetings become official than Ken cancelled pending orders for eight of his leading accounts in Jacksonville and switched all of them to American, a move that was duly noted in West Chester, Pennsylvania, the new headquarters for Norcross since leaving Madison Avenue in New York City. When Tom Blades, the Vice President of Sales at Norcross, saw the cancellations representing eight lucrative outlets in Florida, he was alarmed.

"Do you think this is the extent of the damage Ken will cause?" Blades asked Jim Norman.

"Son, it ain't even started yet," Jim answered darkly. He knew Ken Simpson well both professionally and personally. Even Jim's family knew Ken. Ken even had become a favorite with Jim's son, Mark, who as a child had enjoyed playing soldier and found gifts of genuine fatigues, canteens, pistol belts and the like from Ken enthralling. Jim himself knew well the heart of the old soldier and he was right; the damage had only just begun. Within a week, more than twenty more accounts were cancelled and presumably switched to American and there would be more, many more, in the weeks ahead.

At the same time, Ken was having his own personal difficulties as well. His long marriage to his childhood sweetheart, Sue, was in the process of disillusionment though the painful parting would still be months away.

"When I married her, she was every bit the lady," Ken said. "But life has a way of dealing things, some of them unpleasant. And I didn't help the situation. I was gone much of the time and had not played a big role in raising our children. I always seemed to be getting home after they had gone to bed and leaving the next morning chasing work before they ever got up."

Furthermore, Ken's work ethic made his relationship with his children, particularly Kenny, difficult at best. "I was a lousy parent," Ken said in biting self-criticism. "Kenny and I talked about that when he was a middle-aged man. I told him that my own father never supported us and was never around even though he was already a school teacher at the age of eighteen.

"My father had left his family behind and was no role model for me. So the only thing I knew was making money and, unlike my father, my goal was always to make enough money to support my family."

Yet, Ken was a tough task-master when he was home with his children during their waking hours and, once again, used his own life experiences as his guides.

"For example, when I was a kid, I would never run from a fight. But, Kenny wasn't wired that way. I remember making Kenny walk up the street on the wrong side because there were bullies up the street and his inclination was to avoid them. I never believed anyone could make you walk across the street if you didn't want to cross it. So, I made Kenny face the bullies." The exercise did not bring father and son closer together emotionally.

The relationship between father and older son also did not improve when Ken grudgingly gave Kenny permission to drive his new Porsche supposedly to a nearby convenience store where Kenny and some of his teenage buddies were known to gather.

"Go there and straight back home," Ken warned his son. "I don't want you driving around with your buddies in the car." Kenny indicated that he understood his father's conditions and drove away from the family home.

In less than half an hour, the phone in the Simpson home was ringing.

"Mister Simpson," the male voice on the other end of the line was saying, "I live down here on the highway and your new

Porsche is on my front lawn on its roof."

Stunned, Ken rushed to the scene of the accident. Kenny and one of his teenage friends had been in the car when, apparently because of excessive speed, it had gone out of control and flipped. Neither boy seemed injured but Ken put both of them into his car and hurried to the hospital to have them checked out. "I had to make sure there were no hidden injuries," he said. "The last thing I needed at the time was a big insurance claim."

Ken would within weeks, however, finally succumb to Kenny's plea for a car of his own and the younger Simpson had his eyes on a particular 1958 Chevrolet. But Ken decided a Nash Rambler was a more conservative choice and purchased the iconic vehicle for his son. But clearly, Kenny considered himself more of a Chevy man than a Nash man.

"We have never been close," Ken said of his relationship with his older son in 2010. "But our relationship is better today and it is clear that he has done a good job with his family."

In a real sense, Ken's family would most often be the people with whom he worked. "People who worked for me were the people who were close to me," Ken said in a moment of introspection. "But, I had trouble tying the knot with my family."

If Ken's relationship with Sue was teetering on the brink, his relationship with American Greeting was never a high priority for his new company. "They didn't know what to do with me, but they paid me for almost a year," Ken said.

Indeed, Ken had switched large pockets of his Norcross business to American in the aftermath of his firing. Yet Ken had a light workload when it came to calling on store managers and selling potential new accounts. There was never any push to unleash Ken's sales abilities that American had felt so keenly as a competitor.

Ken was left with time on his hands and an urgency to find a way to make up the difference in compensation from the level he had achieved at Norcross and the salary at which he was hired by American. Almost in a thinking-out-loud sort of way, Dave Hodgkiss, who had been one of Ken's salesmen at Norcross, mentioned that selling horse feed could be the answer. Dave had some expertise on the subject and was particularly impressed with a product made available to horse farmers and sportsmen under the Falstaff label.

Ken had thought Dave's suggestion that horse feed could be a lucrative commodity a curious comment and pressed for more information. It was clear that Dave had considered the possibility more than merely causally. The best horse feed available in Florida, where there were plenty of fine horses, Dave said, came under the brand name Falstaff, and was a subsidiary of the brewery by the same name. In the Sunshine State, Falstaff feed was available only in the Sarasota area.

"It's the best horse feed a farmer or a rancher can buy for his horses," Dave told Ken. "It's fourteen percent protein and the horses love it and it's good for them."

Ken had heard enough. He cleared out his home office, rented a U-Haul truck and trailer and he and Kenny drove to Sarasota. They drove back to their Jacksonville home with thirteen tons of Falstaff horse feed, all in fifty-pound bags.

"Here I was, with an office filled with horse feed, and I didn't even know anybody who owned a horse," Ken said with a smile in 2010. So, Ken hit the highway driving up and down rural roads in Duvall County and even into the thoroughbred country that stretches south of Gainesville in the Florida interior. "Every time I spotted a horse, I stopped and tried to find its owner."

Ken knew only one way to sell his thirteen tons, the same way he had sold greeting cards. He would provide more service than the local feed store would or could offer.

"I made a deal with the horse owners," he said. "I would provide the best horse feed money could buy, and I would put it into the farmers' feed sheds and I would keep the feed sheds stocked. The farmers would never have to worry about that part of the operation again."

"All you've got to do is open the fifty-pound bags and feed it to the horses. And pay me," Ken would tell the horsemen as he quoted a price that would give him a profit of about fifty cents a bag.

Ken was in horse feed business and the money was beginning to roll in. With Ken continuing to search the back roads for business on the weekends and working for American Greetings during the week, word of his new venture was spreading across North Florida.

After picking up his first load in Sarasota, Ken began contracting with long-haul truck drivers bound from Florida, usually loaded with citrus, to the Chicago area. Instead of searching for other loads for the return trip, they would take on twenty tons of Falstaff horse feed in the Illinois city and return to Jacksonville every Friday where the fifty-pound bags once again would be off-loaded into a warehouse Ken had quickly rented when his feed business began to grow well beyond his former home office.

It was a whirlwind business venture, however, and it died when the brewing company withdrew from the horse feed business leaving Ken with customers he no longer could supply. "When I lost Falstaff as the supplier," Ken said, "the happiest people in North Florida were the Purina people."

"So I bought my own eighteen-wheeler," Ken said. He hired drivers and began scheduling runs for them hauling citrus to northern destinations from Chicago to New York. Occasionally, Ken would ride with the drivers on their long hauls and on at least one occasion took the wheel of the big rig as a relief driver. It was easier to get premium horse feed for a time than to find reliable drivers. Eight big rig jockeys were in Ken's employ in the year he was with American. Though the horse feed aspect of the business had been sound, it was not enough to bolster the operation of the big rig. Ken lost $20,000 in a year and sold the truck.

Almost from the beginning of his relationship with American Greetings, frustrations were building. Nine months in,

Ken still was feeling like a greeting card salesman who just happened to sell horse feed. But, those two worlds were beginning to shift. Had Falstaff not discontinued the horse feed line, would Ken have become a feed salesman who also happened to sell cards?

Falstaff's withdrawal from the business had made it a moot question. Ken's role with American had become unquestionable when on a single day he moved eight outlets to American. In doing that, Ken once again had outlined the service the managers and owners could expect. "I agreed to certain service levels with the companies and American refused to abide by those agreements."

It now was clear that a future with American was not in the cards. But, other factors were in the works that would finally once again restore Ken as a warrior in the greeting card industry.

Ken was about to get a telephone call from English Bennett, a man who once had worked for Ken at Norcross. Gibson Greeting Cards' Southeast regional manager Frank Lubrecht was interested in discussing the possibility of Ken's return to the card business in a very active way, English said. It was a contact that could hardly have come from anyone better connected at Gibson than Frank; Frank's brother-in-law, Dick Eubanks, was the Chief Executive Officer at Gibson and his blessing could be strongly implied.

"Would you talk to him?" asked English who apparently had been the man who had stoked Lubrecht's (and presumably Eubanks') interest in the old Norcross renegade.

"Sure, English. I'll talk to anybody," Ken said.

A Gibson Guy

As a man who had carved out his own niche, if only briefly, in the horse feed business in Florida, Ken was a pretty good greeting card salesman in the opinions of most upper level management in the industry. So when Ken drove to his appointment with Frank Lubrecht in Orange Park, a southern suburb of Jacksonville located in Clay County, on that pleasant day in January 1976, he knew why he had been asked to the meeting and it wasn't to discuss the proper protein balance in horse feed.

On the drive to the picturesque bedroom community surrounded on the east and south by the waters of Doctors Lake, Ken considered what he knew of Gibson, including the fact that the company at the time was considered third in the industry behind Hallmark and American, with Norcross a distant fourth.

"I knew that Gibson was number one in the country in serving businesses that wouldn't grow," Ken said critically in 2011. Though he wasn't sure such an appraisal would be of benefit in his talks with Frank, Ken was pointed in his critique of Gibson when the subject was broached early in his meeting with Gibson's Southeast manager in Orange Park. And Frank had not disagreed with Ken's analysis.

"What do you think should be done about that?" Frank

asked.

"I think you should get rid of those businesses that won't grow and find some that will," Ken responded.

"Could you make that happen?"

"Certainly," Ken responded.

"Would you be interested in coming to work for Gibson?" Frank asked.

Though he had expected the question, Ken did not answer quickly. "It depends," he finally parried.

"On what?" Frank asked.

"Well, it depends on how much freedom I would have to run my part of the business aggressively and, of course, what you are willing to pay me to do it."

Without question, these were answers from Ken that Frank had expected. "We'll offer you $20,000 a year and a bonus," Frank said. It was, Ken thought, not a get-rich-quick salary, yet it was one that was acceptable in the market in the early days of 1976, especially if Gibson would stand by its bonus promise for the long haul.

"What will the bonus be based on?" Ken asked.

"On the business you bring to Gibson," Frank answered. "In other words, the bonus will be based on what you generate for Gibson."

"So, you can pay me a percentage of the business I create for Gibson? Can you really do that, even if I am very successful?"

"Yes, sir," Frank answered unequivocally.

"And what's the job?"

Ken would be the district manager for all of Florida, South Georgia and Mobile, Alabama, Frank said. It was an industry footprint that Ken knew well and which Ken thought was perfectly poised for growth, especially by a company such as Gibson that had a lot to offer but almost no aggressive representatives in the field to make it work. In that regard, Ken was well ahead of the curve in understanding the business and the differences between Norcross, for whom he had worked for thirteen years, and Gibson, the company he may now join. To Ken, compared to Gibson, Norcross had been limited in its scope in the industry.

"Norcross sold greeting cards, and that was it. That's all there was," Ken said in 2011. "But Gibson had the total package – greeting cards, gift wrap, gift bags, and other paper products. Gibson had the complete package, from a product point of view. But it was my impression that Gibson wasn't coming close to using what it had available to its best advantage." Ken was confident that he knew how to parlay that untapped Gibson strength to major advantage.

"You've got a deal. You just hired yourself a district manager," said Ken, reaching across the table to shake hands with his new boss. Ken was ready to launch his own program in the Southeast and immediately would begin to surround himself with familiar and trusted faces.

The first call he would make once the meeting with Frank had come to an end was to his old friend, Ron Campbell, whom Ken had hired at Norcross in 1968 and who quickly agreed to become one of Ken's managers under the Gibson banner. "I trusted Ron," Ken said years later, "and he turned out to be the best hire I ever made. He was the best operations man I ever knew. I would make commitments to clients that seemed impossible sometimes, and Ron would get it done.

"Details don't amuse me. But Ron would take a job that required a lot of detail and he'd just work it to death." The Simpson-Campbell alliance would last for the rest of Ken's corporate career and would become the most dynamic in the greeting card industry.

Though English Bennett, then the Gibson representative in Birmingham, had obviously given Frank an accurate picture of Ken, his former boss at Norcross, it is likely that not even Frank Lubrecht fully understood the transformation of a company and an industry he had just put into motion.

It may be that Morry Weiss, the top executive at American, knew what was now likely to unfold, however.

Within a week, Ken flew to Cincinnati, headquarters city for Gibson Greeting Cards, to meet with company officials for the first time. As he unpacked his suitcase in his hotel room, the telephone on the nearby side table jangled to life. Weiss was on the line.

In retrospect, Ken thought it a strange conversation. It seemed clear to Ken that American had hired him almost a year earlier not to sell greeting cards, but to eliminate him as the spirited thorn-in-the-side competitor for American he had been when he had worked for Norcross. As an American employee himself, Ken had merely marked time for almost a year selling few greeting card accounts in North Florida while selling horse feed and overseeing the driving of citrus north in his eighteen-wheeler. His having a business on the side seemed of no concern to American, as long as Ken wasn't causing havoc as competition for American.

Now, though, Weiss seemed to be saying that Ken's defection to Gibson was a major blow to him personally.

"I am really disappointed in you," Weiss said on the phone. "I would have thought you would have consulted me before you took the job with Gibson."

Weiss' opening comment caught Ken by surprise. Ken was thankful that American had been there to hire him after his ambush firing at Norcross. But there seemed little tying him to the company beyond his gratitude. Indeed, in the months that payroll checks had been arriving from American, Ken had seen Weiss but one time "and there was no reason to expect that he had special interest in what I could do for American," Ken said.

"Can you think of any scenario at all under which you would come back to American?" Weiss challenged Ken seemingly opening the door to a wide range of possibilities.

Ken was silent for a moment as the question raced through his mind. "No, I really can't," Ken finally answered.

"Well, you're a big boy and it's your decision," Weiss responded. There the brief conversation had ended but not Weiss' effort to derail Ken's employment with Gibson. A day later,

American was on the phone again, this time to officials at Gibson. In that telephone conversation with Gibson, American demanded that Gibson fire its newest district manager because, it was claimed, he was under contract to American.

"Which was true," Ken said in 2011. "It was a contract that prohibited me from operating in the same area for another company for a year after I no longer was employed by American." Indeed, Gibson had hired Ken to manage the very area for which Ken theoretically had been responsible in his months with American, seemingly in violation of his contract. Ken's sphere of influence would be in the Mid-West, a Gibson official informed American.

In order to validate that response, Gibson quickly added the Mid-West Region to Ken's realm of responsibility. American pursued the legal question no further.

Now, what Ken considered the passive nature of Gibson's sales force became an annoyance to Ken. In considering the challenge that lay ahead of him, Ken realized that in fourteen years of existence in the card business, he had become acquainted with only one member of the Gibson sales staff. He had never encountered another Gibson salesman in the field in all that time. It was a realization that haunted Ken as he prepared for his role in a district Gibson sales meeting scheduled in late winter 1976 in Orlando. Getting ready for that meeting was not unlike the painstaking preparation he had made for his work on Hill 449 in Korea; Ken knew the lay of the land and he was ready to move. There would be nothing timid about his approach.

There had been what Ken had seen as a gratuitous reunion quality to the sales force meeting at the beginning. Old salesmen were renewing acquaintances, asking about family and spending time retelling old tales. Finally, with the meeting underway, Dean Sampson, Gibson's national sales manager, introduced Ken as the newest district manager and it was Ken's turn to address the gathering of salesmen who now would answer to him. "I had something to say," Ken remembered, "and even though it was my first sales meeting with Gibson, I never thought about trying to tone down what I would say."

It became clear immediately that Ken Simpson wasn't in Orlando to enjoy the late winter warmth and to socialize with the people who worked for his new company, some of them for decades. From the beginning, he spoke bluntly.

"I've been in the field in the card business for fourteen years now," he told the Gibson field staff, "and I've never met any of you. I've never seen you out there. I've been there every day, but I've never seen any of you there.

"Well, ladies and gentlemen, it is a different day for Gibson, at least in Florida and parts of Georgia and Alabama. We're going after the business and we'll be successful. In fact, I am here to win and to be successful. Nothing else will be acceptable. We're going to be out there working the territory as never before. We're going after everything, mom and pop operations, but also the big chains. We don't have to roll over and give up the big accounts to anyone.

"Now you can come along with me or you may decide not to come along. It's up to you and I don't give a damn what you decide, but the people who work for me are going to be successful."

Ken had finished his brief talk. The room had fallen silent. No one marked the time or the date on the calendar, but it was a defining moment not only for Ken, but for Gibson and the greeting card industry as a whole.

When the meeting had drawn to a close, Ken and Dean Sampson walked together from the room. Little was said until Dean quietly remarked, "I've never attended a sales meeting like that before."

Dean's words were not news to Ken Simpson.

Ken had discovered and then capitalized on a little-known precept of the greeting card industry at the time. It was possible to create relationships with retail outlet managers that would develop based more upon service provided than in brand recognition. At the time, the Hallmark name, for example, was not impossible to overcome as a competitor.

"Ken was committed to serving the customer," Ron Campbell said in 2011. "Ken would offer services that the big two, Hallmark and American, either wouldn't or couldn't. And the big two knew that whatever region Ken was working was a region where they were going to have a fight on their hands."

Ken was not the sort of manager, Ron said, who did his work tied to a desk in an air-conditioned office. "He knew everything that was going on, every contact his people were making and what was at stake," Ron said.

"All the area managers, like me, who worked for Ken were expected to keep him informed. We were to call Ken every Sunday evening to go over what was coming up early in the week and to discuss any problems we thought might come up. I had the Daytona Beach area at the time, and I was on salary plus expenses, and my home telephone bill always seemed to run between $400 and $500 a month. And most of that was for calls to Ken, mostly on Sunday night.

"I would begin trying to call Ken about six on Sunday evening and many times I would get busy signals," Ron said. "I knew that meant he was talking to some other manager who worked for him. There were Sundays when I wouldn't get through to Ken until around midnight, but I wasn't going to bed without getting that call through. It was all about service."

From the beginning at Gibson, Ron knew Ken well enough to know that servicing the account was the key. Now, Ken was about to begin cashing in on his earlier relationships, especially with Eckerd Drugs through Harry Roberts. Because of Ken's limited role with American, the Eckerd stores he had won when he was with Norcross still had not been switched to American. The Eckerd outlets soon would be moving, but not to American.

Already, Ron was on the phone to Milton (Andy) Anderson with whom he had worked at Norcross. In the phone conversation, Ron had told Andy that Ken would be moving the Eckerd accounts to Gibson "so, if you don't mind, you can bring the files on those accounts over to me." It was a rare, bold move, but one that would have eventually fallen into place even if Andy had resisted the request.

Andy, who would later also join Ken under the Gibson banner, complied delivering the Eckerd files from Norcross to Ken's office and to Ron. Gibson to that point had never aggressively gone after the chain operation business. Indeed, almost by design, it seemed, Gibson had avoided competing for the business of retail chains in its geographic footprint. Now, within the first year with Ken as district manager in the Mid-West, Florida, South Georgia and in the Mobile, Alabama, area, Gibson would begin serving many outlets for the burgeoning drug store chain. Many others would follow in the months and years ahead and, indeed, would become the backbone of the Gibson Greeting Card Company for years.

On the part of the Gibson map controlled by Ken, the world was changing rapidly and the change was not very appealing for most of the Florida sales force that had attended the Orlando meeting. Defections and resignations were coming in every day, and as quickly as one resignation arrived on Ken's desk, another former or current Norcross employee who knew well the Simpson style was hired as the replacement. Many of the new Gibson staff members were people who had been Ken's fellow salesmen at Norcross and were pleased to be on board with another company and with their former salesman in charge. Quickly, Ken was assembling his own sales machine, especially in Florida.

In fact, by early summer, only three key members of the Florida sales force in place at the time of Ken's hiring remained employed by Gibson, and two of those three were tenuous at best. One of the three had at one time been a district manager himself and had a long history of more than twenty years with the company. But that, too, was about to end. When the man informed Ken that he had plans to vacation in Alaska, Ken had advised against it.

"You won't be taking that vacation with my permission," Ken informed the man who once held the job Ken now occupied. "If you go to Alaska with the situation we have going on here in Florida right now, your job won't be here when you get back."

"He went to Alaska," Ken said in 2011. "He had no job when he got back."

Yet another salesman with a long history with Gibson failed to attend a mandatory sales meeting at a Howard Johnson's motel near Miami. When Ken inquired about the missing member of his force, he was informed that the man had an installation in Boca Raton that day and was attending to that. When the meeting had ended, Ken drove to the Boca Raton store where he found his salesman sitting alone in an empty retail shop apparently awaiting a shipment of fixtures and product that had not yet arrived.

Ken's visit was short and to the point.

"Didn't you know I had called a sales meeting in Miami?" Ken asked.

"I knew," the man answered. "But I needed to get this installation done."

"What installation?" Ken responded as he felt his anger rising. "You're just sitting here in an empty store."

"There must have been a mix-up," the man said weakly.

"You have a choice," Ken said to the startled employee. "You can resign. You can retire. Or I will fire your ass. You decide. Right now!"

The man retired on the spot.

Some viewed Ken's presence in the first year with Gibson as something of a reign of terror. Others saw it differently and, indeed, people with whom Ken had worked successfully in the past were anxious to rejoin their old boss with Gibson. It was the sort of transformation of that part of the company Ken had hoped would occur. And the transformation had come even more rapidly than Ken had expected.

Still, years later, and in the clear respective of looking back, Ken was astonished that he had the latitude to change the company as he did. "It still amazes me that Gibson would just turn me loose and let me have my head the way they did. I wound up firing everybody in the state except one man, and I never thought about whether that was a problem or not. The only man I didn't fire was John Lubrecht, the boss' son who had the Orlando area. And it wasn't because he was Frank's son; John was the smartest man in the region. I didn't enjoy firing people, but I was determined to have an operation that would be successful.

"There also is another way of looking at what was going on. By being so aggressive and working to increase the volume, we wound up saving a lot of jobs.

"But I recognize now that I really was ruthless. I was cleaning house in Florida and nothing was going to stop me unless they fired me." But Gibson apparently could not afford to terminate the renegade. He was changing the playing field for the card business in Florida and Gibson was clearly benefitting fiscally. When the dust had settled on his first year with the company, Florida had moved to No. 1 in sales volume increase for Gibson.

Indeed, in the year just prior to Ken joining Gibson, the district recorded $1.5 million in sales volume. In Ken's first full year, it topped $2.5 million in what was primarily new business. At the same time, businesses that would not grow were being terminated which, Ken said, "was damn near all" of the existing business he had inherited at Gibson. Ken envisioned a sizable bonus as a result only to find that Gibson was drastically limiting that part of the commitment it had made to its new district manager. Ken was awarded a modest bonus with an equally modest pay raise.

Both Ken and Gibson had begun a journey in which there would be no turning back. "When I worked for Gibson, it was the most success I ever had," Ken said as he looked back in retirement. In 1976, the memorable years for Ken had only just begun.

Just Friends

If Ken struck fear in the hearts of reluctant salesmen who were in place when he was hired as a manager by the Gibson Greeting Card Company, the effect he had on business owners and managers was just the opposite. It was not unusual for Ken to become friends with his clients. Though some of those friendships would last a lifetime, Ken's own personal life was not marked with closeness to his immediate family. While Ken was reshaping the greeting card landscape in Florida for Gibson, his marriage was falling apart. Indeed, Ken's marriage to Sue was past rescue when Ken loaded a desk and typewriter into a trailer he had used for hauling horse feed and moved out of the family home in Jacksonville. He moved to Treasure Island on the West Coast of Florida not far from St. Petersburg from where he would manage his gold mine of a territory under the Gibson Greeting banner. Sue filed for divorce which became final in 1977, and Sue and Sam, the couple's youngest child, moved back to Wake Forest, North Carolina.

While Ken was perhaps vilified by former Gibson salesmen who disdained a more aggressive approach to the greeting card market, he was adored by store owners and managers, including Frances Atkinson who, with her husband Frank, owned Atkinson Drugs in Jacksonville where they had Ken and the Norcross card line in their store. Once, when Frances and Frank attended a trade show and stopped by the Gibson booth, they met Bert Rovens. Rovens was then a Gibson vice president and when he began pitching the Gibson line to the Atkinsons, Frances quickly placed his chances of doing business with the company into perspective.

"We can talk about anything in the store except for my card section. I love my card man," she said, referring to Ken and the service approach he had brought to the Atkinson business. No one was going to dislodge Ken from that involvement with the drug store operation. Atkinson Drugs was not an exception in that regard; in Ken's business life, that sort of loyalty was more frequently the rule than the exception.

That loyalty underscored the unique relationship Ken had with clients and that relationship became the cornerstone of his greeting card success, Ken's long-time operations manager Ron Campbell said. "I came from retail," Ron said in 2011, "and I first encountered Ken when he was trying to sell my father on Norcross for my father's Happy House store. We had Hallmark and a company named Rust Craft, which is no longer in business, in our card section. Ken wanted Norcross there with Hallmark and when he made his pitch, I didn't think we could do it. I pointed out that if we went with Norcross, we would have to pay heavier freight charges for having product shipped in to the store.

"Ken reached into his pocket and brought out some money and put it in my hand. 'That's for the freight,' he said. And that made a lasting impression on me and we wound up with Norcross as our primary card provider.

"It was clear that Ken knew as a salesman what I knew as a retailer, that service is often more important than price or terms."

What neither knew at the time was that a relationship that would last far beyond retirement for each had been put into motion. "We became brothers," Ron said.

By the time Ken was hired by Gibson, his business acquaintance with Nancy Falkenheiner and her husband, Charles, the owners of Just Cosmetics, had been in place since the Norcross years and the accounts were now with American Greetings.

More than a year into building his career with Gibson and in essence rebuilding the card industry on the East Coast, especially in Florida, the lucrative Just Cosmetics accounts remained with American. Ken knew that American was not then and really had never been committed to the service levels that made Ken successful with his clients. Just Cosmetics was featured in twenty-eight Belk-Lindsey stores in Florida and half of those had very profitable card sections.

"Nan," Ken said, using the shortened name by which Nancy Falkenheiner was known, "became my biggest account in 1977" and took over Just Cosmetics after the death of her husband. Through the first year with Gibson, Ken thought about the greeting card bonanza that Just Cosmetics represented and hoped that someday it would become a part of the growing Gibson profile in Florida. But Ken made a decision that friendship in that case was more important than business and he would not push Nan in that regard. He never brought up the possibility of moving the account to Gibson in conversations with the woman who would become one of Ken's best lifetime friends.

"I wouldn't try to sell her until she was ready to ask me to take over the (card) business," Ken said. He knew that Nan was well aware of the drastic difference in service with and without Ken involved and Ken believed that eventually his long-time friend would seek that more desirable service level once again. Ken was right. When Nan finally broached the subject of moving Just Cosmetics to Gibson and asked him to take charge of her card department, Ken was ready to move. Just Cosmetics once again quickly became one of his largest accounts and would remain with Ken for years to come.

If anything, Ken's relationship with Just Cosmetics confirmed the personal friendship between Nan and Ken to an even more permanent degree. She retired in 1986 after selling the Just Cosmetics franchises outright to Belk-Lindsey.

(Nan Falkenheiner remained a close friend. Nan died in 2001 and a marker acknowledging the long friendship has an honored place in the Simpson memory garden near the crest of Walker Bald.)

Officers who had out-ranked Ken during his military days, including many of those in command positions, sometimes had been keenly aware that controlling this warrior had not always been an easy task. In more than a decade and a half in the greeting card business, higher management had discovered the same thing about this man with a passion for serving his greeting card customers. In both cases, it was clear that Ken was in the battle to win, whether from a military or a corporate point of view.

"In the greeting card business, Ken was great at solving problems, even if he had to throw money at it to arrive at the solution," Ron Campbell said. "It wasn't always what upper management would have done, but by the time upper management found out about Ken's solutions, it was usually too late to do anything else."

Tom Cooney, Gibson CEO 1978-1986 (1984)

One man who learned of Ken's personality the hard way was Thomas M. Cooney who was fifty-nine years old when he succeeded Dick Eubanks as Gibson Greetings' chief executive officer in early 1978. Cooney, a former candy company executive, had been selected by CTI Financial Corp., the owner of Gibson Greetings since 1964, to turn the company's earnings around. The card section of Gibson had shown losses in revenue for six consecutive years when Cooney arrived. Cooney intended to begin reversing the company's fortunes by learning about how the company worked from the grassroots up. When Cooney heard that Ken soon would be pitching Jefferson Super Stores, a small chain of large retail outlets serving South Florida from Boca Raton to Miami, Cooney decided he would participate in the effort and flew to Miami.

Ken had never met the man who had been hired to lead Gibson back to corporate profitability, but he knew of Cooney's reputation. "He was a head knocker," Ken said years later. "He didn't mince words and he was as tough as they come.

"He had been hired to grow the company and he wasn't too big for any kind of job. That was clear. Which is why he had come to Miami to help sell Jefferson."

If knowing as much about Ken were deemed important by the new Gibson boss, Cooney would arrive in Miami at a distinct disadvantage.

Cooney and Ken had barely become acquainted when the meeting with Jefferson management began. Cooney did much of the talking, and he decided to emphasize a point that came as a troubling surprise to Ken. Cooney hammered home his view that Gibson Greetings offered clients such as Jefferson Super Stores a level of service the quality of which was, according to Cooney, unequalled in the business.

"Our service is great, better than any in the business," Cooney flatly proclaimed. "Isn't that right, Ken?" Though a plan for the sales pitch to Jefferson had not been discussed beforehand, Cooney obviously had expected Ken to pick up on the theme perhaps, and that he would choose to postulate. When Ken's response came, Cooney was clearly stunned. Years later, Ken said that by passing the proverbial baton his way, Cooney had left Ken with a problem. "I knew Gibson's service wasn't the best in the country, and it really wasn't that great," Ken remembered. Would he now give credence to something that, in Ken's mind, was grossly flawed?

Ken paused briefly and gathered his thoughts. Then instead

of underscoring Cooney's claim to Jefferson management, Ken spoke first directly to his boss.

"Tom, I'm a district manager for Gibson. Mine is just one district in the company. I can't talk about the other districts, but I can talk about my district, which is the district in which the Jefferson Super Stores are located. And in my district we have great service, certainly better than anybody else in the country." Ken left it at that. Cooney smoldered.

When the meeting had ended, Ken knew that Cooney was clearly upset. "He didn't like me very much," Ken said. "He could have fired me, but I wasn't worried about that. I had been fired before." Firing did not come, nor did friendliness replace the coldness between the two men for some time to come.

There was still an uneasy peace between the two men when in late 1978 Cooney summoned Ken to company headquarters in Cincinnati. Was this to be Ken's moment of reckoning from the Jefferson fiasco? Ken had hoped that incident was now behind the two men and, indeed, no serious damage had been administered to the potential client relationship; Jefferson was among Gibson's new accounts and they were not complaining about the service Ken was providing. Still, Ken wasn't certain why he was being called into the big office.

Ken mentally noted on his arrival at corporate headquarters that the analysis of Cooney's personality had apparently not changed. "He was still a hard man who wasn't afraid of other hard men," Ken said.

"Sit down," Cooney virtually commanded Ken when Ken had entered the executive office. Cooney got quickly to the point. "We need a regional manager in Texas and I was hoping you'd take the job," Cooney said.

Ken's mind raced. Was this Cooney's version of an exile to Siberia? "How much does it pay?" Ken asked.

"I think we can talk about a fifteen percent raise," Cooney responded. (At the time, Ken's salary at Gibson had risen to $24,000 annually.)

In some ways, Ken knew the company as well as Cooney and he knew that the Texas region had traditionally been a low producer for Gibson. It would be difficult, Ken thought, to survive in Texas or anywhere else on the raise being offered barring a sudden rush of clients to the Gibson banner. Ken also knew that though he had hitchhiked across the Texas Panhandle in a blizzard many years earlier, he was acquainted with almost no one in the big state. "I didn't have a house there and I didn't know anyone there at the time," Ken said, remembering his quick consideration of the job offer from the Gibson CEO. He knew, as well, that the move to Texas would be expensive and was unlikely to be covered by the raise he was being offered.

"Tom," he finally answered soberly, "there's just no way in hell I can go to Texas for a fifteen percent raise." He wasn't even sure the move would have been a wise one at 100 percent.

"You hungry?" Cooney asked.

"Maybe a little," Ken responded.

"Let's go to lunch."

The session in Cooney's executive suite had lasted less than five minutes.

Cooney must have, in some quarter, admired the blunt personality of his man, Ken, in Florida. Cooney himself was at the top of the Gibson hierarchy for more than a decade and answered to four different owners. Of what became the revolving door at the ownership level, Cooney once was quoted, "The way we operate, it doesn't much matter who owns our stock as long as they are not intrusive."

Perhaps not even Ken could have stated it more clearly or bluntly. At least in that way, the two were not very different. The credo for each man seemed to be: Just get out of my way and let me do my job.

The arrival of Cooney as the CEO was the biggest change at the top for Gibson since CIT Financial Corp. had acquired the company in 1964. But bigger changes were ahead. In the first of those changes, RCA acquired CIT Financial in 1980 and thus became Gibson's parent company.

Only two years later, former Treasury Secretary William Simon organized a leveraged buyout of the greeting card company. According to one publication in the mid-1980s, the deal put Simon and his partners in the "get-rich-quick hall of fame" when their $1 million stake in the company ballooned to $184 million in additional shares virtually overnight when they took the company public. It was the largest leveraged buyout in Wall Street history at the time.

If Gibson was going through major changes in the late 1970s and early 1980s, Ken's role too was shifting, though not to Texas. Cooney had not been reluctant to make changes in the regional managerial level of the company almost from the beginning. For Cooney personally, whether Ken was qualified for a promotion was questionable; he had turned down the Texas assignment.

Ken's qualifications were not questionable for Bert Rovens, a company vice president, and when the important Northeast Region needed a new leader, Rovens recommended Ken.

Bert Rovens, VP of chain sales, "Gibson's best," according to Ken (1984)

"I'm not sure he's the man we want there," Cooney responded to his trusted vice president.

"Bert knew me," Ken said in 2011. What Rovens knew was that Ken was the most dynamic man Gibson had in the field. At almost any level of the company below the executive suite, Ken was already a star. If Cooney had been hired to reverse the fortunes of Gibson

Greetings, he was beginning to win that battle thanks in no small part to Ken Simpson, and Rovens knew how important Ken was to the future success of the company.

"He's the man we need in Washington," Rovens told Cooney.

"Are you that sold on the guy?" Cooney pressed.

"Absolutely," Rovens answered, pronouncing the word in clear syllables for emphasis.

"Well, promote him," Cooney instructed Rovens, seeming to bestow on his vice president the authority he had not had to that point.

Already, a trusting relationship had developed between Ken and Rovens, a man Ken considered the best salesman Gibson had, and Ken considered Rovens a strong ally and supporter. As was the case with Ron Campbell, Ken's friendship with Bert Rovens still was going strong in the spring of 2011.

The Washington Region included all of the Northeast United States except for New York and spread east-to-west from Norfolk, Virginia, to Cleveland and included the cities of Washington, Philadelphia and Pittsburgh and all the smaller dots on the map scattered throughout that section of the country.

The region also included a string of seventy-five Revco Drug stores in and around Pittsburgh and Cleveland and through the countryside between the two cities. And the "Everything Up" approach service to Revco, a concept that Ken had pioneered going back to his Norcross days, had not been a great success. Upper management, including Cooney, had adopted the program even if some of the salesmen in the field lagged behind in its implementation. "I had to find out why it wasn't working," Ken said. He scheduled his first sales meeting in the region to address the Revco service, and the meeting was short, to the point and was vintage Ken Simpson.

"May-Cohen's in Florida was a big account," Ken rationalized. "And 'Everything Up' had worked great there. So I knew if we could make the biggest accounts work better with the concept, we could also make the littlest accounts and everything in between work just as well."

At the meeting at which Ken appeared for the first time in the role of regional manager, he quickly dispelled any notion that the concept of "Everything Up" was negotiable. "You have a choice," he told the assembled Gibson employees who had primary responsibility for the Revco accounts. "You can make 'Everything Up' work or we'll bring in somebody who will." It was clear that Ken knew the names and phone numbers of former employees and co-workers from the Norcross and American years who fully believed in the "Everything Up" program.

"You're on notice," Ken said, concluding his very brief remarks. "You've got your ass on the line. Make 'Everything Up' work or you'll be replaced by someone who will."

Almost overnight, "Everything Up" began to work so well that Ken never had to try to inspire compliance again with his sales force. So committed was Gibson to the concept that it rigged a display at a trade show many of its customers would attend. The display featured a bank of traditional Gibson greeting card fixtures, each with display racks above and with three lower drawers. Through a mechanical arrangement, the drawers would open and close to a staccato beat as if by magic revealing that each drawer was empty, confirming the low inventory and the logic that customers' money would not be tied up in inventory that was not on sale. It was the message Gibson wanted to get to its customers, and Ken was the primary messenger. Among the customers that understood the significance to the "Everything Up" program was Sam Walton, founder of the merchandising giant Wal-Mart.

By the end of 1979, Ken's new region had become the top producing region in the country, which was considered a remarkable achievement in so short a time, and Ken was only just beginning. For his performance, Tom Cooney gave Ken a $6,000 raise.

When Cooney notified Ken that his salary was being

increased significantly, it was yet another signal that the long-ago difficulty of that first meeting in Miami in selling Jefferson Super Stores had become nothing more than an interesting memory. There also was a sense that the two strong-willed men had learned to appreciate each other, in part because in some ways they were more alike than not.

"I really admire Tom Cooney," Ken said in March 2011. "He was the hardest working CEO I ever knew. And he was a man who could and would speak his mind, and that was just fine with me."

Thanks in large part to both Cooney and Ken, Gibson was prosperous. For Cooney, the specter of six consecutive red-ink years that he inherited when he arrived at Gibson also was in the past. And Ken, the man who would not lie to back up his boss years earlier in Miami, was the major contributor to that success. Even more good times were ahead. Ken's own history with Eckerd, which began in his Norcross years, was beginning to pay off in a major way. Impressed by the service and the performance Ken had generated for Eckerd while at Norcross, the burgeoning drug store chain was ready to turn over 100 more stores to Ken and to Gibson, all in the Atlanta area.

It would be a monumental job of introducing Gibson into the Eckerd profile in Atlanta, but Ken had the perfect "right arm" for the chore, his associate Ron Campbell.

The Gibson Years

In order to bring as much stability to the effort that soon was to be launched in Atlanta with Eckerd Drugs, Gibson Greetings added the Georgia metropolitan area along with the remainder of the Southeast United States to Ken's sphere of responsibility. In essence, Ken had replaced Frank Lubrecht, the man who had hired him for Gibson. Though newly installed in the District of Columbia, Ken quickly began planning a move to Atlanta. Ken was the logical choice to head up the project; Eckerd, for which he perhaps was the only choice, had moved to Gibson because of its history and its success with Ken. Ken soon would find that more changes lay ahead.

The first of those was born out of curiosity.

Among Gibson employees who answered to Ken was Bunny Greenall, wife of John Greenall. John had been one of Ken's first customers years earlier when Jim Norman had dispatched Ken to Jacksonville to take charge of Norcross' North Florida district where Ken would launch his card-selling career.

"I had heard a curious thing about Bunny and the company car," Ken said. "I had heard that once she got to Maggie Valley (North Carolina) she had to leave the company car at the (Maggie Valley Country) club and take another vehicle to her home on Quail Ridge.

"I had to see that for myself." On July 4, 1981, Ken visited the Greenalls in their log cabin home tucked away at the end of a torturous gravel mountain road and at the pinnacle of a distant crest of the Blue Ridge Mountain range. It was a residence that was beautifully decorated on the interior and also offered a breathtaking view of the valley below and Lake Junaluska, the pristine setting for the headquarters of the Methodist Church in Western North Carolina, so that navigating the difficult mountain cart path seemed well worth the effort.

"I was so impressed immediately by where John and Bunny lived that I said to them that this is where I'm coming to live. It was love at first sight," Ken said. Within two weeks, Ken had purchased his own building lot on the flank of Walker Bald along the same ridge but at a slightly higher elevation, and he knew that a home perched on the side of that mountain would have a view similar to that of the Greenall's. Within months, a small log cabin built from a kit and measuring twelve feet by sixteen feet would emerge along the steep hillside. It would begin with only a bathroom, a great room and an open fireplace and would grow in the years ahead to become a large log cabin with a warm hearth for a traveling man. It was the place Ken and Ruth, married since 1980, would call home by 1983. The road to the building spot indeed was precarious, even more treacherous than that which somewhat tenuously connected the Greenalls to the world, but it was not a deterrent to Ken. If necessary, he decided that he too would leave his company car parked near the clubhouse in the valley.

Already, Ken knew his heart and his hearth would be in Maggie Valley, but he now was involved in a move to Atlanta where he established a one-man regional office which would become his operating base. In 1980, soon after Ken took over the region, one of his first meetings was with Landy Laney, president of Ingles Supermarkets, a prominent grocery chain with stores in six states and with its headquarters and distribution center located in Black Mountain, North Carolina. Gibson had just been eliminated as one of the two greeting card vendors supplying Ingles because of what

Laney considered poor service, and American Greetings had taken over all but one of the formerly Gibson-supplied Ingles stores. High on Ken's list of priorities in his new region was an attempt to win back the Ingles account, and he began with a visit to Laney's office.

Laney was pointed in his assessment of Gibson and the card business overall. In his time as the president of Ingles, Laney had developed no loyalty to any particular card company and, indeed, rated the service his company had traditionally received as unsatisfactory.

"If a card man's performance was what he promised," Laney told Ken in their first meeting, "he would have all of Ingles' business."

It was the comment Ken had hoped to hear.

It took more months for Gibson to regain the ground it had lost in the Ingles chain, but within a year Laney allowed a foot in the door once again for Ken and Gibson and with it an implied challenge to establish credibility with Ingles. The challenge was not lost on Ken. He established a new district and placed its headquarters in Maggie Valley and from there he would concentrate the Gibson effort on the Ingles chain.

Confirmation that Gibson had achieved credibility where Laney had seen none before came quickly when the Ingles president placed the entire Ingles chain in Ken's Gibson camp. It was the beginning of a successful and lasting relationship between Ingles and Ken.

But now, Ken had a major challenge facing him, the installation of Gibson fixtures and cards in 100 Atlanta area Eckerd Drug locations and the removal of existing stock and fixtures, mostly those of American Greetings. And it had to be done in thirty days, and with minimal interruption at individual locations. Ken knew that the fact that each Eckerd installation was virtually identical to all the others was a matter of good fortune; each installation would consist of fifty-six running feet of fixtures laden with Gibson products made ready for shoppers at a lightning pace. Ken outlined the challenge to Ron Campbell, his Director of Operations and a Gibson manager along Florida's northeast coast.

Ron took the assignment as a challenge and began by posting a large map of the Atlanta area on one wall of the apartment he had rented in the Georgia city. On the map, he marked every Eckerd location scheduled to be re-fitted with the Gibson card section. In time, each location also would bear the notation that the installation had been successfully completed.

Early in the operation, company CEO Tom Cooney flew in from Gibson headquarters in Cincinnati to look in on the most unique and ambitious installation plan in greeting card history in the United States. He remained mostly in the background seldom speaking, looking over shoulders, frequently nodding his approval of the Campbell plan. His contribution was to appoint Billie Campbell "house mother" for the Gibson employees living temporarily in the apartment that served as headquarters, and then he flew back to Cincinnati apparently pleased that the operation was in capable hands.

Ron augmented the Gibson team members with temporary workers, some of whom returned to work the project day after day, a development Ron had not anticipated but one that immeasurably placed the ambitious thirty-day plan within reach. The combination of Gibson talent and hired help was critical and it was successful with the logistical details coming from Ron.

"The key was to make sure the new fixtures were delivered early on the day of installation," Ron said years later. Any delay in that aspect of the operation and the whole schedule would have been irretrievably compromised. "It became very important to secure the commitment of trucking companies and, if necessary, of individual drivers to make precise on-time deliveries and that wasn't always a simple thing to achieve," Ron said. "We didn't want the fixtures arriving early so that we had to find a place to store them until we were ready for them, and we sure didn't want them coming late while teams sat around waiting because if that were to happen we would be losing valuable time. Cooperation and coordination was very important.

"For a time, we also were able to do it in cooperation with American. Their people would show up and get their fixtures out as we were going in with the Gibson line," Ron said. The early plan was to do three to four conversions a day so that at the end of thirty days, the card sections in all 100 Eckerd stores would belong to Gibson.

"We got really good at doing it in a hurry," Ron said. So good, indeed, that the Campbell squad didn't need the full thirty days to complete the installation of Gibson in all 100 stores.

"It was at the time the biggest thing any card company had ever done," Ron said in 2011.

For Ken, the completion of the Atlanta project was fulfilling, but he considered it just another triumph in his private goal to do his part to grow Gibson to become the second largest greeting card company in the country behind only Hallmark, and perhaps eventually challenging the king of the industry.

"I was doing my best to catch American," Ken admitted in 2010. But in an interview of a prospective new employee then working for American and who was in a position to know, a comparison of volume came up. "I was surprised," Ken said. "Here I was trying my best to catch American, and I found out we were already ahead of them, certainly in the southern part of the country."

Like taking a hill in Korea, Ken now was driven to solidify the Gibson position in the battle for the favor of the card-buying public. He would yet have his best chance to do that along the Potomac.

By the spring of 1984, Ken had been named assistant vice president of sales for all of Gibson's operations east of the Mississippi River. It was a promotion that brought him to company headquarters in Cincinnati. Ken bought a house only three blocks from Gibson headquarters, so close indeed that employees motoring through his neighborhood in driving to and from work could determine if Ken was home by whether his car was parked in his driveway. He worked at the company headquarters through the week and he would drive home to Maggie Valley every weekend.

Ken had been reporting to his office at corporate headquarters for less than a year when a conversation with Vice President of National Chains Pinky Halvorson, a close friend of company CEO Tom Cooney, brought yet another change, but in title only. In the course of the conversation, Ken had a question for Pinky.

"Pinky, what's the difference," Ken began, "between being a vice president and being an assistant vice president?"

"I don't really know," said Pinky who apparently had never before been asked to ponder such a question. "But I know how to find out. I'll be right back."

Ken (left) with Pinky Halverson, Gibson VP of chain sales (1984)

Pinky was gone about twenty minutes and in that time apparently had relayed Ken's question to Cooney. "I've got your answer," Pinky announced triumphantly when he returned to speak to Ken. "There is no difference. You're being promoted to vice president of sales, and you'll still have everything east of the Mississippi, just as you do now."

The question also had at the same time brought promotions to vice presidencies to Sam Facciola, who would still oversee Gibson operations west of the Mississippi, and Mike Tobin who would continue to direct the administrative end of the company.

Ken came to understand that the Atlanta accomplishment, impressive as it was, was merely a dress rehearsal for an even bigger similar assignment, this one coming in 1985.

By then, Ken, still living in Cincinnati through the week, had expanded his habit of driving instead of using airline travel to move about his region that spanned the country from the Mississippi River east and from Canada to the Florida Keys. But one of his most important trips was only the three blocks from his Cincinnati home to his office. Bud Fantl, the chief operating officer of Peoples Drug Stores, and other company executives had arrived at Ken's and Bert's invitation to Cincinnati to discuss the possible shift of all 165 District of Columbia area outlets to Gibson. Ken and Bert had made progress in the talks and finally a Peoples official asked Ken how long it would take to convert the entire chain in the D.C. area to Gibson.

"Ninety days," Ken said boldly, perhaps basing his response on the success with Eckerd in Atlanta.

Fantl, who apparently expected something closer to six months, was incredulous. "Are you sure?" he pressed.

"Ninety days," Ken repeated. "We can do the whole package in ninety days."

It was a sale, but it came with the understanding that every Peoples Drug store would be selling Gibson products within ninety days of a project starting date agreed upon by both Peoples and Gibson. And, as had been the case with the Eckerd operation in Atlanta, there must be minimum interruption in each store as the conversion was taking place.

Following the successful sales pitch with Fantl and his managers in Cincinnati, Ken got into his car and began the long drive from Cincinnati to Maggie Valley. As he drove on through the night through Kentucky and Tennessee and finally into the mountainous end of North Carolina, the euphoria of having landed the big account began to wane as Ken began to have some worrisome doubts that it really would be possible to meet the

Peoples goal of converting every store – all 165 of them - in only ninety days.

He argued with himself as he drove. "There's no way any company anywhere could do that," he said to the darkness. "I was a damned fool to tell them we could do it.

"Why, we probably couldn't do it if we brought everybody in the region in to D.C. to convert the Peoples stores," he chided himself.

The thought was a "Eureka!" moment for Ken. "Wait a minute!" he said out loud. "That's the way we'll do it! We'll bring everybody who works for me in and get it done." When Ken arrived home near midnight, he went to his telephone and called Ron in Florida.

"We got the Peoples accounts in Washington, 165 stores. Gotta get it done in ninety days. Are you up for it?"

"Sure," Ron quickly answered with a confidence he didn't really feel in the middle of the night.

"The only way we can do it, Ron, is to bring everybody in the region in."

There he left the planning to Ron. It would, Ken said, be three-times-Atlanta in difficulty, and it would be a project far beyond anything any other card company in America had ever attempted, including Gibson. By the time the Washington project had been successfully completed, Ron would make a name for himself as a logistics genius in the company and Ken would prove once again that there was no job too big for people who worked for him to tackle.

Even before the sun peeked in on a new day, Ron was at work on the ambitious D.C. project, making plans, searching out potential land mines. He quickly understood that the challenges his yet-to-be-assembled teams would face would be several times more difficult than Atlanta had been, just as Ken had said.

"We recognized that from day one. As bad as Atlanta traffic can be, Washington traffic is far worse. So we had to take that into account," Ron remembered. The devil would be in the details, he knew. For example, mobile dumpsters would have to be brought in on tight schedules, "but I realized right away that we then would be dealing with entities not only in the District, but Virginia and Maryland when it came to disposing of the material we were replacing." Ron eventually would have to carry a ready supply of cash just to pay the varying disposal fees day by day. But when it became clear that the cost of the dumpsters was threatening the budget for the project, Ron discovered that it was more economical to rent U-Haul trucks, assign a Gibson employee to drive and two temporary workers to man the dump detail.

This time, Gibson employees being brought in, most of them for a week at a time, would be housed in a hotel and among them would be an employee out of Atlanta named Laura Hill, a former X-ray technician who had been hired by Ken.

"We worked hard through the day, and in the evening it was great sharing a meal or a visit with other Gibson employees from other parts of the eastern United States," Laura said.

The expert organizer Ron had turned out to be made certain that every detail was taken into account, and the most minutely organized aspect of the operation turned out to be Ron's own schedule. From the moment he had answered that middle-of-the-night telephone call from Ken, Ron was determined to overlook nothing and came to realize that the role of the coordinator would be critical. And he knew he was the coordinator.

"I thought about what it was going to take for me to do my job and I found I had to wake up every morning at 4:44 a.m.," he said. Not 4:45, nor 4:40. At exactly 4:44 a.m. "The reason that was important was that I had to get to the hotel where our people were, I had to pick up the temporary crew, we had to double-check with store managers, and I had to supervise transportation arrangements to that day's first installations. That meant we had to be on the road from the hotel to the sites of the first conversions of the day no later than 8 a.m. and there was all that traffic to deal with. With all the preparations that had to be made on a daily basis, that meant that the latest I could sleep was to 4:44 in the morning."

Calculated into the schedule was training time in the proper way to use tools required to erect the new fixtures as they were going into the store not only for new temporary workers, but for Gibson employees as well. Ken had a history of hiring women employees at a rate far greater than managers in other segments of the company, which meant that "we had to train an awful lot of girls in how to use the tools we had, and some of the men, too, for that matter," Ron said.

Complicating the procedures Ron put in place was that, unlike in Atlanta where one Eckerd was very much like all the other Eckerd stores in space and layout, no two Peoples stores were alike. Card sections varied in size and positions in the store almost as much as perhaps would have been the case had each store been independent. A one-size-fits-all plan that had been useful in Atlanta would have quickly collapsed in Washington.

In every case, it was necessary for yet-to-be-assembled fixtures to arrive on the day of installation, and getting the cooperation of truckers and their companies was even more of a challenge than had been the case in Atlanta. To overcome that hurdle, Ron turned to the operations department at Gibson and that department's history with over-the-road carriers was critically important in making that aspect of the plan work.

"I came to realize that one of the keys also was to follow up and follow through," Ron said.

"Nothing was ever too big for Ron to tackle," Ken said in 2011. And, as had been the case in Atlanta, all the Peoples Drugs outlets in the D.C. area were converted to the Gibson brand in less than ninety days.

By the time the Washington project had been successfully completed, Ron had made a name for himself as a logistics genius in the company. But some of the memories of the D.C. installations would remain with him in an interesting way.

"To this day," Ron said in 2011, "I sometimes awaken at exactly 4:44 in the morning."

Ron Campbell had remained Ken's operations manager and his star in the company also seemed likely to be on the rise until he joined Ken, Cooney and Pinky in a dinner meeting at Maggie Valley Country Club at the base of the mountain where Ken and Ruth were living in the expanding log cabin. In the course of the evening, someone broached the subject of Gibson's new "overlay" program, which in effect contained promotional merchandise which were considered more sellable early in the season than the seasonal cards. When the featured season arrived, all the merchandiser had to do was lift away the plastic display containing the promotional cards and the seasonal cards were already in display array beneath.

"I'm not sure I'm sold on the overlays," Ron said during the brief discussion. It was an off-the-cuff remark, but one that threatened to be a potentially career-changing moment. It left Tom Cooney, who believed passionately in the "overlay" program, red-faced. The tone of the dinner meeting had been abruptly altered.

It was a comment that would haunt Ron for a time and for the moment had caused damage to Ron's chances of being promoted up the line despite his remarkable work in Atlanta and Washington. It would take an unlikely moment for Ken to rescue Ron's chances of promotions.

Ken's opening came in a meeting of Gibson upper echelon at The Breakers in Palm Beach when the company brass was seeking ways of insuring the continued growth it was enjoying along the South Florida coast from Palm Beach to Miami.

Everyone at the meeting agreed that a strong director was needed for the Miami district.

"You got anybody who could handle that job?" Pinky asked Ken.

It was the opening Ken needed.

"I don't have anyone good enough to do that job," Ken responded. "The best man I've got is Ron Campbell and he hasn't been good enough to get a district of his own yet. So, if Ron Campbell isn't good enough, then I don't have a man who's worth a damn. So, no, I don't have anyone."

In Ken's unique way, he had just given Ron the highest recommendation he could have offered, and Pinky understood the underlying message in Ken's sarcasm.

Pinky once again excused himself from the meeting and made his way to Tom Cooney's suite. When he returned he announced to Ken, "Ron's good enough to handle the South Florida district."

"I didn't want Cooney to make Ron a district manager. I just wanted him to admit Ron was good enough to be a district manager," Ken said to Pinky. "Ron is worth more to me as an operational manager and we've got sixty Gray Drugs to install in the South Florida area." Cooney once had gotten over the anger he felt after his initial meeting with Ken years earlier, and now he apparently had gotten beyond Ron's unfortunate assessment of the "overlay" program that had come at the meeting at Maggie Valley.

Once Ron took over the installation of Gray Drugs, he began to write letters once a week to Tom Cooney informing him about progress on the installations in South Florida. The letters solidified his standing with the company in a way perhaps nothing else could have.

"Once Ron started writing those letters," Ken said years later, "Mr. Cooney never questioned him again."

Ken (right) and his Director of Operations Ron Campbell (date unknown)

Months later, Ken's relationship

with the upper management of Peoples Drugs came into question, though only briefly. The drugstore chain discovered that one of Ken's employees, who had responsibility for maintaining the card section at an outlet in Norfolk, Virginia, was falsifying the return of Gibson seasonal stock from that location. Not only would the altered figures impact the drugstore, they also would enhance production figures that went to Gibson's corporate offices to the point that his bonus pay would be greater. When the drugstore confronted the Gibson representative about the alleged scam, the man responded that Ken was aware of what he was doing.

Ken's quick temper already was legendary throughout the Gibson empire. Now he wasn't in a mood to admit complicity in a scheme by one of his employees. With anger raging within, Ken climbed into his car and drove from Maggie Valley, North Carolina, to Norfolk with the intention of not only personally firing the man, but of taking him to task, perhaps even physically, for leveling false charges against him.

For almost seven hours and 439 miles he drove, and his anger had abated not at all by the time he arrived at the man's home and pulled into the driveway.

Slamming the door of his car behind him in anger, Ken stormed to the house and burst through the front door uninvited. He called the man's name and found that the man quickly had barricaded himself into a bedroom at the rear of the house.

"I had come to do him harm," Ken remembered years later. "But he had the door locked and I couldn't get to him, and that was probably a good thing.

"Then it hit me. Here I had come bursting into this man's house and I'm standing at a bedroom door yelling at him and threatening him. I could be in big trouble."

Finally, confirming that the man now was no longer an employee of Gibson, Ken returned to his car, started the engine, struggled with his anger once again and drove the 439 miles back to Maggie Valley.

Gibson and Peoples calculated the loss and Gibson wrote a check to Peoples in repayment.

It was only the second, and last time, that Ken's honesty had been called into question. The first had been when Norcross bosses questioned his integrity when he was fired, and now the second by a man trying to cover his own wayward tracks in Norfolk.

Saving Grace

By the time of the leveraged buyout of Gibson by former Secretary of the Treasury William Simon and his group in 1983, Ken understood that upper management had, in a general way, been uncertain how to control him as the man in charge of the Gibson effort in the eastern United States. It was truly a case of some of his company's upper management not wishing to live with Ken, but fully aware that he was so productive and was responsible for a large portion of profits that it also could not live without him.

Proof that there was wisdom in understanding Ken's considerable impact on Gibson's bottom line would in the decade of the 1990s be conclusively confirmed.

One of Ken's bosses, Benjamin Sottile, was aware of the ruffled feathers Ken left with upper management and even marveled at it. "I never saw an organization like this," he once said. "Everybody who works for Ken likes him or loves him; everyone Ken worked for couldn't stand him."

Ken understood that love-hate relationship, but both he and Tom Cooney had come to appreciate the forthright nature of the other and the talent each brought to the table. When Sottile, an executive with Revlon, replaced Cooney as president and chief operating officer in 1986, it was the start of another solid working situation with the man in charge for Ken, even though he discovered that the two top executives saw their roles in diametrically opposite ways.

"Tom was a hard worker," said Ken in a 2011 appraisal. "He'd work as hard as anybody. Ben, on the other hand, didn't like to work and told us so. He said at an early meeting that he didn't like to work hard which meant that we would have to work hard so he wouldn't have to."

For twenty years, Gibson CEO's Cooney and Sotille found Ken to be a strong company man. It was the management level of the company between the CEO and that of the vice presidents of sales who apparently resented the "loose cannon" personality not easily harnessed.

"Ken Simpson was the most unique man in business I ever encountered, and I was involved in seven companies in my time," Sotille said. "The common way to get ahead in business and climb the corporate ladder is by doing everything you can to please the people above you and by abusing the people under you.

"Ken was the absolute opposite of that. He frequently abused the people above him on the corporate ladder and did everything he needed to do to make the people working for him happy. Almost everybody who ever worked for Ken loved him and, like Ken, would do anything to make us a better company.

"Let me put it this way: Ken was the George Patton of the sales force. He didn't take anything off anybody. He was a take-no-prisoners kind of guy working in the corporate world.

"When everybody else was wishy-washy and indecisive, Ken was a no-nonsense guy, a get-the-job-done kind of guy no matter what the job was."

The results, Sotille said, were in the numbers. "National companies usually divide the country up into five regions – East, Midwest, West, Southwest and Southeast," Sotille said. "Traditionally, the Southeast is the weakest of the regions. It's tough to introduce something new in the Southeast and expect it to be a hit right away. It takes a lot longer in the Southeast. That's because attitudes in the Southeast are, well, more laidback. So, for most companies, the Southeast is always the weakest region.

"But it wasn't with Gibson. It was the strongest region, better than New York or Chicago or Los Angeles. And there was one reason it was the strongest for Gibson – Ken Simpson. It was like his Korea of the business world and once again he was a great soldier.

"I understood that," Sotille continued. "My own background was military/business."

Yet, keeping a soldier such as Ken had been on the front line of the wars the card companies fought was no easy task, Sotille said. Just as had been the case in Korea, friendly fire in the business world also could be professionally lethal. In Ken's case, friendly fire wasn't always very friendly in his years of selling greeting card products. Ken's shield for a time in the face of corporate friendly fire seemed to be Sotille himself.

"In the time I was at Gibson, Ken had five different people (company presidents) he had to report to," Sotille said in 2011. "Every one of them came to me at one time or another asking me to fire Ken.

"More than once, Ken came to me and thanked me for saving his job and protecting him. But I kept telling Ken that I never did that. I never saved his job; he did that. In every case when the man he answered to asked me to let him go, I answered that, yes, I was willing to do that. But I would tell them that before I do, all you have to do is be ready to bring the man into the company who can do what Ken does for Gibson.

"I knew I'd never have to fire Ken because there was never another one like him out there. In all my years, I never ran into another man like Ken. He was one of a kind and his loyalty to the company was incredible. He had this 'can do' attitude that was amazing. No matter the task you put in front of Ken, you knew he was going to find a way to do it and his attitude permeated the whole company."

For Sotille, Ken was both a dream employee and a nightmare – a nightmare because "his boss might tell him to do something and if Ken thought it was foolishness, he'd forget about it and go out and do things his way." And a dream, Sotille said, "because as the CEO you have to worry about sloppy management, sexual harassment, expenses and a whole range of things, but I never had to worry about Ken when it came to that sort of thing."

Ken himself finally decided to find an exit from the ivory tower and a return to the open road where he traditionally had done his most effective work for the company.

He found his opening when Sottile became Gibson's chief executive officer in 1987. Ken offered to return to the field and therefore to the road leaving Sam Facciola, who still was in charge of company business west of the Mississippi, alone in the role of vice president of sales.

"Sam's got the west," Ken said in his talks with Sotille, "and I've got the east. I have the most volume and we're both vice presidents. It's a strange setup and when you take a look at it, I'm confident you're going to change it.

"When you do change it, I want to go back to the field. I won't need office space in Cincinnati. I'll just go back to Maggie Valley and run the eastern part of the country from there."

Ben agreed to the new alignment and named Ken senior regional vice president of sales. Ken was free to move permanently to Maggie Valley. His log cabin was growing to a comfortable size and he rented a house in downtown Waynesville nearby and renovated it for use as his office and his center of operations. He hired Marlene Jolley as his secretary. From Waynesville, Ken continued to work major accounts throughout the eastern half of the country and to pursue new business.

As a year-around resident of Maggie Valley, Ken knew he would from time to time have to deal with ice and snow on his return to the log cabin at more than a mile in elevation.

"There were nights when I wasn't able to drive all the way up to Simpson Lane (the mountain street where the log house was located). Sometimes I could get as far as the north side," Ken said, "and I'd have to leave the car and walk the rest of the way up the mountain."

There was, however, the night he returned to Maggie Valley from a business trip and began the drive up the mountain. As he moved along, it was clear that the snow was growing progressively deeper the higher he moved up the winding road. Finally, he could progress no further. He left his car and began to attempt the final mile by making his way through snow that varied from two to three feet in depth.

"I was in pretty good shape in those days," Ken said. "But I will never forget that night." Ken pushed his way through the snow until he felt heavily fatigued. He then would lie in the snow until his breathing returned to normal, then he continued.

"I did that all the rest of the night," Ken remembered. "Climb through the snow for a while, and lie down to catch my breath." Finally, near first light, he made it along the flatness of Simpson Lane and pushed his way into the warmth of the log cabin.

"What took you so long?" Ruth asked as she brushed the sleep from her eyes.

Ken didn't respond.

Back in the home office in Cincinnati, storm clouds of another sort were beginning to gather for Gibson.

One of Gibson's leading accounts was the Phar-Mor drug store chain, a Youngstown, Ohio, company founded by Michael I. (Mickey) Monus and David S. Shapira in 1982. The chain's business model was based on an approach Ken himself had developed at Gibson, the deep discount program which is dependent upon selling large quantities of merchandise with small profit margins.

The deep discount approach itself was flawless provided volume could be increased markedly. "Under the deep discount program," Ken once calculated, "you can increase revenue by fifty percent if you can sell three times as much merchandise as stores selling at full price. If you increase sales fourfold, profit will double by comparison."

Randy Barfoot, the director of non-foods for Winn-Dixie with whom Ken soon would do business, placed the deep discount theory in its most simple terms: "We found out that it was better to make a nickel three times than a dime one time."

It is an approach that is not without danger, however. "If you double or triple your volume, you're a victor," Ken said simply. "If you don't, you lose the business."

Ken never came close to losing business on the deep discount program and his theory worked well and meshed with the Phar-Mor philosophy so seamlessly that sales of Gibson product "was growing like a wild fire," Ken said in 2011. All of the close to 100 Phar-Mor stores each had made room for huge greeting card sections and quickly collectively topped the $1 million mark in volume. In the months ahead, that figure would soar much higher.

"All along, I had a feeling something wasn't right, though," Ken said, and he knew any problems Phar-Mor had were not from the deep discount program.

Ken's intuition was on the mark. In 1992, Phar-Mor declared bankruptcy. The most serious charge involved in the collapse was that Monus and his chief financial officer, Patrick Finn, were accused of embezzlement. It was charged that they had hidden losses and moved about $10 million from Phar-Mor to the World Basketball League which Monus had founded. Phar-Mor quickly became a company rife with scandal including an alleged attempt at jury fixing once Monus' case came to court. Finn was sentenced to thirty-three months in prison and Monus, who was also tried on jury tampering charges and acquitted, was handed a sentence of nineteen years, seven months which later was reduced to eleven years.

But the damage was far-reaching, including the human toll represented by the displacement of 5,000 Phar-Mor employees, and a prosecutor estimated that the total loss to investors exceeded $1 billion. The case was profiled in a PBS documentary entitled "How to Steal $500 Million."

The collateral losses for Gibson alone topped $30 million and the card company teetered on the brink of collapse itself as a result. "And we got off relatively easy," Sotille said, "compared to other companies that were supplying Phar-Mor. When the troubles began, Phar-Mor was paying us and I got on the phone with Mickey Monus and told him that the Phar-Mor account was a significant one for us and I urged him to keep paying us" despite the mounting money problems the Ohio company faced.

"Mickey said he would, and he did keep paying us until the bankruptcy court froze everything."

Phar-Mor finally emerged from bankruptcy in 1995, but in the three years the company was in bankruptcy, retail giants Wal-Mart and Target had begun building new stores around the country and almost all of those new giant retail outlets included pharmacies. That development led to Phar-Mor's final demise in 2002 when Giant Eagle purchased its remaining assets in bankruptcy court.

From the beginning, the Phar-Mor collapse in scandal was easily large enough to cause fiscal tremors through Gibson's upper echelons, and one of the ways Sotille sought to soften the blow to the card company he now headed was to voluntarily cut his own salary. He offered to reduce his compensation by twenty percent, but the board of directors would not accept that level of commitment, but agreed to a five percent reduction. "I wasn't a hero," Sotille said in 2011. "Let's face it, most CEO's make a lot of money and they can afford to give back if it's needed. The thing I'm still very proud of is that every member of Gibson management to a man agreed to reductions in salary similarly."

In total, while the cuts in executive salaries were significant, they were not enough alone to save the company against the pressure of the Phar-Mor failure.

Once again, as had been the case with other customers including Eckerd and Peoples, Ken and his staff seemed to be the men on white horses riding to the rescue. This time, with Sotille playing an important role, the salvation came in the form of Ken's work with Winn-Dixie Director of Non-Foods Randy Barfoot and a massive agreement with Winn-Dixie to place Gibson products in all 1,200 of the company's grocery stores, most of them in the Southeast United States. It was a move that in some ways dwarfed the tie-in with Phar-Mor.

The Gibson/Winn-Dixie marriage began with a plan by the grocery chain based in Jacksonville, Florida, to alter if not discontinue offering greeting card and related products in their stores. At the time of the decision, Gibson operated sections in two of the chain's twelve divisions with Hallmark and American splitting the remaining ten. For Sotille, the writing on the Winn-Dixie wall was that the grocery chain could be mulling a decision to eliminate greeting card sections from its retail offerings altogether.

Barfoot said in a 2011 interview that little consideration had been forthcoming in Winn-Dixie's inner circle of management of eliminating greeting cards altogether. "Actually, we weren't thinking about getting out of the card business," he said. "We just never had really gotten into it perhaps the way we should have.

"We were taking a look at all of our non-foods inventory," Barfoot remembered. "Up to that time, card display fixtures were revolving upright spinners that usually contained about eight rows of six or seven cards. There might be two or three of those in a store, and that was it."

At the same time, he said, with Sam Walton serving as a board member, Winn-Dixie was beginning to think about growing into much larger retail space in the form mostly of new store buildings. "When that happened, we knew we would have more gondolas for merchandising, and perhaps bigger ones," Barfoot said.

The question became one of determining how greeting cards, and all other non-food items, would fit into the chain's bigger, brighter look in its new outlets and whether those items would be able to be conformed to the computerization, including tracking and billing inventory, that already was underway.

Barfoot said the saturation of computerization in the

grocery industry, "if nothing else, provided a strong tailwind" for Winn-Dixie's stronger tie-in with Gibson and Ken.

Ken had three major factors in his favor when it came to the question of whether he could persuade Barfoot and Winn-Dixie to take an even deeper plunge with Gibson. Importantly, he had developed a rare friendship with Randy Barfoot. "He also had an idea how to do what we needed to get done when it came to card offerings in our stores," Barfoot said. And the third thing that worked strongly in Gibson's favor was the lethargy being shown Winn-Dixie by both American and Hallmark at the time.

"Both American and Hallmark were indifferent to spending any time and effort on supermarkets," Barfoot said. "When we would visit their booths at trade shows and tell them we were from Winn-Dixie, it became clear that we were wasting their time."

But when talks with Ken began, Barfoot said turning to a sports metaphor, "I shut my eyes and swung, and it turned out to be a home run."

"The problem for Winn-Dixie was that the beer man and the bread man and the milk man came in on a daily basis and left their products and left a bill with it," Sotille said. "Card companies, on the other hand, kept the section well-stocked and sent a statement about ten days into each new month. That worked fine for card companies, but it wasn't very compatible with Winn-Dixie's accounting procedures."

The difference in billing and supply procedures, Sotille feared, could eventually lead to the end of card sales in growing Winn-Dixie stores.

With prejudice, both Sotille and Ken saw the possibility of discontinuing the line as an unsatisfactory alternative, one that the chain would soon regret if it became reality, and Sotille arrived in town ready to support his best salesman in trying to save the account more than to, in the beginning, augment it. His argument to Barfoot was difficult to discount.

"Historically, big grocery chains are not known for making a lot of money," Sotille said in 2011. "But they do shovel a lot of money around. If they handle $6 billion a year, their profit may be only $100,000, for example. They handle a lot of money, but they don't traditionally make a lot of money."

"So," he asked Barfoot, "why get rid of the cards? Greeting cards make up one percent of your business, but they account for ten percent of your profit. Instead of getting rid of what really is your best profit item, why not fix it?"

Barfoot, Sotille and Ken discussed the issues facing Winn-Dixie at length and came up with a difficult plan. "We'd do it the same way as the beer, bread and milk companies," Sotille remembered in 2011. It was the birth of what became known throughout the card company as "front door delivery" and grew to include a refurbishing program for fixtures instead of paying higher prices for replacements.

"We're going to make this work," Sotille told Barfoot. "But Ken and I don't want to go to the trouble to figure out how to make it happen, then watch Hallmark or American walk right in and say, 'We can do the same thing.'

"If we make it work, we want to be in every Winn-Dixie in the country."

Barfoot extended a handshake. "Make it work and it's yours," he said.

In 2011, Barfoot said that the determining factor in Gibson's favor had been simple. "Ken Simpson," he said. "You couldn't find a better man when it came to coming up with something new. Ken's a genius.

"There were times when he and I would sit around talking and I'd tell him about something that I would like to have happen but doubted that it was possible. Ken would usually tell me he can get that done. I'd ask him how long it would take and he'd say, 'Oh, about a week, Randy.' I'd tell him that I wasn't sure that was possible. But within a week, the project would be done.

"Trust. That was very important to me and it still is. I trusted Ken Simpson. I knew I had the special privilege of a warm hand at the top of management, and he was the same on his side. If I committed to something with Ken, I wouldn't stop until the chairman of the board made me. And Ken was the same. He was never afraid to go to the top, the very top, at Gibson to get something done.

"It was a wonderful partnership.

"Maybe other people didn't know Ken as well as I did. But Ken was a very important asset to me. Every once in a while, I'd need to go to Piccadilly (Cafeteria), get me some turnip greens and cornbread and humble myself down and really listen to what Ken had to say. He really is a genius. When the smarter person is on the other side of the desk, and if you really listen, thirty minutes is more valuable than six months in school."

Making a new Winn-Dixie system work wasn't a locked-in probability in Sotille's eyes. It would take a different way of thinking, even for a veteran like Ken. As Ken drove his boss back to the airport for the return trip to Cincinnati, the two talked about the challenge.

"I don't know how you're going to do it, but we've got to make it work," Sotille said. He left the problem with Ken.

Years later, the Gibson CEO said he wasn't overly concerned about how it would work. "I knew Ken Simpson," he said. "And I knew that if there was a man in America who could pull this off, it would be Ken."

For his part, Ken knew the only man in America who could best work with him to transform Ken's and Sotille's commitment to Winn-Dixie into the best solution. Once again, Ron Campbell entered the picture as Ken's logistical guru, and together the two old associates began planning. "All I know is that Ken wound up setting up warehouses to serve just the Winn-Dixie people, and bought trucks to make it work," Sotille said. Once everything was quickly in place, the trucks loaded with Gibson stock began rolling before sunrise every morning heading for Winn-Dixie stores, just like beer, bread and milk trucks were doing.

And the plan worked.

Ken had made the plan work, in part, by returning once again to one of the keys to his success years earlier when he was but a rookie salesman for Norcross. "Getting product to store shelves can be an expensive proposition," Randy Barfoot said. "In many cases, the product is delivered to the store and placed in a storage room where manifests are verified that there are the number of cases in the delivery as it says there are.

"Then somebody else has to open each case and make sure it contains the product in the quantity it should be. But we're not finished there. After that, someone has to take the product to the aisle and place it on the shelf in a way that customers can find it – like products with like products, and so on.

"It costs money to do all that, just to get a product to the customer.

"But what Ken was offering was to bring the cards in – front door delivery – and place them in the aisles of our stores," Barfoot continued. "Then someone from Gibson would come in and open all the boxes, check their contents, place the cards in an attractive way on the fixtures and would make sure the display remained attractive, and I didn't have to pay labor costs on all that. Ken's company would take care of that.

"And if Ken Simpson said he could do that, I knew Ken Simpson not only could do that, but I could depend on it happening. In all my years with Winn-Dixie, I didn't allow myself to get very close to very many of our suppliers, but I trusted Ken and he never let me down."

Ken in a sense was an original thinker in a business world in which imitation was sometimes seen as the essence of professionalism. Even before the words became a catch-phrase, Ken was thinking outside the box when it came to serving his customers. Ron Campbell had learned that, Nan Falkenheiner knew it, Harry Roberts at Eckerd Drugs understood it and so did almost everyone who had ever done business with Ken. Ken was a problem solver and, perhaps more importantly, an innovator.

It was the spirit of innovation that led to "Everything Up" and "front-door-delivery."

When a labor strike shut down the flow of product from Gibson's warehouses in Kentucky, the only retail outlets that continued to receive inventory through the period of the labor strife were customers served by Ken in the Southeast United States.

Ken's solution was to once again become a trucker. He rented large panel trucks and he and various people who answered to Ken in the Gibson organizational chart drove to company warehouse facilities in Kentucky and personally kept the supply lines open to customers in his region.

"None of us knew anything about warehousing on that scale," Ken said years later. "But we sure learned. We learned how to pull our own orders, do the paperwork and load everything into the trucks."

For days, the only shipments laden with greeting card company products rolling east and south out of Kentucky were those being handled by Ken and his workers. And they were on the road constantly during the work stoppages by union workers. Ken was not particularly anti-labor, but he was very strongly pro-customer, a fact not lost on Randy Barfoot.

The Gibson/Winn-Dixie marriage began with twenty stores scattered in a wide swath across the Southeast from Greenville, South Carolina, to Richmond, Virginia, and was instantly a hit with the grocery chain's upper management. As revenue from Gibson doubled and tripled what the company's card sections were previously doing, installations could not take place rapidly enough. Gibson spread through the chain like euphoria.

The Winn-Dixie conversions were taking place so rapidly that Gibson, still feeling the Phar-Mor backlash, sent the company attorney to talk with Ken to make sure everything was legal. It was a case of the company perhaps over-reacting to the still-troubling news about Phar-Mor. Ken, who had never created litigation problems for Gibson, took the prying by the visiting attorney as a personal affront that seemed to question his very integrity and he bristled at the lawyer's questions.

"We've got nearly 700 stores already selling product," Ken said pointedly to the lawyer, "and all the rest are ready to go forward. Now, we can take 1,200 stores, or we can give them back the 700."

The lawyer packed up his briefcase and flew back to Cincinnati. "I knew we weren't going to give them back," Ken said in 2011.

If Sotille needed verification that the system was a boon to Winn-Dixie, it came in a phone call months later from A. Dano Davis, the chain's CEO, Barfoot's boss and the latest in a long line in the Davis family tree to control the company even though it was by then traded publicly. Davis told Sotille that a delegation from Proctor & Gamble had made an appointment and had visited him in the executive offices in Jacksonville.

"He said that the Proctor & Gamble people spent ten minutes setting up their screens for their presentation and all the suits were getting ready to do their things," Sotille recalled. "Proctor & Gamble was so big that their people could intimidate a lot of chain store executives and make demands that nobody else would attempt.

"Mr. Davis said that they began by reminding him that Proctor & Gamble was easily his most important and largest supplier. But before they could go any further, Mr. Davis stopped them.

"'You're not even our biggest and most important supplier from Cincinnati,' Mr. Davis told them. When they found out that number one was the Gibson Greeting Card Company, it changed the whole atmosphere of the meeting."

The Winn-Dixie account was so massive that "it was the thing that saved Gibson after the Phar-Mor collapse," Ken said.

"There's no doubt about it," Sotille said. "Ken and Winn-Dixie saved us."

At the end of the first year with a limited number of stores on line, the volume from Winn-Dixie sales settled in just short of $15 million. By the time the move to Gibson had swept through all twelve divisions of the grocery chain, the volume touched $117 million a year. In the subsequent year, revenue from Winn-Dixie topped $127 million.

Using Barfoot's metaphor, Winn-Dixie no longer was earning the three nickels instead of the dime; it now was earning five and six, and even sometimes seven nickels instead of a solitary dime in profit.

"It's pretty hard to go broke when you're beating your previous profit by one and a half times and more," Barfoot said.

"Phar-Mor was the thing in its day," Ken said, "but our tie-in with Winn-Dixie saved the company." It also created a lasting friendship between Ken and Randy Barfoot who have remained in touch since both retired.

End of the Line

With Ben Sotille having moved up to the top spot on the company organizational chart, there was a vacancy in the office of president, and it was a coveted position for several members of the Gibson management team, including Dwayne Tabor, a vice president in sales.

"Dwayne was a smart man," Ken said, "and he wanted to be president, and he should have been president." When positioning was taking place for the job, however, Tabor missed a chance to rally other key Gibson people, including Ken, to his cause.

When Ralph J. Olson became the president instead, Tabor confirmed his intention to leave the company.

"You're a smart man," Ken told him. "But it's a damn shame that as smart as you are, you weren't smart enough to use me." (After leaving Gibson, Tabor found success as the president of a company specializing in home security.)

Who would become president of Gibson Greeting Cards and thus his boss was no great distraction for Ken. He knew his place with the company was in the field and he was continuing to work the eastern half of the country from his Maggie Valley and Waynesville base of operations.

At the time Sotille was considering whom his new president would be, Ken was considering who his new clients would be. In late 1992, Bob Ingle, the founder and chief executive officer of the Ingles Supermarket chain, became interested in the deep discount program Ken had put into place in Winn-Dixie stores. Bob Ingle called Ken seeking details of how the plan would work for his business empire. He was convinced that the Ingles stores would be a perfect fit and in 1993 Ken began a deep discount program for the greeting card departments in all Ingles stores. Now Gibson had yet another client and another source of revenue in trying times. Ken's relationship with Ingles would be an enduring one. (Ken's friendship with Bob Ingle continued until Ingle's death on March 6, 2011, during the writing of this book.)

Ken flanked by CEO Ben Sotille (right) and VP of Sales Dwayne Tabor (1988)

With the addition of Ingles and the relationship with Winn-Dixie, Ken and the people who worked for him were on a roll. The dust from the Phar-Mor implosion had barely settled when in a conversation with Ralph Olson, the new Gibson president, Ken forecast a banner year for the portion of the company that geographically remained under his control. And he was willing to bet on it.

Ken and Robert P. Ingle, Ingle's Supermarkets founder and CEO (2002)

"Next year," he told Olson, "I expect to come in with $100 million in sales." It was a goal to which it was believed no one in the card-selling business had ever aspired, and Olson himself considered the possibility to be extremely unlikely.

"That's selling a lot of cards," he responded.

"I'll tell you what," Ken said, "if I can come in with $100 million in sales, will you buy me a new company car?"

It was a bet Olson apparently thought he would easily win, though Gibson itself would be the big winner if he had to buy the car. "You've got it," Olson responded.

When the sales had been totaled for 1993, Ken's region had brought in $112 million and Olson ordered a new sports car for Ken who became known for achieving Gibson's first-ever $100 million region.

Ken's relation with Olson, however, would come to an explosive end and would underscore the uneasy relationship he had with second-level management.

During a sales meeting, Olson had told Sotille privately that problems were developing for Gibson in its relationship with Safeway, the grocery store chain centered mostly in the western United States, but with one division in Ken's region in the Washington, D.C., area.

"But, Ralph," Sotille said to his president, "why haven't I heard anything about this already from Ken?"

"He's covering it up," Ralph charged. "Ken is the problem, and they just don't want to work with Ken anymore." It was unsettling news for Sotille and he decided to act quickly to gather information to determine if there indeed were a problem and, if that proved to be true, whether Safeway could be saved.

The sales meeting at an end, Ken drove his two bosses to the airport to catch their flight back to Cincinnati. Sotille sat in the front passenger seat and Ralph Olson took his place just behind Sotille. It was the perfect time, Sotille reasoned, to bring up the Safeway account and to begin learning what was at the root of the matter.

"Ken, how's it going with the Safeway account?" Sotille

began as though merely making conversation.

"Fine," Ken responded proudly. "We're ahead of schedule in getting everything installed. I'd say it's going well, and we've got a solid relationship with the management there."

Sotille allowed only the sound of the automobile to intrude for but a moment.

"Well, that's not what I hear," he said.

Ken seemed stunned. "What do you hear, Ben?" he asked, his voice still even.

"I hear we're in real trouble there and it looks like we're going to lose the account."

"Who told you that?" Ken asked as the first wave of anger swept over him.

"Ralph," Sotille answered.

Even though he was driving, Ken turned and looked at Ralph in the rear seat. The car, traveling near sixty miles an hour, swerved though only slightly. Now Sotille could see the anger in Ken's face.

"What the hell are you talking about?" Ken asked Olson angrily. "You're a liar, Ralph. How'd you hear a thing like that?"

Olson responded that the warning had come from an employee at Safeway. And Ken felt fresh anger boiling inside.

"Ralph, the man's a clerk," he bristled. "He's got nothing to do with the Safeway account and isn't in management. Are you going around now and getting your information from clerks? You're just talking crap now, Ralph. Why don't you ask somebody who knows something about the account?"

"Relax, Ken," Sotille interjected. "Just relax and drive."

Ken drove on toward the airport, but in his anger drove past the airport exit that he had taken dozens of times in the past and had to wind his way along neighborhood streets to return to the airport area. The three men were cloaked in tense silence for the remainder of the circutious ride. At the airport, Sotille was delivered to his gate for his departure and, still silently, Ken drove Ralph on to another departure point.

Neither Ralph nor Ken said anything to defuse the situation.

"This is not over," Ralph said to Ken as he picked up his bags at the curb and headed for the check-in counter.

Over the weekend in his North Carolina mountain home, Ken began to second-guess his angry response. It was possible, he concluded during his quiet deliberations, that he perhaps would not survive as a Gibson employee after his firey outburst to Ralph and in Sotille's presence. On Monday morning, Ken drove from Maggie Valley to corporate headquarters in Cincinnati and found Olson in his office. He apologized for his outburst.

"I'm sorry I said all that, Ralph, because I should have more respect for the office you occupy in this company than that," Ken said, being careful, however, not to be seen as yielding on the Safeway question.

"Thank you, Ken," Olson responded. "I'm glad you came in and said that." Though it was not stated, Ken assumed that Olson was weighing action to be taken against the company's most productive salesman, possibly even asking Sotille to fire him. It would not have been the first such occasion, nor the last.

But the apology did not end the incident. In another part of the building that morning, Sotille went to the account for the answers he needed. He placed a phone call to upper management at Safeway to ask if the relationship remained mutually pleasant and profitable without sharing any information about the angry verbal confrontation between Ken and Olson on the subject. Sotille was assured that Safeway was pleased with its association with Gibson and had no intention of removing the card company from the grocery chain's aisles.

Within days, Olson resigned as Gibson's president "for personal reasons."

By 1995, Gibson had been a publicly held company for a dozen years and with hostile takeovers becoming common occurrences, the company was not immune to pressures from other corporate suitors. For a time, Gibson's board considered "multiple offers", including one from American Greetings based in Cleveland, but was able to rebuff each of them.

In an ironic turn of events, Ken's work with Winn-Dixie had saved Gibson from following Phar-Mor into bankruptcy. Now American, he learned, wanted to take over its competitor, Gibson Greeting Card Company, principally because American now wanted the lucrative Winn-Dixie tie-in.

As long as Ken and Randy Barfoot of Winn-Dixie called the shots, the only way another company could break through was to find a way to acquire all of Gibson.

Indeed, American would try yet again in early 1996 when Ben Sotille was released as Gibson's CEO to negotiate a purchase of the company. Gibson refused, this time citing possible antitrust issues such a deal perhaps could trigger, and American bowed out yet again.

Now, with Sotille gone, long-time Gibson employees feared that Gibson, the company that had the ignominious honor of playing a major role in launching Wall Street's leveraged buyout craze, may be facing its own demise. Those feelings were not without validation. In April 1997, Frank J. O'Connell, known to be a corporate raider, became Gibson's new chairman.

Gibson was on its death bed at the hands of corporate raiders. And though Ken only suspected it for some time, it became clear that his own association with the greeting card company to which he had given so much also was in danger of breaking.

On the personal front, Ken's fifteen-year marriage to Ruth had ended in divorce in 1995. Ken had personally designed and had built a small penthouse on the same ridge of the mountain on which his first log home had taken shape, and he moved into the new living quarters.

In late summer of 1995, Ken moved out of the place that now would be known as The Penthouse and into the house at the crest of Walker Bald in a lease arrangement. He then purchased the home with a 180-degree view of the Appalachian range whenthe snow was on the ground in the early weeks of 1996. The house was considered only a summer home at the time, one that would be rebuilt over the next few years into a fine, expansive home which Ken calls The White House.

Among the features of the home at the time Ken bought it was a wide front porch facing east with a spectacular view of the mountain range from which one could understand the name, Blue Ridge. It was to that front porch that Ken and Tom Behymer, a fellow Gibson executive, retreated when Tom came to town for a visit just before the Fourth of July 1996. Tom was spellbound by the beauty of the place and the scenery that rolled far to the horizon all around him, and the two men talked.

"We talked about everything," Ken remembered in 2011. They talked about the good times and the difficult times for Gibson through the previous two decades, about people both had known in the business and Ken gave Tom a capsule history of his life to that point atop Walker Bald. They discussed a bleak future they envisioned for Gibson Greetings.

Now he awaited the *coup de grace*, but it did not come. There was silence between the two men. Finally, Tom spoke again. "I can't do it," he said softly. "Firing you makes no sense. I just can't do what I was sent here to do."

Tom returned to Cincinnati and to Gibson headquarters, his mission not fulfilled. At the end of the year, Tom was retired. When Ken closed his Waynesville office in 1997, he continued to work from his home where he held many meetings with members of his staff.

Ken would survive. Gibson would not.

Death for the company came in agonizing strokes. Gibson closed its manufacturing plant and contracted its printing to other companies. It sold its 180-store Paper Factory to the company's management team. In May 1999, it cut 110 workers from the payroll and the board adopted a poison pill, a controversial defensive strategy that can place members of the board in financially

Nan Falkenhainer with (left to right) Ken, Randy Barfoot and Frank Lubrecht (1996)

advantageous positions in the event that a hostile takeover were to emerge. It meant that any suitor would be unable to leverage the company by seeking to buy controlling stock from groups of shareholders directly and would, instead, be required to deal first with directors.

On November 3, 1999, Gibson agreed to be acquired by American Greetings, a deal brokered by Frank J. O'Connell, for $163 million, or $10.25 a share, down from eighteen dollars per share American had offered in 1996. The man who sat at the bargaining table on behalf of American was Morry Weiss who once had hired Ken as a way to significantly reduce competition from other card companies.

The deal immediately impacted the 400 employees at Gibson's Amberley Village headquarters in Cincinnati, and 500 more in the company's distribution centers in Berea and Kenton County, Kentucky. Not included in those numbers were the hundreds of Gibson employees in the field, some of whom continued to work under the American banner.

(O'Connell would go on to other fields. He later took over Indian Motorcycle Corporation, the oldest motorcycle company in the United States, and presided over its liquidation as well.)

Four months after the sale to American was announced, in March 2000, Ken retired. Among those attending Ken's retirement party in the spring of 2000 was former Gibson CEO Tom Cooney. The engraved crystal bowl Tom presented to Ken at the party occupies a place of honor in the house atop Walker Bald. Also attending Ken's retirement party was Randy Barfoot, his former partner at Winn-Dixie.

Ken's secretary Marlene Jolley with district manager John Greenall, Ken's first customer (1996)

Ken and Laura, who would become his third wife, welcomed Siamese cat sisters Thelma and Louise as permanent residents in their mountaintop home and soon brought home a new German shepherd puppy and named him Simpson.

Winn-Dixie VP Marilyn Bush (left) with Ken and her mother, Nan Falkenhainer (1992)

Epilogue

The combination of health issues that required surgery and the challenge of digging through years of memories perhaps inescapably left Ken Simpson in a reflective mood by the time the last question was asked in the process of preparing this manuscript. It was as though those memories had been there all along, as of course they had been, but he had not bothered to fully draw back the curtain to revisit the good times and the tough times in his own life at one sitting figuratively.

These days, Ken's favorite chair is a comfortable Queen Anne placed at a round table beside a telephone that he uses to keep in touch with many of the people who have been important in his life. The chair sits beside a large window in what Ken calls "the north room," and beyond the window and rolling into the hazy blue distance is all the beauty of the Western North Carolina mountains.

The late Anne Kennedy, the Wake Forest High School teacher who once arranged to have Ken expelled from school for fighting, bestowed a special name for the mountaintop home during one of her treasured visits before she died on June 5, 2011.

She called it "Ken's Kingdom," which it truly is.

"What beauty!" I said during one of the final interview sessions with Ken at the "White House." "I know you must never grow tired of seeing it."

"It is beautiful," he agreed, yet not turning to gaze once more upon the panorama. "But, you know, I almost never see it.

"I know it's beautiful and it's spectacular. But when you live in the mountains like this, maybe you just get used to it and after a while you don't think about the beauty all around you until somebody drives up here for the first time and is blown away by the spectacular views. Then you take another look. And you smile."

Taking a look at his life was much the same. By the time we had reached the late stages of what must have seemed endless interviews and question after question, Ken had taken a look at the scenes of his life that were there all along. As with all of us, there are regrets, but seemingly very few for this man who has been a fighter virtually every day of his life and, certainly from a health standpoint, still is.

Laura Simpson (2005)

"Well, in looking back, I guess you could say that I really did do it my way," he said, borrowing as so many have from the Frank Sinatra hit song. Any other way would not have been Ken Simpson.

The consolation Ken finds in having done it his way is that the number of people who were gainfully employed because he became a strong force in the greeting card industry – salesmen, managers, clerks, warehousemen, cargo carriers, printers, and long ago ladies working for one dollar an hour in the beginning – cannot be calculated. "All I know is that a lot of people had jobs because of what we were doing," Ken says now.

Ken's and Laura's most treasured keepsake is a thick ring binder notebook filled with letters and poems from people with whom he worked, letters written to mark Ken's retirement. They include personal notes that speak to Ken's style of leadership and to the fact that, as Ken says, "if anyone up the line wanted to do anything about anybody who worked for me, they knew they would have to deal with me first. Nobody was going to fire anyone under me without firing me first." The letters invariably speak of the pride the writers had in joining Ken in reaching for success.

On Ken's 80th birthday, he received the same greeting card from two different former employees, Marilyn Bush, Ken's vice president for Winn-Dixie and Nan Falkenheiner's daughter, and his long-time Director of Operations Ron Campbell. It reads:

In a world that does its best
to make us a little fuzzy
around the edges,
some people still manage
to have bold outlines.
They know who they are,
what they're about,
what they alone can give.
And just like them,
the gifts they share are bold,bright, beautiful.

Inside the card are these words:

You're someone who doesn't compromise
on being the person only you could be,
someone who doesn't hold back
on sharing the gifts only you can give.
And especially today,
I, for one, just want to say
thank you, thank you, thank you …

Photogenic Simpson (2005)

Ken's favorite poem in the notebook filled with admiration for the man is the well-known "Man in the Glass." The poem, which has been an inspiration to generations of men, was placed there by Laura.

"You changed the world for me and so many others," Laura wrote at the end of the poem. "You will never have trouble with 'The Man in the Glass.'"

There perhaps are times when Ken wonders if he was successful enough. He frets these days about some of the things almost all of us worry about. Among those points of concern is whether he has been a good steward in providing for Laura in the event she survives him. When Simpson, his regal German shepherd of championship blood, seemed to be developing hip problems common to the breed, the compassion of the man was inspiring. And when cat sisters Thelma and Louise come to meow good morning, his is a gentle pat on the head. For the two, that seems almost enough. Almost.

He remains at the age of eighty-two an executive in a scaled down way; Laura is the Chief Operating Officer of the two-person operation that requires attention, but not so much that it interferes with her insistence that she have time to prepare wonderful meals for Ken every day and for guests when they come to the mountain.

And Ken keeps his thick personal listing of telephone numbers at his fingertips and frequently calls people with whom he shared life as both a military fighting man and a take-no-prisoners business man. Not often enough, he says, some of them also find their way past the "Chicken Turnaround" and to the crest of Walker Bald. Ken remains loyal to those who were loyal to him.

His love of automobiles remains in his heart, but health issues have robbed him of times behind the wheel of his twelve cylinder 1999 Mercedes, a twelve-year-old marvel of a machine still with only about 20,000 miles on the odometer. It still shines as though it arrived from the dealership only yesterday.

Laura's mother died in the early weeks of 2011 after a courageous battle with Parkinson's. Bob Ingle, the founder and CEO of the grocery chain in Western North Carolina that bears the family name, died a few weeks later. Mr. Ingle believed in Ken and his passing filled the old fighter with sadness and left Ken with the loss of a good friend and short a luncheon buddy. "Bob Ingle was a brilliant man," Ken said.Ken has had moments of misgiving about cooperating with an effort to chronicle his life in this book; he frets occasionally that he will be seen as a man capable of great anger and one possessing little patience for men of a different passion. Yet, through it all, what seems to come best into focus is the loyalty and the generosity of this rare man.

And whether the focus is on wars fought or business battles waged, he remains yet one of America's great fighting men with a view of his world that stuns and enthralls the senses. And perhaps compared to many of us, he seems at peace with "The Man in the Glass."

When you get what you want in your struggle for self
And the world makes you King for a day,
Just go to the mirror and look at yourself,
And see what THAT man has to say.

For it isn't your father or mother or wife
Who judgment upon you must pass;
The fellow whose verdict counts most in your life
Is the one staring back from the glass.

Some people may think you're a straight-shootin' chum
And call you a wonderful guy,
But the man in the glass says you're only a bum
If you can't look him straight in the eye.

He's the fellow to please, never mind all the rest
For he's with you clear up to the end,
And you've passed your most dangerous, difficult test
If the man in the glass is your friend.
You may fool the whole world down the pathway of years
And get pats on the back as you pass,
But your final reward will be heartaches and tears
If you've cheated the man in the glass.

Peter "Dale" Wimbrow Sr. (1934)
1895-1954

The cat Simpsons, Thelma (top) and Louise (2001)

About the Author

Wilt Browning is a former newspaper editor and sports columnist, and is the winner of a number of journalism awards including North Carolina Sports Writer of the Year, which he won five times. This is his seventh book.

Now retired from the newspaper business, Wilt lives in Kernersville, North Carolina, and has remained busy as a writer since he penned his final sports column for the *Asheville Citizen-Times*. For almost twenty years, he was sports columnist and for a time sports editor for the *Greensboro News & Record*, and covered the Braves in the team's first six seasons in Atlanta for the *Atlanta Journal*. He also has written for the *Charlotte Observer*, the *Greenville News* in South Carolina, and the *Topeka Capital and State Journal*.

In a six-year period out of the newspaper business, Wilt worked in the front offices of two National Football League teams, the *Atlanta Falcons* and the *Baltimore Colts*, both as public relations director.

Wilt is a native of Easley, South Carolina, but he and his wife, Joyce, have made their home in North Carolina since 1977. They are the parents of five children and eight grandsons.

Other books authored by Wilt are *Linthead, Saying Goodbye, The Rocks, Deadly Goals, Come Quittin' Time* and *Do They Play Football in Heaven?*.

Wilt can be reached at *wbrowning@triad.rr.com*.

About the Cover

The cover of Warrior was created by Dave Shaffer from a concept offered by the author. The elements of the cover represent the sweep of years in the life of Ken Simpson. The right side of the image was taken from a snapshot of First Lieutenant Simpson taken in Korea when Ken was 23 years old. The left side is from a photo shot in the early autumn of 2010 when Ken was 81.

Index

Index

CPSIA information can be obtained at www.ICGtesting.com
Printed in the USA
BVOW02s1842280514

354760BV00002B/175/P

9 780984 632060